S0-ASF-004

Contents

Frommer's®

PORTABLE
Dominican Republic

3rd Edition

by Darwin Porter & Danforth Prince

Here's what critics say about Frommer's:

"Amazingly easy to use. Very portable, very complete."

—*Booklist*

"Detailed, accurate, and easy-to-read information for all price ranges."

—*Glamour Magazine*

Wiley Publishing, Inc.

Published by:

WILEY PUBLISHING, INC.

111 River St.
Hoboken, NJ 07030-5774

ISBN: 978-0-470-14567-8

Editor: Marc Nadeau
Production Editor: Eric T. Schroeder
Cartographer: Guy Ruggiero
Photo Editor: Richard Fox
Anniversary Logo Design: Richard Pacifico
Production by Wiley Indianapolis Composition Services

For information on our other products and services or to obtain technical
support, please contact our Customer Care Department within the U.S. at
800/762-2974, outside the U.S. at 317/572-3993 or fax 317/572-4002.

Wiley also publishes its books in a variety of electronic formats. Some con-
tent that appears in print may not be available in electronic formats.

Manufactured in the United States of America

5   4   3   2   1

List of Maps

ABOUT THE AUTHORS

As a team of veteran travel writers, **Darwin Porter** and **Danforth Prince** have produced titles for Frommer's, including guides to Italy, France, the Caribbean, England, and Germany. A film critic, columnist, and broadcaster, Porter is also a Hollywood biographer. His most recent releases are *Brando Unzipped*, documenting the private life of Marlon Brando, and *Jacko: His Rise and Fall*, the first complete biography ever written on the tumultuous life of Michael Jackson. Prince was formerly employed by the Paris bureau of the *New York Times* and is today the president of Blood Moon Productions and other media-related firms.

AN INVITATION TO THE READER

In researching this book, we discovered many wonderful places—hotels, restaurants, shops, and more. We're sure you'll find others. Please tell us about them, so we can share the information with your fellow travelers in upcoming editions. If you were disappointed with a recommendation, we'd love to know that, too. Please write to:

Frommer's Portable Dominican Republic, 3rd Edition
Wiley Publishing, Inc. • 111 River St. • Hoboken, NJ 07030-5774

AN ADDITIONAL NOTE

Please be advised that travel information is subject to change at any time—and this is especially true of prices. We therefore suggest that you write or call ahead for confirmation when making your travel plans. The authors, editors, and publisher cannot be held responsible for the experiences of readers while traveling. Your safety is important to us, however, so we encourage you to stay alert and be aware of your surroundings. Keep a close eye on cameras, purses, and wallets, all favorite targets of thieves and pickpockets.

FROMMER'S STAR RATINGS, ICONS & ABBREVIATIONS

Every hotel, restaurant, and attraction listing in this guide has been ranked for quality, value, service, amenities, and special features using a **star-rating system**. In country, state, and regional guides, we also rate towns and regions to help you narrow down your choices and budget your time accordingly. Hotels and restaurants are rated on a scale of zero (recommended) to three stars (exceptional). Attractions, shopping, nightlife, towns, and regions are rated according to the following scale: zero stars (recommended), one star (highly recommended), two stars (very highly recommended), and three stars (must-see).

In addition to the star-rating system, we also use **seven feature icons** that point you to the great deals, in-the-know advice, and unique experiences that separate travelers from tourists. Throughout the book, look for:

Finds	Special finds—those places only insiders know about
Fun Fact	Fun facts—details that make travelers more informed and their trips more fun
Kids	Best bets for kids and advice for the whole family
Moments	Special moments—those experiences that memories are made of
Overrated	Places or experiences not worth your time or money
Tips	Insider tips—great ways to save time and money
Value	Great values—where to get the best deals

The following **abbreviations** are used for credit cards:

AE	American Express	DISC	Discover	V	Visa
DC	Diners Club	MC	MasterCard		

FROMMERS.COM

Now that you have this guidebook to help you plan a great trip, visit our website at **www.frommers.com** for additional travel information on more than 3,600 destinations. We update features regularly to give you instant access to the most current trip-planning information available. At Frommers.com, you'll find scoops on the best airfares, lodging rates, and car rental bargains. You can even book your travel online through our reliable travel booking partners. Other popular features include:

- Online updates of our most popular guidebooks
- Vacation sweepstakes and contest giveaways
- Newsletters highlighting the hottest travel trends
- Online travel message boards with featured travel discussions

The Best of the Dominican Republic

Sugar-white beaches, inexpensive resorts, and rich natural beauty have long attracted visitors to the Dominican Republic. But at the same time, a not-entirely-deserved reputation for high crime, poverty, and social unrest has scared away many travelers. So which is it: a poverty-stricken country rife with pickpockets and muggers, or a burgeoning destination of beautiful beach bargains?

The answer, of course, is a little of both. The people of the Dominican Republic are among the friendliest in the Caribbean, and the hospitality here seems more genuine than in more commercialized Puerto Rico. The weather is nearly perfect year-round, and the Dominican Republic's white-sand beaches are some of the Caribbean's finest. Punta Cana/Bávaro, for example, is the longest strip of white sand in the entire region.

Safety *is* still a concern here, but that shouldn't dissuade you from planning a vacation to the Dominican Republic. Crime consists primarily of robberies and muggings, and most of it is limited to Santo Domingo (although the north-coast resorts around Puerto Plata and Playa Dorada are not as safe as they should be). There is little incidence of violent crime against visitors, however. Follow simple common-sense rules of safety, and you should be fine. Lock valuables in your hotel safe, carry only a reasonable amount of cash or (better yet) one or two credit cards, and avoid dark deserted places, just as you would at home.

(***One note:*** Men traveling alone here will find themselves solicited more often by prostitutes than anywhere else in the Caribbean. Prostitutes are at their most visible and aggressive in such relatively unmonitored tourist zones as Cabarete and within the bars and lounges of most of the deluxe hotels of Santo Domingo, especially the Jaragua.)

The combination of low prices and scenic tropical terrain has made the Dominican Republic one of the fastest-growing destinations in the Caribbean. Bargain-hunting Canadians, in particular, flock here in droves. Europeans arrive by the planeloads in summer. Don't expect the lavish, spectacular resorts that you'll find in Puerto Rico or Jamaica, but do expect your vacation to be that much less expensive.

Although referred to as "just a poor man's Puerto Rico," in reality the Dominican Republic has its own distinctive cuisine and cultural heritage. Its Latin flavor is a sharp contrast to the character of many nearby islands, especially the British- and French-influenced ones.

Columbus spotted its coral-edged Caribbean coastline on his first voyage to the New World and pronounced: "There is no more beautiful island in the world." The first permanent European settlement in the New World was founded here on November 7, 1493, and its ruins still remain near Montecristi in the northeast part of the island. Natives called the island Quisqueya, "Mother Earth," before the Spaniards arrived to butcher them.

Nestled amid Cuba, Jamaica, and Puerto Rico in the heart of the Caribbean archipelago, the island of Hispaniola (Little Spain) is divided between Haiti, on the westernmost third of the island, and the Dominican Republic, which has a lush landmass about the size of Vermont and New Hampshire combined. In the Dominican interior, the fertile Valley of Cibao (rich, sugar-cane country) ends its upward sweep at Pico Duarte, the highest mountain peak in the West Indies, which soars to 3,125m (10,253 ft.).

Much of what Columbus first sighted still remains in a natural, unspoiled condition. One-third of the Dominican Republic's 1,401km (871-mile) coastline is devoted to beaches. The best are in Puerto Plata and La Romana, although Puerto Plata and other beaches on the Atlantic side of the island have dangerously strong currents at times.

Political turmoil kept visitors away for many years, but even that is a thing of the past. Almost from its inception, the country was steeped in misery and bloodshed, climaxing with the infamous reign of dictator Rafael Trujillo (1930–61) and the ensuing civil wars (1960–66). But the country has been politically stable since then, and it is building and expanding rapidly. The economic growth hasn't benefited everybody equally, though. The country is still poor, even by Caribbean standards. Every day, many Dominicans risk their lives crossing the 87km-wide (54-mile) Mona Passage, hoping to land in Puerto Rico before attempting to slip into the United States.

The greatest threat to the Dominican Republic these days comes from hurricanes, which periodically flatten entire cities. The major resorts have become adept at getting back on their feet quickly after a hurricane. Still, if a hurricane hits the country before your trip, you might want to call ahead and make sure your room is still standing.

1 The Best Beaches

The most tranquil beaches are those on the western side of the D.R., particularly Boca Chica or those along the southern coast of La Romana and Bayahibe. Beaches that front the Atlantic—notably at Punta Cana, La Samaná, and Puerto Plata—are likely to have more turbulent waters on and off throughout the winter months, although conditions are idyllic on many a day, even from December through February.

- **Playa Boca Chica**   There is good and bad news here. The beach of immaculate fine sand is still one of the best in the Caribbean. The gin-clear waters are protected by coral reefs, making Playa Boca Chica one of the most family-friendly of all the strips of sands in the D.R. Now the bad news: The beach lies 30km (19 miles) east of Santo Domingo, and, as such, is the virtual Riviera for the teeming masses of this overcrowded city. Lined with coconut palms, the wide beach was a brilliant stroke of nature, but man-made intrusions have ruined a lot of its backdrop with pizza stands, cafes, bars, tacky souvenir stalls, and blaring music all day long. See chapter 4.

- **Punta Cana/Bávaro Beaches**   One of the world's greatest beach strips is centered at Punta Cana and Bávaro on the eastern coast of the Dominican Republic. This stretch of beachfront goes on for 32km (20 miles) and is renowned for its all-inclusive resorts, the largest concentration in the Caribbean. The beaches here are wide, filled with golden sand, gorgeous, and safe for swimming all year. See chapter 6.

- **Cayo Levantado**   On the peninsula of Samaná, along the east coast of the Dominican Republic, this island near the mouth of Bahía de Samaná lies 7km (4⅓ miles) southeast of the town of Samaná. It can easily be reached by boat. Once on this island, beach lovers will find three beautiful strips of white sand, but little in the way of facilities. A tropical forest covers much of this hill-studded island, and when not enjoying the beach, you can go hiking along trails that are cut through the jungle-like vegetation. Cayo Levantado was known to TV watchers in the '70s as the famous Bacardi Rum island, featured in commercials. See chapter 7.

- **Playa Rincón**   On the eastern shoreline of the Peninsula Samaná, Playa Rincón is consistently hailed by *Condé Nast Traveler* as one of the 10 top beaches in the Caribbean, and we agree that it deserves such an accolade. Set against the 600m (1,969-ft.) cliffs of Cape Cabrón, the beach is hard to reach, but once you're here you can wander a Robinson Crusoe tropical paradise of white sands—just don't expect any facilities. There's plenty of color in the sea—vivid turquoise, blues, and greens that are safe for swimming and ideal for snorkeling. See chapter 7.
- **Playa Dorada**   This is the most celebrated beach along the Amber Coast and the site of a large concentration of all-inclusive resorts. The golden or white sands along its Atlantic Ocean waters—often turbulent—have been discovered, and how, so don't expect to be alone on the beach. Instead of depending on beach facilities, most patrons of Playa Dorada use their beachfront hotels for food, drink, toilet facilities, and changing rooms. Water-skiers and windsurfers alike take delight here. Because the waters of this beach front the Atlantic, waves can be a bit high in winter, the waters a bit rough for swimming. Guests at all the Playa Dorada resorts have free access to the beach. See chapter 8.

2 The Best Attractions

- **Altos de Chavón,** La Romana   This is a re-creation of a 16th-century Spanish village, lying near the famous Casa de Campo resort at La Romana along the southern coastline. It is a true living museum—part artisans' colony, part tourist diversion. Its highlight is a Grecian-style amphitheater. It's also one of the best places in the Dominican Republic to shop for handicrafts. See chapter 5.
- **Zona Colonial,** Santo Domingo   Comprising nearly a dozen city blocks, this is what remains of the first European city in the Americas, and many of its monuments have been well preserved. Old Santo Domingo was the seat of Spanish power in the West Indies and was the port of that country's conquest of the Western Hemisphere. Wandering its cobblestone streets and exploring its old churches and monuments is to step back into history. At every turn, you see something historic, such as Calle Las Damas, the first paved street in the Americas. See chapter 4.

- **Alcázar de Colón,** Santo Domingo   In the Colonial Zone of the old city, this fortress was built for Columbus's son, Diego, and his wife, who was the niece of King Ferdinand of Spain. Diego ruled the colony in 1509 and made this his residence. This is also the palace-fortress where he entertained the likes of Cortés, Ponce de León, and Balboa. See chapter 4.
- **Parque Nacional Los Haïtises,** Samaná Peninsula   On the southern tier of Samaná Peninsula, this sprawling park is the second-most visited in the country, covering 208 sq. km (78 sq. miles) and spanning 24km (15 miles) west from Boca de Inferno to the head of Río Barracote. It's a mangrove swamp that's home to some 112 bird species and nearly 100 plant species. Caves of the original inhabitants, the Taíno Indians, remain to be explored. See chapter 7.

2

Planning Your Trip to the Dominican Republic

Golden- or white-sand beaches shaded by palm trees and crystalline waters teeming with rainbow-hued fish—it's all just a few hours' flight from the East Coast of the United States.

To the southeast of Cuba, the Dominican Republic shares the island of Hispaniola with the less-developed and dangerous Haiti.

Spicy food, spicier merengue, and the gentle, leisurely lifestyle of the islands draw increasing thousands to the Dominican Republic every year. Most of these visitors are middle-class Americans, Canadians, and Europeans. Except for the Casa de Campo, the D.R. is a moderately priced island—not a pocket of posh like St. Barts and Anguilla that draw movie stars or else CEOs. Its long, palm-lined *playas*—or beaches—such as Punta Cana, Boca Chica, Bávaro, and Playa Dorada have become world famous.

But the one thing that is making the beach-loving world take notice of the island is its spectacularly affordable prices, especially those charged at its all-inclusive resorts.

Frugal travelers from Canada and America, and from such European countries as Britain, Germany, Spain, Switzerland, Italy, and France, have combined forces to make the Dominican Republic the most popular country to visit in the Caribbean.

1 Regions in Brief

SANTO DOMINGO   Originally called Nueva Isabela and once Ciudad Trujillo (named after the despised dictator), the capital of the Dominican Republic was founded in 1496 by none other than Bartolomé, the brother of Columbus. Today, Santo Domingo is a thriving and sprawling metropolis of some 2.5 million people.

One of the fastest-growing cities in the Caribbean, it still retains much of its Spanish flavor in its colonial zone. Other than San Juan, it also offers the largest concentration of museums in the Caribbean. What it doesn't have is a beach. So, come here for sightseeing and shopping, but for the sands head to Boca Chica and Juan Dolio (see below). These, however, are not the best resorts in the D.R. For those you'll have to go elsewhere. Our suggestion is to spend 2 days in the D.R. capital and then the rest of your vacation time at a resort of your choice. A preview of the major possibilities will follow.

BOCA CHICA & JUAN DOLIO   To the immediate east of Santo Domingo, these twin beach resorts open onto one of the most beautiful stretch of beaches on the east coast, known for their powdery white sands and shallow waters, safe for swimming. Fun in the sun begins approximately 31km (19 miles) east of Santo Domingo, but only a 5-minute drive from Las Américas International Airport, serving Santo Domingo. Many Europeans call the area "Playa St. Tropez," as it evokes the fun-loving port on the French Riviera. Even with its hordes of visitors, St. Tropez is still chic. Juan Dolio and Boca Chica are most definitely not chic. Lying immediately east of Boca Chica, the fast-rising Juan Dolio boasts even more hotels than Boca Chica, most of them all-inclusives.

Boca Chica had its golden age during the heyday of dictator Trujillo. Wealthy residents built vacation homes here and used it as a weekend escape. This allure lasted until the 1970s when rising resorts, especially Playa Dorada in the north, threatened the popularity of Boca Chica.

Today Boca Chica has lost much of its allure, even though the great beachfront is still here. It's filled with rather lackluster hotels offering some of the cheapest package deals in the Caribbean in winter.

Restaurants and bars have become very touristy, and on weekends the scene takes on a bit of madness, as thousands of residents of Santo Domingo descend on the beach, placing a heavy burden on the limited facilities. Restaurants and bars have taken on a very touristy aura; prostitution, both male and female, is clearly evident.

Playa Boca Chica, as lovely as it is, is one of the most overrun in the D.R. Instead of tranquillity, you will often hear the blasting sounds of a mariachi band.

As for Juan Dolio, you could skip it completely and not suffer great deprivation. It is more a tourist development by the sea instead of a real town. The beach here stretches for 5km (3 miles) and the many hotels and resorts are among the worst in the D.R.

Many of these date from the 1980s when a building boom occurred here. However, after 9/11 there was a great fall-off in business. Because it doesn't have the allure of other emerging resorts in the D.R., many of these hotels have closed or else look as if they haven't made any improvements since Ronald Reagan was president of the United States. Our advice: Skip it and head for golden sands elsewhere. However, if, because of time restrictions, you are based in Santo Domingo and want to slip in some beach time, head to Boca Chica over Juan Dolio.

LA ROMANA/BAYAHIBE These twin resorts, so different in character, lie east of Santo Domingo along the southeastern coast, a 2-hour drive from Santo Domingo, although you can fly to the area's small airport as well. Compared to the overbuilt Punta Cana, a virtual Miami Beach strip of hotels, La Romana and Bayahibe are very different.

La Romana is dominated by one resort, Casa de Campo, one of the grandest in the Caribbean. With its deluxe hotel rooms and private villas, plus two Pete Dye–designed golf courses, the 7,000-acre (2,800-hectare) Casa de Campo is reason enough for many visitors to fly to the D.R. in the first place. It is a destination unto itself.

Casa de Campo remains the dowager of D.R. resorts, although it has been supplanted by newer, more cutting-edge resorts such as those at Punta Cana. Casa de Campo still retains a loyal clientele and wins new converts every year.

Casa de Campo also lies next to the single greatest tourist attraction of the D.R., Altos de Chavón, the re-creation of a 16th-century Spanish village that is amazingly realistic. It's part museum, part artisans' colony. It's also a great place to go on a shopping expedition, where you can purchase many of the paintings and crafts produced on the spot, including jewelry and macramé.

The actual town of La Romana remains the sleepy backwater it always was. It is almost devoid of tourist attractions and serves mainly as a refueling stop for visitors to the area.

Bayahibe, lying 30km (19 miles) east of La Romana, didn't exist until the late '90s. That's when hotel developers were drawn to its pristine beachfront. The area is just now being developed with some all-inclusive resorts, attracting those who want to explore this part of the D.R. but can't afford the high tariffs of Casa de Campo.

If you select one of the few hotels at Bayahibe, you'd better like it, because you'll be spending a great deal of your time on the grounds or on the beach in front of your hotel.

Go to La Romana or Bayahibe if you want to avoid the crowds flocking to Puerto Plata and Punta Cana. From both La Romana and Bayahibe, you can explore two intriguing offshore islands (Saona and Catalina), both with pristine white sandy beaches and also a national park, Parque Nacional del Este. Some of the beaches in the area, unlike those at Boca Chica, you'll have virtually to yourself.

PUNTA CANA & BAVARO This is the Cancun of the D.R. Nowhere in the Caribbean is there such a concentration of resorts, most of them all-inclusives. These resort developments dominate what has come to be known as Costa del Coco or "The Coconut Coast." There are more than 32km (20 miles) of powder-white sandy beaches, among the longest stretch of such beachfront in the world. The beaches edge up to crystal-clear waters, and this coastal land is an upmarket resort, filled with government-rated four- or five-star hotels.

Comparisons with other resorts, particularly Puerto Plata/Playa Dorada in the north, are inevitable. The big difference is that Punta Cana exists just for tourists, whereas the resorts in the north involve you more in Dominican life. Except for hotel staffs, chances are you won't be exposed to anybody but other tourists in Punta Cana.

After arriving, you're taken to your hotel in a shuttle bus where you will swim, eat, breathe, and hang out with other tourists, mainly American, Canadian, French, English, Spanish, and Italian, but also from some countries in South America. At the end of your stay, you board a shuttle bus to take you back to the airport.

Bávaro, the name of one of the best beaches in the Caribbean, has come to designate the district north of Punta Cana, site of some of the best all-inclusives in the D.R.

There is far less rain in Punta Cana than at Puerto Plata. Punta Cana's "dry" beaches are wider than those in the north. Staffs at hotels in Punta Cana have been moved here—often away from their families—from other parts of the country. They are placed into company housing and are eager to escape back to their towns or villages whenever possible. Staffs at Puerto Plata have been born in the region and tend to be friendlier and more welcoming than those in the more isolated Punta Cana, many of whom express resentment at being uprooted from home and hearth and sent to an isolated part of the D.R. to serve at the pleasure of the endless stream of visitors.

The infrastructure of Punta Cana is newer and fresher, but local life doesn't exist. Punta Cana is strictly a hedonist's retreat, attracting those who want sun and often sex and don't particularly want to see the natural attractions that exist elsewhere on the island.

But, oh, those beaches and those endless buffets. Don't expect to lose any weight. The food and drink flow.

PUERTO PLATA & THE AMBER COAST The northern shoreline of the Dominican Republic launched massive tourism to the D.R. back when Punta Cana was a lonely beach strip. Its center is Puerto Plata, named "port of silver" by Columbus. The Amber Coast nickname comes from the rich deposits of amber ore discovered along this coast. The waters of the Atlantic wash up on its beaches of golden sand. The tourist development here since the 1980s has been remarkable, and overbuilding is rampant. To the immediate east of Puerto Plata is Playa Dorada, lying about halfway between the Haitian border and Samaná Peninsula. To the immediate east, in Sosúa, is the fast-rising resort of Cabarete, the windsurfing capital of the Caribbean. "It's our Malibu," is what one local told us.

Puerto Plata lies on the more verdant—and rainier—north shore of the island. But when the rain comes, it arrives suddenly and doesn't last long. Puerto Plata's beaches aren't as wide as those in Punta Cana, but recent improvements have made them better. In 2006, the government dumped tons of sand onto the beaches to replace what was lost to hurricanes.

Unlike Punta Cana, Puerto Plata has an urbanized feel, with an economy based not just on tourism.

Immediately to the east of Puerto Plata is Playa Dorada, the name of one of the best beaches in the D.R. and also a gated compound of resorts, most of them all-inclusives. Here you get all the elements to appeal to visitors—dance clubs, casinos, golf, a shopping center, restaurants, and bars.

More and more visitors are abandoning the more manicured grounds of Playa Dorada and continuing east to Sosúa, a former Jewish settlement. It had a flourishing sex industry in the 1980s before the onslaught of the AIDS epidemic. The prostitutes are still there, although the sex industry has slowed down considerably.

Visitors who head for Sosúa are attracted to the raffish aura of the town, a lively, vibrant spot, but not the most tranquil retreat in the D.R. Its beach is spectacular, however, a kilometer of golden sand set against a backdrop of coconut trees. Sosúa is patronized by an older crowd, mostly North Americans and Europeans.

A much younger and athletic group of visitors heads for Cabarete, even farther to the east of Sosúa. Far less developed than either Sosúa or Puerto Plata, it too opens onto a beautiful beach of white sand fronting a lovely, wide bay. Its windsurfing is not only the best in the Caribbean, but maybe the world.

In the 1990s it was transformed from a fishing village into a tourist town of hotels, restaurants, bars, souvenir shops, and cafes. At night the bars resound to the music of merengue and salsa, even reggae. It's still a "one-road town" and has none of the elements or the refinements of Playa Dorada or Punta Cana.

SAMANÁ   Of all the resorts recommended in this guide, the towns of the Samaná peninsula in the northeast of the D.R. contain the wildest and most savage landscape of all, with a focus on scuba diving, underwater life, and whale-watching. Its beaches are also the least crowded of all the major D.R. resorts. It is also the remotest destination and the hardest to reach. This peninsula once provided a haven in the 1820s for escaped American slaves. In its national park, Los Haïtises, inscriptions from the early settlers, the Taíno Indians, have been discovered. From January to March (more or less) the humpback whales of the Atlantic Ocean come here to breed and rear their newborn calves. The peninsula stretches for 48km (30 miles), lying about 120km (75 miles) northeast of Santo Domingo. The terrain consists of lush, forested hills along with banana and coconut plantations. Since the '90s, tourism has begun to take root, centering about Las Terrenas, the town of Samaná, and Las Galeras.

The resorts of Punta Cana will give you a sanitized view of Dominican life. Samaná is the real deal. Except for a few scattered inns and small hotels, major hotel development did not begin here until the post-millennium.

If you go to Samaná within the next few years or so, you'll get a taste of the Caribbean as it used to be.

How the Resorts Stack Up Against Each Other

	LA ROMANA/ BAYAHIBE	PUNTA CANA/ BÁVARO	SAMANÁ PENIN- SULA	PUERTO PLATA & PLAYA DORADA
General Ambience	Good	Good	Good	Good
Quality of Beaches	Good	Outstanding	Fair	Good
Elegance	Excellent	Good	Poor	Good
Tastefulness & Sophistication	Good	Fair	Poor	Fair
The Dining Experience	Good	Good	Fair	Good
The Honeymoon Experience	Excellent	Good	Fair	Excellent
Transportation to & from the States	Fair	Fair	Poor	Fair

Traveler Beware: The Uneasy Border Between Haiti & the D.R.

The troubled land of Haiti shares the island of Hispaniola with the Dominican Republic. Many residents of the D.R., mired in poverty, flee their homeland every year, risking dangerous sea voyages on rickety boats to the nearby U.S. territory of Puerto Rico. Once here, they can eventually make their way to the mainland of the U.S. and perhaps a more prosperous life.

To Haitians, mired in even greater poverty, the D.R. can appear like the promised land. The poorly patrolled border between the D.R. and Haiti has long been a source of conflict and even attacks and counterattacks.

The most notorious bloodbath occurred in 1937 when the dictator Gen. Rafael Trujillo ordered that the D.R. be "cleansed" of Haitians. Soldiers and citizens alike slaughtered at least 20,000 Haitians, most of them sugar workers. The aptly named Massacre River along the two countries literally overflowed with blood.

Conflicts are still raging in the post-millennium era. As late as 2005, some Haitians were beheaded by machetes. Dominicans have been known to go on a rampage, burning dozens of shacks in Haitian ghettos on D.R. soil.

Since very few visitors ever cross from the D.R. into Haiti by overland route, these dangerous border flare-ups will rarely concern the average visitor. All of the major D.R. resorts are far removed from the dangerous border.

2 Visitor Information

In the United States, you can contact the **Dominican Republic Tourist Information Center** at 136 E. 57th St., Suite 803, New York, NY 10022 (© **888/374-6361** or 212/588-1012); or at 848 Brickell Ave., Suite 405, Miami, FL 33131 (© **888/358-9594** or 305/358-2899; fax 305/358-4185). In Canada, try the office at 2080 Crescent St., Montréal, Quebec H3G, 2B8, Canada (© **800/563-1611** or 514/499-1918; fax 514/499-1393); or at 26 Wellington St. E., Suite 201, Unit 53, Toronto, Ontario M5E 1S2, Canada (© **888/494-5050** or 416/361-2126; fax 416/361-2130). Don't expect too many specifics.

In England, there's an office at 20 Hand Court, High Holborn, WC1V 6JF (© **020/7242-7778**).

On the Web, check out **www.godominicanrepublic.com**.

MAPS   Maps of the Dominican Republic are not of good quality for the most part. However, unless you're planning to do detailed visits to remote areas (highly unlikely), you won't need the type of Michelin maps available in, say, France.

The D.R. government distributes free maps to visitors, and they are available at airport terminals upon your arrival, at hotels, at tourist offices, and at other places frequented by visitors. They are called *Mapas Turísticos,* and they highlight not only Santo Domingo but all the major resorts covered in this guide, including Puerto Plata, Samaná/Las Terrenas, Punta Cana/Bávaro, and La Romana/Bayahibe.

Unless you're planning specialty travel, these detailed regional maps should suffice. On one side is a general overview map of the D.R. itself, where you can determine the location of your resort in the country as a whole. For motorists, the overview map also highlights the major routes of access to your resort.

TRAVEL AGENTS   Travel agents can save you time and money by uncovering the best package deals, airfare, and rental-car rates. Most are professional, but the occasional unscrupulous agent may push deals that bag the juiciest commissions, so shop around and ask hard questions. Arm yourself with the information in this book, and don't let anyone pressure you into a vacation that's not right for you.

If you enlist a travel agent, use one that's a member of the **American Society of Travel Agents (ASTA),** 1101 King St., Suite 200, Alexandria, VA 22314 (℃ **703/739-2782;** www.astanet.com). Call ASTA or visit their website for a list of members in your area.

3 Entry Requirements

ENTRY REQUIREMENTS   Entry requirements can and do change, so the savvy visitor should check with the nearest Dominican embassy or consulate at least 6 weeks prior to departure. As of January 1, 2008, all persons, including U.S. citizens, traveling between the U.S. and Canada, Mexico, and the Caribbean by land or sea are required to present a valid passport or other documents as determined by the local Department of Homeland Security. This passport requirement applies to the Dominican Republic. Upon arrival at their port of entry, visitors must also purchase a RD$333 (US$10/£5.10) tourist card to enter. Keep the receipt. Otherwise, you'll have to pay the fee again upon your departure from the D.R.

Before leaving home, make two copies of your documents— including your passport and your driver's license, your airline ticket, and any hotel vouchers—and leave them home with someone.

PASSPORTS   For information on how to get a passport, go to "Passports" in the "Fast Facts" section of this chapter—the websites listed provide downloadable passport applications as well as the current fees for processing passport applications. For an up-to-date, country-by-country listing of passport requirements around the world, go to the "Document Requirements" Web page of the U.S. State Department at **http://travel.state.gov**.

MEDICAL REQUIREMENTS   For information on medical requirements and recommendations, see "Health," p. 24.

CUSTOMS   For information on what you can bring into and take out of the D.R., go to "Customs" in the "Fast Facts" section of this chapter.

For entry requirements to the D.R., check out **http://travel. state.gov/travel**.

4 When to Go

High season in the Dominican Republic is from mid-December to mid-April. The weather is perfect for beach conditions, in that it's usually dry, and the temperatures are moderated by cooling trade winds blowing in from the northeast. Sometimes a few days can be windy under cloudy skies, but these periods often come and go quickly.

In some ways, April is the most idyllic month, with perfect weather before the heat of summer comes in May. In spite of the heat, many Europeans prefer a summer visit.

Rainy season is from late May until late November. That doesn't mean, however, that it rains every day. Often the showers come in short bursts, followed by clear skies and plenty of sun.

If you want to know how to pack just before you go, check the Weather Channel's online 5-day forecast at **www.weather.com** for the latest information.

HURRICANES   The curse of Dominican weather, the hurricane season, lasts—officially, at least—from June 1 to November 30. But there's no cause for panic: Satellite forecasts give enough warning that precautions can be taken.

To get a weather report before you go, check the **Weather Channel** on the Web at **www.weather.com**.

Average Temperature & Rainfall in Santo Domingo

	Jan	Feb	Mar	Apr	May	June	July	Aug	Sept	Oct	Nov	Dec
Temp. (°F)	76	76	77	79	80	81	81	81	81	80	79	77
Temp. (°C)	24	24	25	26	27	27	27	27	27	27	26	25
Rainfall (in.)	2.2	1.7	1.9	3.0	7.0	6.1	6.1	6.4	6.8	6.5	4.4	2.5
Rainfall (cm.)	5.6	4.3	4.8	7.6	17.8	15.5	15.5	16.3	17.3	16.5	11.2	6.4

DOMINICAN REPUBLIC CALENDAR OF EVENTS

For an exhaustive list of events beyond those listed here, check http://events.frommers.com, where you'll find a searchable, up-to-the-minute roster of what's happening in cities all over the world.

January

New Year's Eve   No place is more fun to be in the Caribbean than Santo Domingo on New Year's Eve. Thousands of merrymakers gather along the Malecón (actually Av. George Washington) to celebrate the coming year. Along this sea-bordering boulevard, bands blast merengue and other music throughout the night. At midnight, fireworks explode and sirens go off. The party continues until daybreak.

New Year's Day   The merrymaking continues on New Year's Day in the town of Bayaguana, lying northeast of Santo Domingo. Here the annual **Festivales del Santo Cristo de Bayaguana** include street dancing, singing, various folkloric activities, a procession through town, and the inevitable Mass.

Epifanía   Also called Día de los Santos Reyes, this nationwide event is celebrated throughout the Dominican Republic. Every town and village marks the end of the Christmas holidays. Santo Domingo has the most interesting observances, with processions through town starring the Three Wise Men. As they sleep, children are given gifts by their parents. January 6.

Día de Duarte   Juan Pablo Duarte is hailed as the father of the Dominican Republic. Duarte executed a bloodless coup against Haiti, asserting his country's independence over their western neighbor. The date was February 27, 1844. Duarte's birthday, on January 26, 1814, is celebrated with gun salutes in Santo Domingo. A carnival is staged in such cities as Santiago, Samaná, San Pedro de Macorís, and La Romana. January 26.

Dominican Holidays

January 1	New Year's Day
January 6	Epiphany/Three Kings Day
January 21	Our Lady of Altagracia
January 26	Duarte Day
February 27	Independence Day, Carnaval
March/April	Maundy Thursday, Holy Friday, Easter Sunday
April 14	Pan-American Day
May 1	Labor Day
July 16	Foundation of Sociedad la Trinitaria
August 16	Restoration Day
September 24	Our Lady of Mercedes
October 12	Columbus Day
October 24	United Nations Day
November 1	All Saints' Day
December 25	Christmas

February

Carnaval This is the biggest event on the Dominican calendar, and it's widely celebrated preceding and including Independence Day, February 27, which often falls around Lent. In Santo Domingo, the big event is 2 or 3 days before February 27, but festivities range around the country in all the towns and cities. Expect spectacular floats, flamboyantly costumed performers, and lots of street dancing, rum drinking, and street food. The masks worn by the participants symbolize good and evil. Some 30,000 merrymakers parade along the Malecón in Santo Domingo.

April

Semana Santa This observance of Holy Week hardly rivals Seville's in Spain, but it's the best in the Western Hemisphere. The week surrounding Easter is marked by islandwide pageants, processions, and celebrations. Many towns and cities burn in effigy a grotesque representation of Judas Iscariot.

June

Espíritu Santo The island's African heritage is much in evidence during this observance. Although an islandwide event, the most intriguing celebrations take place in the town of Villa Mella near

Santo Domingo. The festivities are marked by the playing of African instruments such as Congo drums. First or second week of June.

July

Festival del Merengue Slightly less raucous than Carnaval, a blast of merengue music fills the night along the Malecón in Santo Domingo the last week of July. Festivities continue into the first week of August, coinciding with the observance of the founding of Santo Domingo on August 4, 1496. Artisan fairs are just part of the agenda, along with a gastronomic festival, but it is the live merengue music that attracts participants by the thousands. The world's top merengue musicians and dancers attend this wildly crazed event.

August

Fiesta Patria de la Restauración Restoration Day is celebrated on August 16 islandwide, commemorating the regaining of Dominican Republic independence from Spain in 1863. Parades, live music, street fairs, and other events reach their crescendo in the two main cities of Santo Domingo and Santiago.

October

Puerto Plata Festival Like the Merengue Festival, this is the major cultural event on the northern coast of the Dominican Republic, a weeklong festival that brings the best of bands— merengue, blues, jazz, and folk concerts—to Fuerte San Felipe at the end of the Malecón. Troupes from all over the island come here to perform traditional songs and dances, along with salsa, merengue steps, and African spirituals. Expect parades, costumes, and food fairs. In October, but dates vary.

Descubrimiento de América The so-called "discovery" by Columbus of America on October 12, 1492, is no longer celebrated as a grand event in many parts of the Western Hemisphere. The explorer's arrival on an already inhabited continent brought death, destruction, and disease to much of the Caribbean. Because of the D.R.'s strong link to Spain, the festivities in Santo Domingo reach their peak with celebrations at the tomb of the explorer at Faro a Colón and at the Cathedral of Santo Domingo.

5 Getting There by Plane

Most visitors arrive in the Dominican Republic as part of a package deal that includes airfare. Travel agencies will inform you of the best deals, land-and-air packages that cut costs substantially. For the best discounts, refer to "Package Deals," below. At slow periods of the year, this package deal is tantamount to a giveaway.

Most flights into the country are routed through Miami (flight time from Miami to Santo Domingo is 1¾ hr.). Flying time from New York is 4 hours, and only 30 minutes from San Juan, Puerto Rico.

Most charter flights from Canada originate out of Toronto, taking 4½ hours to reach the D.R. From many cities in western Europe, flying time to Santo Domingo ranges from 8 to 10 hours.

American Airlines (© 800/433-7300; www.aa.com) offers the most frequent service—at least a dozen flights daily from cities throughout North America to either Santo Domingo or Puerto Plata. Flights from hubs like New York, Miami, or San Juan are usually nonstop. American also offers some good package deals.

If you're heading to one of the Dominican Republic's smaller airports, your best bet is to catch a connecting flight with **American Eagle,** American's local commuter carrier. Its small planes depart every day from San Juan for airports throughout the Dominican Republic, including Santo Domingo, Puerto Plata, La Romana, and Punta Cana.

Continental Airlines (© 800/231-0856 in the U.S.; www.continental.com) has a daily flight between Newark and Santo Domingo.

US Airways (© 800/221-0133; www.usairways.com) flies daily from Philadelphia to Santo Domingo. The airline also offers flights from Charlotte, North Carolina, to Punta Cana on Monday, Wednesday, Friday, and Saturday.

JetBlue Airlines (© 800/JETBLUE; www.jetblue.com) flies from New York to the Dominican Republic, and **US Airways** (© 800/221-0133; www.usairways.com) also flies from New York to the island. In addition, **Delta Airlines** (© 800/221-1212; www.delta.com) flies from both New York and Miami to the Dominican Republic.

Spirit Airlines (© 800/772-7117; www.spiritair.com) flies from New York's La Guardia to Santo Domingo and Punta Cana and also has flights from Atlanta, Atlantic City, Chicago, Detroit, Fort Lauderdale, Providence (Rhode Island), Washington D.C., Myrtle Beach (South Carolina), Boston, Tampa, Orlando, Los Angeles, and Las Vegas.

Iberia (© 800/772-4642 in the U.S.; www.iberia.com) offers daily flights from Madrid to Santo Domingo, making a brief stop in San Juan.

Be warned: Arriving at Santo Domingo's Las Américas International Airport is confusing and chaotic. Customs officials, who tend to be rude and overworked, may give you a very thorough check. Stolen luggage is not uncommon here; beware of "porters" who offer to help with your bags.

6 Money & Costs

In general the Dominican Republic is one of the most affordable destinations in the Caribbean—hence, its great popularity. Ten U.S. dollars still buys at least something on the island.

The catch is to plan a vacation way in advance. If you just show up, you'll be charged the "rack rate," and some of these deals can be expensive. However, if you book at an all-inclusive resort, with a package that includes both airfare and accommodations, you can live at a rather moderate per-diem cost, even though staying at a government-rated four- or five-star hotel. Many of these package deals, offered even in winter, can amount to as little as RD$2,100 (US$63/£32) per person per day.

Even if you do arrive independently, you can often find lodgings—and rather decent ones at that—for as little as RD$1,000 (US$30/£15) a night in a double room. Many meals cost only RD$350 (US$11/£5.40) if you avoid expensive items such as lobster or steak.

Cigars are plentiful and cheap, especially if you stick to those made in the D.R. Cuban cigars are still moderate in price here compared to most of the world. However, if you purchase a Cuban cigar, smoke it in the D.R. Americans are not allowed to bring Cuban cigars back to the United States.

If you're watching your pesos, stick to such national drinks as rum or the local beer, *El Presidente*. If money is no object, all the first-class hotels and bars sell expensive imported liquor, such as Scotch. The high import taxes hoteliers or bars pay are reflected in the price of your drink.

THE DOMINICAN PESO, THE U.S. & CANADIAN DOLLARS, & THE BRITISH POUND

The Dominican monetary unit is the **peso (RD$),** which is made up of 100 centavos. Coin denominations are in 1, 5, 10, 25, and 50 centavos, and 1 peso. Bill denominations are in RD$5, RD$10, RD$20, RD$50, RD$100, RD$500, and RD$1,000.

At press time, the prevailing exchange rate between the peso and the most frequently traded currency, the U.S. dollar, was RD$33=US$1 (or RD$1=US3¢). Canadian dollars and British

---

Heads Up: A Note on Pricing

Nearly all hotels in the Dominican Republic list their rates in U.S. dollars, while most restaurants and shops deal with both U.S. and Dominican currencies. Accordingly, our hotel listings will reflect only U.S. dollar prices, while our restaurant, shop, and attractions listings will include Dominican peso prices followed by the U.S. dollar and British pound conversions—that is, if the establishments quote in pesos. Many establishments in popular resorts quote prices only in U.S. dollars.

---

pounds are less frequently traded and, in most cases, are accepted only at banks and at very large hotels. Just before press time for this edition, the British pound traded at approximately RD$65=£1 (or RD$1=1.5p) and the Canadian dollar traded at RD$29=CD$1 (stated differently, RD$1=CD3.5¢).

Note to British Readers: In some cases within this chapter, we've converted U.S. dollars directly into British pounds, and when that was the case, our texts reflect the prevailing exchange rate as US$1.90 =£1 (stated inversely, US$1=53p).

Remember that currency conversion rates can and will change during the lifetime of this edition, as reflected by a complicated roster of political and economic factors, so check the rates from time to time as a means of staying abreast of the cost of your holiday.

CREDIT CARDS   Credit cards are another safe way to carry money. They also provide a convenient record of all your expenses, and they generally offer relatively good exchange rates. You can withdraw cash advances from your credit cards at banks or ATMs but high fees make credit card cash advances a pricey way to get cash. Keep in mind that you'll pay interest from the moment of your withdrawal, even if you pay your monthly bills on time. Also, note that many banks now assess a 1% to 3% "transaction fee" on **all** charges you incur abroad.

Visitors should limit their use of personal credit cards because of credit card fraud and may wish to consider coordinating their trip with their credit card company so that only hotel bills or other specified expenses may be charged. Credit cards should never leave the sight of the cardholder, in order to prevent the card's information from being copied for illegal use. It is advisable to pay close attention to credit card bills following a trip to the Dominican Republic.

TRAVELER'S CHECKS   Although there are ATMs at most banks in the D.R., and at other locations as well, some prudent travelers still carry traveler's checks for emergencies in case there is some malfunction with their ATM cards, which can happen anywhere in the world. Hotels, of course, accept traveler's checks as they would American dollars. You can buy traveler's checks at most banks. They are offered in denominations of $20, $50, $100, $500, and sometimes $1,000. Generally, you'll pay a service charge ranging from 1% to 4%.

The most popular traveler's checks are offered by **American Express** (© 800/807-6233 or 800/221-7282 for cardholders—this number accepts collect calls, offers service in several languages, and exempts Amex gold and platinum cardholders from the 1% fee), **Visa** (© 800/732-1322—AAA members can obtain Visa checks for a $9.95 fee, for checks up to $1,500, at most AAA offices or by calling © 866/339-3378), and **MasterCard** (© 800/223-9920).

Be sure to keep a record of the traveler's checks' serial numbers separate from your checks in the event that they are stolen or lost. You'll get a refund faster if you know the numbers.

American Express, Thomas Cook, Visa, and **MasterCard** offer **foreign currency traveler's checks,** useful if you're traveling to one country or to the Euro zone; they're accepted at locations where dollar checks may not be.

Another option is the new prepaid traveler's check cards, reloadable cards that work much like debit cards but aren't linked to your checking account. The **American Express Travelers Cheque Card,** for example, requires a minimum deposit, sets a maximum balance, and has a one-time issuance fee of $14.95. You can withdraw money from an ATM (for a fee of $2.50 per transaction, not including bank fees), and the funds can be purchased in dollars, euros, or pounds. If you lose the card, your available funds will be refunded within 24 hours.

ATMs   ATMs are linked to a huge network that, most likely, includes your bank at home. **Cirrus** (© 800/424-7787; www.mastercard.com) and **PLUS** (© 800/843-7587; www.visa.com) are the two most popular networks. Most islands have ATMs, though they may be hard to find outside the main towns.

Be sure to check the daily withdrawal limit before you depart, and ask whether you need a new personal identification number (PIN). *Warning:* The use of ATMs should be minimized as a means of avoiding theft or misuse. One local ATM fraud involves sticking photographic film or pieces of paper in the card feeder of the ATM so that an inserted card becomes jammed. Once the card owner has concluded that the card is irretrievable, the thieves extract both the jamming material and the card, which they then use illegally.

CASH It's always a good idea to carry around some cash for small expenses, like cab rides, or for that rare occasion when a restaurant or small shop doesn't take plastic, which can happen if you're dining at a neighborhood joint or buying from a small vendor. U.S. dollars are accepted everywhere. Perhaps $100 in cash (small bills) will see you through.

7 Travel Insurance

The cost of travel insurance varies widely, depending on the destination, the cost and length of your trip, your age and health, and the type of trip you're taking, but expect to pay between 5% and 8% of the vacation itself. You can get estimates from various providers through **InsureMyTrip.com.** Enter your trip cost and dates, your age, and other information, for prices from more than a dozen companies.

U.K. citizens and their families who make more than one trip abroad per year may find an annual travel insurance policy works out cheaper. Check **www.moneysupermarket.com**, which compares prices across a wide range of providers for single- and multi-trip policies.

Most big travel agents offer their own insurance and will probably try to sell you their package when you book a holiday. Think before you sign. **Britain's Consumers' Association** recommends that you insist on seeing the policy and reading the fine print before buying travel insurance. **The Association of British Insurers** (© 020/7600-3333; www.abi.org.uk) gives advice by phone and publishes *Holiday Insurance,* a free guide to policy provisions and prices. You might also shop around for better deals: Try **Columbus Direct** (© 0870/033-9988; www.columbusdirect.net).

TRIP-CANCELLATION INSURANCE

Trip-cancellation insurance will help retrieve your money if you have to back out of a trip or depart early, or if your travel supplier goes bankrupt. Trip cancellation traditionally covers such events as sickness, natural disasters, and State Department advisories. The latest news in trip-cancellation insurance is the availability of **expanded hurricane coverage** and the **"any-reason"** cancellation coverage—which costs more but covers cancellations made for any reason. You won't get back 100% of your prepaid trip cost, but you'll be refunded a substantial portion. **TravelSafe** (© **888/885-7233;** www.travel safe.com) offers both types of coverage. Expedia also offers any-reason cancellation coverage for its air-hotel packages.

For details, contact one of the following recommended insurers: **Access America** (© 800/729-6021; www.accessamerica.com), **AIG Travel Guard** (© 800/826-4919; www.travelguard.com), **Travel Insured International** (© 800/243-3174; www.travelinsured. com), and **Travelex Insurance Services** (© 800/228-9792; www.travelex-insurance.com).

MEDICAL INSURANCE   Most health insurance policies cover you if you get sick away from home—but check, particularly if you're insured by an HMO. With the exception of certain HMOs and Medicare/Medicaid, your medical insurance should cover medical treatment—even hospital care—overseas. However, most out-of-country hospitals make you pay your bills upfront, and send you a refund after you've returned home and filed the necessary paperwork. And, in a worst-case scenario, there's the high cost of emergency evacuation. If you require additional medical insurance, try **MEDEX Assistance** (© **800/732-5309;** www.medexassist.com) or **Travel Assistance International** (© **800/821-2828;** www.travel assistance.com; for general information on services, call the company's Worldwide Assistance Services, Inc., at © **800/777-8710;** www.worldwideassistance.com). **Canadians** should check with their provincial health plan offices or call **Health Canada** (© **866/ 225-0709;** www.hc-sc.gc.ca) to find out the extent of their coverage and what documentation and receipts they must take home in case they are treated overseas.

LOST-LUGGAGE INSURANCE   On international flights (including U.S. portions of international trips), baggage coverage is limited to approximately $9.07 per pound, up to approximately $635 per checked bag. If you plan to check items more valuable than what's covered by the standard liability, see if your homeowner's policy covers your valuables, or get baggage insurance as part of your comprehensive travel-insurance package.

If your luggage is lost, immediately file a lost-luggage claim at the airport, detailing the luggage contents. Most airlines require that you report delayed, damaged, or lost baggage within 4 hours of arrival. The airlines are required to deliver luggage, once found, directly to your house or destination free of charge.

8 Health

STAYING HEALTHY

Other than an upset stomach or sunburn, most travelers to the D.R. don't experience difficulties with their health. However, before winging your way to the island, you should be aware of some health risks. Most visitors at some point come down with at least a mild case of diarrhea, the *número uno* illness for D.R. travelers.

Travelers to rural areas of the island, especially the provinces bordering Haiti, are at risk for malaria. There is little risk, however, if you stay in the major resort areas such as Playa Dorada or Punta Cana.

Another plague, schistosomiasis, is a parasitic infection found in fresh water in parts of the D.R. Don't go swimming in freshwater rivers. Hepatitis B is also commonplace in the D.R.

What to Do If You Get Sick Away from Home

Finding a good doctor in the Dominican Republic can be a problem once you leave Santo Domingo and the big resorts such as those at Playa Dorada or Punta Cana. You should be in fairly good health before venturing into the hinterlands. Most doctors, once you get one, have been educated in the United States and speak English.

If you suffer from a chronic illness, consult your doctor before your departure. For conditions such as epilepsy, diabetes, or heart problems, wear a **MedicAlert** identification tag (© 888/633-4298; www.medicalert.org), which will immediately alert doctors to your condition and give them access to your records through MedicAlert's 24-hour hot line.

Contact the **International Association for Medical Assistance to Travellers (IAMAT)** (© 716/754-4883, or 416/652-0137 in Canada; www.iamat.org) for tips on travel and health concerns in the countries you're visiting, and lists of local, English-speaking doctors. The United States **Centers for Disease Control and Prevention** (© 800/311-3435; www.cdc.gov) provides up-to-date information on health hazards by region or country and offers tips on food safety.

For information about local hospitals and clinics, refer to "Fast Facts" at the beginning of each chapter.

Warning: Malaria Alert

The Center for Disease Control currently posts a malaria warning for parts of the D.R., especially for the resort areas in Altagracia province. That's the southeastern part of the island country. It is recommended that all travelers to the area, including infants and children, begin taking antimalarial drugs before arriving on island. Chances are you, like thousands of other visitors, will be fine, but why chance it?

To find out about current U.S. Department of State travel warnings about the D.R. or the Caribbean in general, check http://travel.state.gov.

Travel Health Online (www.tripprep.com), sponsored by a consortium of travel medicine practitioners, may also offer helpful advice on traveling abroad. You can find listings of reliable medical clinics overseas at the **International Society of Travel Medicine** (www.istm.org).

9 Safety

STAYING SAFE

Foreigners should review their security practices and maintain a low profile. Protests, demonstrations, and general strikes occur periodically. These disturbances have the potential to turn violent, with participants rioting and erecting roadblocks. In the past, police have used deadly force in response to violent protests. Although these events are not targeted at foreigners, it is advisable to exercise caution when traveling throughout the country. In urban areas, travel should be conducted on main routes whenever possible. Street crowds should be avoided. Additional advice about strikes and other security issues in the Dominican Republic may be obtained from the U.S. Embassy in Santo Domingo or by visiting the embassy's website at **http://santodomingo.usembassy.gov**.

Petty street crime involving tourists does occur, and normal precautions should be taken. Visitors walking the streets should always be aware of their surroundings to avoid becoming victims of crime. Valuables left unattended in parked automobiles, on beaches, and in other public places are vulnerable to theft. Cellular telephones should be carried in a pocket, rather than on a belt or in a purse. One increasingly common method of street robbery is for a person or persons on a moped (often coasting with the engine turned off so as not to draw attention) to approach a pedestrian, grab the cell phone, purse, or backpack, and then speed away.

Traveling with Minors

It's always wise to have plenty of documentation when traveling with children in today's world. For changing details on entry requirements for children traveling abroad, keep up-to-date by going to the U.S. Department of State website: http://travel.state.gov. To prevent international child abduction, EU governments have initiated procedures at entry and exit points. These often (but not always) include requiring documentary evidence of relationship and permission for the child's travel from the parent or legal guardian not present. Having such documentation on hand, even if not required, facilitates entries and exits. All children must have their own passport. To obtain a passport, the child *must* be present— *that is, in person*—at the center issuing the passport. Both parents must be present as well. If not, then a notarized statement from the parents is required. Any questions parents or guardians might have can be answered by calling the **National Passport Information Center** at ℂ **877/487-2778** Monday to Friday 8am to 8pm Eastern Standard Time.

Passengers in private taxis (known locally as *carros públicos*) are frequently the victims of robbery. In some instances, the taxi drivers themselves have been known to rob riders. We know at least one American passenger on a *motoconcho* (motorcycle taxi) has been robbed by the driver. Sometimes crooked taxi drivers will turn down a dangerous street where a robber will jump into the car and steal a victim's wallet or purse. The taxi driver himself might have set up the robbery in advance, perhaps with, say, his brother-in-law. Visitors to the Dominican Republic are strongly advised to take only hotel taxis or taxis operated by services whose cabs are ordered in advance by phone and can subsequently be identified and tracked.

The overall level of crime tends to rise during the Christmas season, and visitors to the Dominican Republic should take extra precautions when visiting the country between November and January.

10 Specialized Travel Resources

FOR TRAVELERS WITH DISABILITIES

The Dominican Republic has done little to open up exploration of their island by persons with disabilities. Getting around the country with its potholed roads is hard enough on a healthy visitor with perfect mobility. A pole-vaulter might find it difficult walking in traffic in Santo Domingo. Your best bet is to work through a travel agent to find a resort hotel suitable for a visit by persons with disabilities. Suitable rooms and grounds are more likely to be found at Playa Dorada or Punta Cana than elsewhere.

Even so, a disability shouldn't stop anyone from traveling. There are more resources out there today than ever before.

Organizations that offer a vast range of resources and assistance to disabled travelers include **MossRehab** (✆ 800/CALL-MOSS; www.mossresourcenet.org), the **American Foundation for the Blind (AFB)** (✆ 800/232-5463 or 212/502-7600; www.afb.org), and **SATH** (Society for Accessible Travel & Hospitality) (✆ 212/447-7284; www.sath.org). **AirAmbulanceCard.com** is now partnered with SATH and allows you to preselect top-notch hospitals in case of an emergency.

Access-Able Travel Source (✆ 303/232-2979; www.access-able.com) offers a comprehensive database on travel agents from around the world with experience in accessible travel; destination-specific access information; and links to such resources as service animals, equipment rentals, and access guides.

Many travel agencies offer customized tours and itineraries for travelers with disabilities. Among them are **Flying Wheels Travel** (✆ 507/451-5005; www.flyingwheelstravel.com) and **Accessible Journeys** (✆ 800/846-4537 or 610/521-0339; www.disabilitytravel.com).

Flying with Disability (www.flying-with-disability.org) is a comprehensive information source on airplane travel. **Avis Rent a Car** (✆ 888/879-4273) has an "Avis Access" program that offers services for customers with special travel needs. These include specially outfitted vehicles with swivel seats, spinner knobs, and hand controls; mobility scooter rentals; and accessible bus service. Be sure to reserve well in advance.

Also check out the quarterly magazine *Emerging Horizons* (www.emerginghorizons.com), available by subscription ($16.95 a year within U.S.; $21.95 outside U.S).

The "Accessible Travel" link at **Mobility-Advisor.com** offers a variety of travel resources to disabled persons.

British travelers should contact **Holiday Care** (✆ 0845-124-9971 in U.K. only; www.holidaycare.org.uk) to access a wide range of travel information and resources for disabled and elderly people.

GAY & LESBIAN TRAVELERS

Although homosexuality is not technically legal in the D.R., a staunchly Catholic country, it is more prevalent in the D.R. than anywhere else in the Caribbean, with the possible exception of Cuba, where many young men and women have turned to prostitution, especially in Havana. Hundreds of men are bisexual in the D.R., and many of the younger, handsomer ones are available on a "gay-for-pay" basis, even though they may have a wife and children waiting for them at home. Sex tourism, even that involving minors, is on the rise in the D.R. and has even made headlines in the *New York Times.*

There isn't much of a gay bar scene outside of Santo Domingo, but cruising is evident everywhere, especially in the regular bars, on the beaches, and along the various *malecón* (seafront) promenades at night.

Nearly all D.R. hotels welcome gay and lesbian clients. Same-sex couples seeking to share a room together should encounter no problem anywhere in the D.R. Discretion, however, is the word. Holding hands or kissing in public will be frowned upon and may invite at least verbal abuse, and dozens of cases of gay bashing are reported yearly.

The **International Gay and Lesbian Travel Association (IGLTA)** (© **800/448-8550** or 954/776-2626; www.iglta.org) is the trade association for the gay and lesbian travel industry and offers an online directory of gay- and lesbian-friendly travel businesses; go to their website and click on "Members."

Many agencies offer tours and travel itineraries specifically for gay and lesbian travelers. **Above and Beyond Tours** (© **800/397-2681;** www.abovebeyondtours.com) are gay Australian tour specialists. San Francisco–based **Now, Voyager** (© **800/255-6951;** www.nowvoyager. com) offers worldwide trips and cruises, and **Olivia Cruises & Resorts** (© **800/631-6277;** www.olivia.com) offers lesbian cruises and resort vacations.

Gay.com Travel (© **415/644-8044;** www.gay.com/travel or www.outandabout.com) is an excellent online successor to the popular *Out&About* print magazine. It provides regularly updated information about gay-owned, gay-oriented, and gay-friendly lodging, dining, sightseeing, nightlife, and shopping establishments in every important destination worldwide. British travelers should click on the "Travel" link at **www.uk.gay.com** for advice and gay-friendly trip ideas.

The Canadian website **GayTraveler** offers ideas and advice for gay travel all over the world.

The following travel guides are available at many bookstores, or you can order them from any online bookseller: ***Spartacus International Gay Guide, 35th Edition*** (Bruno Gmünder Verlag; www.spartacusworld.com/gayguide) and ***Odysseus: The International Gay Travel Planner, 17th Edition*** (www.odyusa.com); and the ***Damron*** guides (www.damron.com), with separate, annual books for gay men and lesbians.

FOR SENIORS

Since most of their needs are taken care of in the all-inclusive resorts, seniors form a large part of the patronage at the resorts of Punta Cana and Playa Dorada. Casa de Campo at La Romana is one of the most preferred destinations in the Caribbean for the senior traveler.

One of the benefits of age is that travel often costs less. Don't be shy about asking for discounts, but always carry some kind of ID, such as a driver's license, if you've kept your youthful glow. Also, mention the fact that you're a senior citizen when you first make your travel reservations.

Members of **AARP,** 601 E St. NW, Washington, DC 20049 (*©* **888/687-2277;** www.aarp.org), get discounts on hotels, airfares, and car rentals, plus *AARP The Magazine* and a monthly newsletter.

11 Sustainable Tourism/Ecotourism

Each time you take a flight or drive a car CO_2 is released into the atmosphere. You can help neutralize this danger to our planet through "carbon offsetting"—paying someone to reduce your CO_2 emissions by the same amount you've added. Carbon offsets can be purchased in the U.S. from companies such as **Carbonfund.org** and **TerraPass** (www.terrapass.org), and from **Climate Care** (www.climatecare.org) in the U.K.

Responsible Travel (www.responsibletravel.com) contains a great source of sustainable travel ideas run by a spokesperson for responsible tourism in the travel industry. For the D.R., this is centered around Punta Cana where eco-tours are conducted to a waterfall and a cave. You can also go on a kayak trip on the River Chavón or else tour the rural landscape between El Seybo and Higüey. Whale-watching, deep-sea fishing, and horseback riding are also available. **Sustainable Travel International** (www.sustainabletravelinternational.org) promotes responsible tourism practices and issues an annual Green Gear & Gift Guide.

You can find eco-friendly travel tips, statistics, and touring companies and associations—listed by destination under "Travel Choice"—at **The International Ecotourism Society (TIES)** website, www.ecotourism.org. Also check out **Conservation International** (www.conservation.org)—which, with *National Geographic Traveler,* annually presents **World Legacy Awards** (www.wl award.org) to those travel tour operators, businesses, organizations, and places that have made a significant contribution to sustainable tourism. **Ecotravel.com** is part online magazine and part eco-directory that lets you search for touring companies in several categories (water-based, land-based, spiritually oriented, and so on).

In the U.K., **Tourism Concern** (www.tourismconcern.org.uk) works to reduce social and environmental problems connected to tourism and find ways of improving tourism so that local benefits are increased.

The **Association of British Travel Agents (ABTA)** (www.abta. org) acts as a focal point for the U.K. travel industry and is one of the leading groups spearheading responsible tourism.

The **Association of Independent Tour Operators (AITO)** (www.aito.co.uk) is a group of interesting specialist operators leading the field in making holidays sustainable.

For information about the ethics of swimming with dolphins and other outdoor activities, visit the **Whale and Dolphin Conservation Society** (www.wdcs.org) and **Tread Lightly!** (www.tread lightly.org).

The organizations listed above offer general information about ecotourism. For more specific adventures in the D.R., several outfitters can hook you up with eco- and adventure activities. The major local activities include mountain biking, surfing, whale watching, white-water rafting, bird-watching, canyoning, hiking, horseback riding, kayaking, jeep safaris, island exploring, and rock climbing. For a general preview of these activities, refer to www.godominicanrepublic.com.

One of the best eco-tour operators is **GreenGO!** (www.alt greengo.com) where bookings are made on land.

Tody Tours (www.todytours.com) is operated by Kate Wallace, who arrived in the D.R. in 1994 as a Peace Corps volunteer and loved the country so much she stuck around. She guides visitors on bird-watching tours and tailors jaunts to the needs of individual clients. Contact her at Calle Jose Gabriel Garcia 105, Zona Colonial, in Santo Domingo (© **809/686-0882**).

12 Getting Around the Dominican Republic

Getting around the Dominican Republic is not always easy if your hotel is in a remote location. The most convenient modes of transport are shuttle flights, taxis, rental cars, *públicos* (multi-passenger taxis), and *guaguas* (public buses).

BY PLANE   The quickest and easiest way to get across a difficult landscape is on one of the shuttle flights offered by **Air Century** (© **809/826-4222;** www.aircentury.com), flying from Santo Domingo to Puerto Plata, Punta Cana, La Romana, Samaná, and Santiago, among other towns. The only catch is that flights are not regularly scheduled, but depend on demand. The airline operates 24 hours a day, 7 days a week.

BY RENTAL CAR   The best way to see the Dominican Republic is to drive. *Motorists drive on the right here.* Although major highways are relatively smooth, the country's secondary roads, especially those in the east, are riddled with potholes and ruts. Roads also tend to be badly lit and poorly marked in both the city and the countryside. Drive carefully and give yourself plenty of time when traveling between island destinations. Watch out for policemen who may flag you down and accuse you (often wrongly) of some infraction. Many locals give these low-paid policemen a RD$100 (US$3.05/£1.55) *regalo,* or gift "for your children," and are then free to go.

The high accident and theft rate in recent years has helped to raise car-rental rates here. Prices vary, so call around for last-minute quotes. Make sure you understand your insurance coverage (or lack thereof) before you leave home. Your credit card issuer may already provide you with this type of insurance; call to find out.

For reservations and more information, call the rental companies at least a week before your departure: **Avis** (© **800/331-1084** in the U.S., or 809/535-7191; www.avis.com), **Budget** (© **800/472-3325** in the U.S., or 809/549-0351; www.budget.com), and **Hertz** (© **800/654-3001** in the U.S., or 809/549-0454; www.hertz.com) all operate in the Dominican Republic. All three have offices at the Santo Domingo and Puerto Plata airports, as well as in downtown Santo Domingo. Avis and Hertz also have offices in La Romana and Santiago, and Avis has one in Punta Cana.

Although the cars may not be as well maintained as those of the big three above, you can often get a cheaper deal at one of the local firms, notably **MCAUTO Rental Cars** (© **809/688-6518**). If you want a car with seat belts, you must ask. Your Canadian or American driver's license is suitable documentation, along with a valid credit card or a substantial cash deposit.

BY PUBLIC TRANSPORTATION   *Públicos* are unmetered multi-passenger taxis that travel along main thoroughfares, stopping often to pick up people waving from the side of the street. A *público* is marked by a white seal on the front door. You must tell the driver your destination when you're picked up to make sure the *público* is going there. A ride is usually RD$6 (US20¢/10p).

Public buses, often in the form of minivans or panel trucks, are called *guaguas* (pronounced "*gwa*-gwas"). For about the same price, they provide the same service as *públicos,* but they're generally more crowded. Larger buses provide service outside the towns. Beware of pickpockets onboard.

Warning: Don't get into an unmarked street taxi. Many visitors, particularly in Santo Domingo, have been assaulted and robbed by doing just that. The minimum fare within Santo Domingo is RD$95 (US$2.90/£1.45). In Santo Domingo, the most reliable taxi company is **Tecni-Taxi** (© **809/567-2010**). In Puerto Plata, call **Tecni-Taxi** at © **809/320-7621.**

13 Package Deals

For value-conscious travelers, packages are the smart way to go because they can save you a ton of money. Especially in the Dominican Republic, package tours are *not* the same thing as escorted tours. You'll be on your own, but in most cases, a package will include airfare, hotel, and transportation to and from the airport—and it may cost you less than just the hotel alone if you booked it yourself. A package deal might not be for you if you want to stay in a more intimate inn or guesthouse, but if you like resorts, read on.

You'll find an amazing array of packages. Some packages offer a better class of hotels than others. Some offer the same hotels for lower prices. Some offer flights on scheduled airlines, and others book charters.

Before booking a charter flight, be aware of the downside. These flights are less frequent than the major airlines and may be cancelled at the last minute for some reason. Refunds are much harder to acquire should the need arise. Expect off-hour departure times. Once you arrive at your destination, baggage claim is often a much slower process. Some charter outfitters have also gone bankrupt, leaving passengers stranded at a destination. Remember to comparison-shop among at least three different operators, and always compare apples to apples.

Most land-and-air packages include meals, and you'll find yourself locked into your hotel dining room every night if your meals are prepaid. Most of the all-inclusives in the D.R. break this monotony by offering a series of different restaurants, ranging from Italian to Chinese, under one roof.

Incidentally, the all-inclusives are among the most upmarket properties on the island. Almost without exception, they tend to be first-class or in a few cases even deluxe. Unless your hotel is run by a recognizable chain, such as Meliá, you can never be sure exactly who owns the resort at which you are staying. It is rumored that drug money in some cases has fueled some of the massive hotel development in the D.R.

If you're seeking a more varied dining experience, avoid, if you can, **AP (American Plan),** which means full board, and opt for **MAP (Modified American Plan),** meaning breakfast and either lunch or dinner. That way, you'll at least be free for one main meal of the day and can sample a variety of the island's regional fare. However, this is often difficult to arrange since most of the major resort hotels in the D.R. book guests on the all-inclusive plan that includes lunch. At certain key times of the year, especially over the long Christmas and New Year's season, AP may be mandatory.

The best place to start your search is the travel section of your local Sunday newspaper. Also check the ads in national travel magazines like *Arthur Frommer's Budget Travel, National Geographic Traveler,* and *Travel Holiday.*

Liberty Travel (© **888/271-1584;** www.libertytravel.com) is one of the biggest packagers in the Northeast, and it usually boasts a full-page ad in Sunday papers.

Another good resource is the airlines themselves, which often package their flights together with accommodations; another good choice is **American Express Travel** (© **800/335-3342;** www. americanexpress.com). Among the airline packagers, your options include **American Airlines Vacations** (© **800/321-2121;** www. aavacations.com) and **US Airways Vacations** (© **800/455-0123;** www.usairwaysvacations.com). American usually has the widest variety of offerings because it's the major carrier to the region.

The biggest hotel chains and resorts also offer package deals. If you already know where you want to stay, call the resort itself and ask if it offers land/air packages.

To save time comparing the prices and value of all the package tours out there, contact **TourScan, Inc.** (© 800/962-2080; www. tourscan.com). Every season, the company computerizes the contents of travel brochures that contain about 10,000 different vacations at 1,600 hotels in the Caribbean, including the Dominican Republic. TourScan selects the best-value vacation at each hotel and condo. Two catalogs are printed each year, which list a choice of hotels.

Just-A-Vacation, Inc. (© 301/559-0510; www.justavacation. com), also specializes in good deals for resorts.

Some of the leading North American tour operators still featuring tours include **GWV Vacations** (© 800/CALL-GWV; www.gwv vacations.com), focusing on package vacations from Boston to Puerto Plata, Punta Cana, Santo Domingo, and La Romana. This is your best bet if you live in New England.

Those wanting more than the usual hotel-and-airfare deal can book a number of adventure tours. The best of these are offered by **Iguana Mama** (© 800/849-4720 or 809/571-0734; www.iguana mama.com), featuring mountain biking, hiking, canyoning, mule treks, and cultural tours.

FAST FACTS: Dominican Republic

Business Hours Most shops and businesses are open Monday to Friday from 8am to 4pm. Those serving the tourist industry are also open on Saturday. Government offices are open Monday to Friday from 7:30am to 2:30pm—that is, officially. In reality, you shouldn't bother showing up until after 9am. Most banks are open Monday to Friday, 8am to 4pm.

Currency See "Money," earlier in this chapter.

Customs Just before you leave home, check with your country's Customs or Foreign Affairs department for the latest guidelines—including information on items that are not allowed to be brought into your home country, since the rules are subject to change and often contain some surprising oddities.

Customs allows you to bring in 1 liter of alcohol, plus 200 cigarettes and gift articles not exceeding a value of RD$2,800 (US$85/£43). Anything over that limit is subject to import taxes.

Returning **U.S. citizens** who have been away for at least 48 hours are allowed to bring back, once every 30 days, US$800 worth of merchandise duty-free. You'll be charged a flat rate of 4% duty on the next US$1,000 worth of purchases. Be sure to have your receipts handy. On mailed gifts, the duty-free limit is US$200. With some exceptions, you cannot bring fresh fruits and vegetables into the United States. For specifics on what you can bring back, download the invaluable free pamphlet *Know Before You Go* online at **www.cbp.gov**. (Click on "Travel," then "Know Before You Go Online Brochure.") Or contact the **U.S. Customs & Border Protection (CBP),** 1300 Pennsylvania Ave. NW, Washington, DC 20229 (© **202/354-1000**) and request the pamphlet.

For a clear summary of **Canadian** rules, write for the booklet *I Declare,* issued by the **Canada Border Services Agency** (© **800/461-9999** in Canada, or 204/983-3500; www.cbsa-asfc.gc.ca). Canada allows its citizens a C$750 exemption, and you're allowed to bring back duty-free one carton of cigarettes, one can of tobacco, 40 imperial ounces of liquor, and 50 cigars. In addition, each day you're allowed to mail gifts to Canada valued at less than C$60, provided they're unsolicited and don't contain alcohol or tobacco (write on the package "Unsolicited gift, under $60 value"). All valuables should be declared on the Y-38 form before departure from Canada, including serial numbers of valuables you already own, such as expensive foreign cameras. *Note:* The C$750 exemption can only be used once a year and only after an absence of 7 days.

U.K. citizens returning from **a non-EU country** have a Customs allowance of: 200 cigarettes; 50 cigars; 250 grams of smoking tobacco; 2 liters of still table wine; 1 liter of spirits or strong liqueurs (over 22% volume); 2 liters of fortified wine, sparkling wine, or other liqueurs; 60cc (ml) perfume; 250 cc (ml) toilet water; and £145 worth of all other goods, including gifts and souvenirs. People age 16 and under cannot have the tobacco or alcohol allowance. For more information, contact HM Revenue & Customs at © **0845/010-9000** (from outside the U.K., 02920/501-261), or consult their website at www.hmrc.gov.uk.

The duty-free allowance in **Australia** is A$900 or, for those under age 18, A$450. Citizens can bring in 250 cigarettes or 250 grams of loose tobacco, and 1.125 liters of alcohol. If you're returning with valuables you already own, such as for-eign-made cameras, you should file form B263. A helpful brochure available from Australian consulates or Customs offices is *Know Before You Go*. For more information, call the **Australian Customs Service** at ✆ **1300/363-263**, or log on to www.customs.gov.au.

The duty-free allowance for **New Zealand** is NZ$700. Citi-zens over age 17 can bring in 200 cigarettes, 50 cigars, or 250 grams of tobacco (or an assortment of all three if their com-bined weight doesn't exceed 250g); plus 4.5 liters of wine and beer, or 1.125 liters of liquor. New Zealand currency does not carry import or export restrictions. Fill out a certificate of export, listing the valuables you are taking out of the country; that way, you can bring them back without paying duty. Most questions are answered in a free pamphlet available at New Zealand consulates and Customs offices: *New Zealand Cus-toms Guide for Travellers, Notice no. 4*. For more information, contact **New Zealand Customs Service,** The Customhouse, 17–21 Whitmore St., Box 2218, Wellington (✆ **04/473-6099** or 0800/428-786; www.customs.govt.nz).

Documents   See "Entry Requirements" earlier in this chapter.

Electricity   The country generally uses 110-volt AC (60 cycles), so adapters and transformers are usually not necessary for American appliances.

Embassies   All embassies are in Santo Domingo, the capital. The **United States** embassy is on Calle Cesar Nicholas Penson at the corner of Leopold Navarro (✆ **809/221-2171**). The embassy of the **United Kingdom** is located at Hotel Santo Domingo, Suite 1108 (✆ **809/472-7111**). The embassy of **Canada** is found at Calle Capitán Eugenio de Marchena 39 (✆ **809/685-1136**).

Emergencies   Call ✆ **911**. See "Hospitals," below.

Hospitals   Medical care is limited, especially outside Santo Domingo, and the quality of care varies widely among facili-ties. There is an emergency 911 service within Santo Domingo, but its reliability is questionable. Outside the capital, emer-gency services range from extremely limited to nonexistent. Blood supplies at both public and private hospitals are often limited, and not all facilities have blood on hand, even for emergencies. Many medical facilities throughout the country do not have staff members who speak or understand English. A private nationwide ambulance service, **Movi-med,** operates in Santo Domingo, Santiago, Puerto Plata, and La Romana; its telephone number is © **809/532-0000** in Santo Domingo and © **1-200-0911** outside Santo Domingo. Movi-med expects full payment at the time of transport.

Internet Access More and more this hookup is available. See individual listings in the chapters.

Language The official language is Spanish; many people also speak some English.

Liquor Laws The official drinking age in the Dominican Republic is 18, but the law is not enforced very well.

Mail A disaster! It's recommended that you not rely on D.R. postal services unless absolutely necessary. It is estimated that the chance of your letter reaching its intended destination is about 50%. International courier services such as United Parcel Service, Federal Express, or DHL are the way to go.

Medical Facilities See "Hospitals," above.

Passports **For Residents of the United States:** Whether you're applying in person or by mail, you can download passport applications from the U.S. State Department website at **http://travel.state.gov**. For general information, call the **National Passport Agency** (© **877/487-2778**). To find your regional passport office, check the U.S. State Department website.

For Residents of Canada: Passport applications are available at travel agencies throughout Canada or from the central **Passport Office,** Department of Foreign Affairs and International Trade, Ottawa, ON K1A 0G3 (© **800/567-6868;** www.ppt.gc.ca).

For Residents of the United Kingdom: To pick up an application for a standard 10-year passport (5-year passport for children under age 16), visit your nearest passport office, major post office, or travel agency, or contact the **United Kingdom Passport Service** at © **0870/521-0410** or search its website at www.ukpa.gov.uk.

For Residents of Ireland: You can apply for a 10-year passport at the **Department of Foreign Affairs Passport Office,** Setanta Centre, Molesworth Street, Dublin 2 (© **01/671-1633;** www.irlgov.ie/iveagh). Those under age 18 and over 65 must apply for a €12 3-year passport. You can also apply at 1A South Mall, Cork (☎ **021/494-4700**), or at most main post offices.

For Residents of Australia: You can pick up an application from your local post office or any branch of Passports Australia, but you must schedule an interview at the passport office to present your application materials. Call the **Australian Passport Information Service** at ☎ **131-232,** or visit the government website at www.passports.gov.au.

For Residents of New Zealand: You can pick up a passport application at any New Zealand Passports Office or download it from their website. Contact the **New Zealand Passports Office** at ☎ **0800/225-050** in New Zealand or 04/474-8100, or log on to www.passports.govt.nz.

Pharmacies Refer to the local listings in the individual chapters. If you're on medication, it's best to bring an adequate supply with you. Don't always count on the local pharmacy being able to fill your prescription.

Safety Refer to the section on "Staying Safe," earlier in this chapter.

Taxes A departure tax of US$10 is assessed and must be paid in U.S. currency. The government imposes a 13% tax on hotel rooms, which is usually topped by an automatic 10% service charge, bringing the total tax to staggering heights. A 12% sales tax on food and drink is assessed.

Telephone The Dominican Republic area code is **809.** Place calls to or from the Dominican Republic as you would from any area code in North America. You can access **AT&T Direct** by dialing ☎ **800/222-0300.** You can reach **MCI** at ☎ **800/888-8000** and **Sprint** at ☎ **800/877-7746.**

Television & Radio More than seven local TV networks, all Spanish-speaking, blanket the island. But most of the English-speaking TV stations in Miami are picked up as well. It's estimated that about 50% of the island's television sets can also tap into satellite programming or cable. Some 150 radio stations feature mostly merengue, bachata, and the nation's national pastime: baseball.

Time Atlantic Standard Time is observed year-round. Between November and March, when it's noon in New York and Miami, it's 1pm in Santo Domingo. However, during U.S. daylight saving time, it's the same time in the Dominican Republic and the U.S. East Coast.

Tipping Most restaurants and hotels add a 10% service charge to your check. Most people usually add 5% to 10% more, especially if the service has been good.

Water Stick to bottled water.

Weather The average temperature is 77°F (25°C). August is the warmest month and January the coolest month, although, even then, it's warm enough to swim.

3

Settling into Santo Domingo

Bartolomé Columbus, brother of Christopher, founded the city of New Isabella (later renamed Santo Domingo) on the southeastern Caribbean coast in 1496. It's the oldest city in the New World and the capital of the Dominican Republic. Santo Domingo has had a long, sometimes glorious, more often sad, history. At the peak of its power, Diego de Velázquez sailed from here to settle Cuba, Ponce de León went forth to conquer and settle Puerto Rico and Florida, and Cortés set out for Mexico. The city today still reflects its long history—French, Haitian, and especially Spanish.

Santo Domingo is one of the Caribbean's most vibrant cities, with a 12-block Colonial Zone to rival that of Old San Juan in Puerto Rico. Come here to walk in the footsteps of Cortés, Ponce de León, and, of course, Columbus himself. Allow at least a day to capture some of the highlights of the old city, such as its Alcázar (a palace built for Columbus's son, Diego).

Santo Domingo is also one of the grand shopping bazaars of the Caribbean, with such "hot" items as hand-wrapped cigars for sale virtually everywhere, along with local handicrafts. Jewelry made of larimar or amber is also much sought after. From gambling to merengue, Santo Domingo is also one of the liveliest cities in the Caribbean after dark. Be careful, however. Most of the Dominican Republic's crime is concentrated in Santo Domingo. Keep valuables in your hotel safe, carry a minimum of cash with you, don't wear flashy jewelry, and, if in doubt, take a cab.

1 Orientation

ARRIVING

Most flights arrive at **Aeropuerto Internacional Las Américas** (© **809/947-2225**), lying 13km (8 miles) east of the city center. This is not a good introduction to the Dominican Republic. Customs officials are often hostile, and retrieval of suitcases from the luggage carousels is cramped, neurosis-inducing, and, if you trip over any of the wheeled carts that passengers push up to the edge of the carousels, fraught with hazards. Once you've survived them, you have to face an array of hustlers waiting to steal your money, grab your luggage (and disappear with it), or else hawk dubious deals on everything from hotel rooms, gypsy cabs, or cheap car rentals. Not only that, but if you're a single man traveling alone, you might be offered a woman for the duration of your trip. If you express no interest, a boy might be offered instead.

Expect a lot of hassle and aggression. It's better to have everything reserved in advance, including your hotel and your car rental, before you face these touts trying to separate you from your money.

At the exit to the baggage reclaim area, you'll see a branch of **Banco de Reservas,** where you can change your currency into Dominican pesos. And once you exit from the security-controlled area inside the terminal, you'll find a handful of ATMs dispensing Dominican pesos. *Note:* Although virtually everyone in the D.R. accepts U.S. dollars as payment for virtually anything, it's hard to actually lay your hands on dollars once you're inside the country. We tend to bring two or three hundred dollars in U.S. cash into the country, safely tucked away, for tips and for the purchase of handicrafts—just because it's easier than calculating everything in pesos and because locals seem to genuinely appreciate the receipt of U.S. dollars.

If you don't rent a car, you'll need to take a taxi. Count on at least 45 minutes to an hour to get from the airport into the center of town. The local taxi union is powerful enough to prevent bus service from operating here. Taxis, available 24 hours, cost about US$35 (£18) for one-way transits for up to four passengers and their luggage into town. Always negotiate and agree on the fare before getting in.

If you're flying into the capital from somewhere else within the Dominican Republic, perhaps Puerto Plata or La Romana, chances are your plane will land at the smaller **Aeropuerto Isabela (© 809/ 947-2297)** in the city's northern suburb of Higüero. A taxi from there to any point within the center of Santo Domingo costs around US$30 (£16). Always negotiate and agree upon the fare before getting in, and be aware that if your hotel is on or near the Malecón, the traffic, especially during rush hour (usually 4:30–6:30pm) is likely to be horrendous.

Motorists who arrive from one of the popular resorts will find it easy to access the central city. If you're coming from the north on Autopista Duarte, the highway becomes Avenida Kennedy at Luperón, which will take you into the heart of Santo Domingo. If you're driving from a resort in the east, follow the signposts marked

CENTRO CIUDAD until you come to the Puente Duarte, a bridge over the Río Ozama. The road at this point becomes Avenida 27 de Febrero. Follow this road to the intersection with Calle 30 de Marzo, at which point you turn left and head for the Zona Colonial, or Colonial Zone.

Chances are you won't be arriving from elsewhere in the Dominican Republic by bus, although the major towns and cities of the D.R. maintain bus links with Santo Domingo. Buses let passengers off at the terminal at avenidas 27 de Febrero and Navarro (© 809/221-4422), at Av. Máximo Gómez 61 (© 809/221-4422), behind the Plaza Central, or at the terminal at Guarocuya 4 (© 809/544-4580), across the street from Centro Olímpico. Taxis are found at all bus terminals to take you to your hotel within the city itself.

VISITOR INFORMATION

A not-very-helpful staff mans the city's main tourist office at the **Secretaría de Estado de Turismo,** Edificios Gubernamentales, avenidas México and 30 de Marzo (© **809/221-4660;** fax 809/682-3806; www.dominicana.com.do). Hours are Monday to Friday 8:30am to 3pm. Much of the information dispensed here—such as it is—is hopelessly out-of-date.

MAPS

A good map of Santo Domingo is imperative for getting around, and vital if you plan to traverse the country by car. The best ones are published by **Mapas Triunfo, Av. Mexico 119, in Santo Domingo** (© **809/566-0959**). A map simply called *Dominican Republic* has a detailed street map of Santo Domingo and a good road map of the country. This map is sold all over the city in gift shops and bookstores and even at newspaper and magazine kiosks.

CITY LAYOUT

To get your bearings, you need to know that no one refers to the city's main artery as **Avenida George Washington.** This is a palm-lined boardwalk open to the sea. The *Guinness Book of World Records* calls it "The Planet's Largest Disco" because of all the clubs found here. Locals call it **El Malecón** (meaning sea wall), and it hugs the edge of the Caribbean for a total distance of 7.9km (5 miles). This is one of the dozen or so major boulevards of the city, and the most important one. Parading along this boulevard at night (beware of pickpockets) is the major nighttime activity of both locals and visitors.

Forget about street addresses. Presumably, buildings are assigned a number, but locals rarely use them. The way to find an address is to tie in a building you're seeking with either a landmark or else the major cross street.

Chances are your hotel will be along the Malecón. For sightseeing, however, most interest focuses on the **Zona Colonial (Colonial Zone),** the heart of the centuries-old city where Sir Francis Drake, and Columbus, once walked.

Running parallel to the Malecón, but inland from the Caribbean, is **Avenida Independencia.** This wide boulevard cuts through the Gazcue sector of town, coming to an end at **Parque Independencia** and its nearby Palacio Nacional, lying just west of Zona Colonial. Parque Independencia is "ground zero" for the denizens of Santo Domingo.

One of the city's most attractive districts is **Gazcue,** lying immediately to the west of Zona Colonial, south of the Avenida Bolivar, and north of the Malecón. This is an upper-middle-class neighborhood with tree-shaded sidewalks. It centers on Plaza de la Cultura, and includes a popular stretch of El Malecón within its boundaries. A number of museums are here, and chances are you'll be visiting the district.

Río Ozama separates the western or right bank of Santo Domingo from the left or eastern bank. Lying directly off the Avenida España, the two districts here are **Villa Duarte** and **Sans Souci,** with most interest focusing on the **Columbus Lighthouse,** which locals refer to as **El Faro Colón,** or **"El Faro."** This monumental and stately-looking lighthouse, whose floor plan was inspired by the form of a giant cross, towers over the western end of **Parque Mirador del Este,** a stretch of woodland spanning the length of the barrios east of the river.

The city's outer barrios won't concern the average visitor. These include **Villa Mella** to the north, a dreary sector of thatch huts and concrete structures which locals call home. Villa Mella is different from the rest of the districts in that most of its population was largely descended from slaves from the Congo, and some of the old Congolese culture still lives on in music, religion, and language. At press time for this edition, a new subway line was in the process of being built, a north-south line that, when completed in what's presently estimated as sometime in 2011 or 2012, will link the Villa Mella neighborhood with El Malecón.

A barrio of more interest to the average visitor is the wealthy, and in some cases, spectacularly wealthy, **Arroyo Hondo,** lying to the immediate northwest and the site of the much-visited **Jardín Botánico,** or botanical gardens. Close to the city's heart, the area gets a lot less upscale the more you travel northward. A short distance to the east of the botanical gardens lies the **Parque Zoológico (zoo).**

GETTING AROUND
BY PUBLIC TRANSPORTATION

From sunup to sundown, public buses serve Santo Domingo. The better-maintained and more orderly buses are those maintained by OMSA. They make stops only at clearly designated bus areas, they are air-conditioned and relatively comfortable, and they charge, for a ride between any two points within the city, RD$10 (US30¢/15p) per person. There's also a network of *guaguas,* privately owned, loosely monitored vans and minibuses which charge only RD$5 (US15¢/8p) per person for rides between loosely defined neighborhoods, almost always without the benefit of air-conditioning. To catch an OMSA bus, head for the nearest bus stop. To catch a *guaguas,* you'll have to stand beside the road and hail one down (as opposed to going to a more orderly and signposted bus stop).

BY TAXI

Taxis aren't metered, and determining the fare in advance (which you should do) may be difficult if you and your driver have a language problem. You can easily hail a taxi at the airport and at most major hotels. *Warning:* Don't get into an unmarked street taxi. Many visitors, particularly in Santo Domingo, have been assaulted and robbed by doing just that. The minimum fare within Santo Domingo is RD$100 (US$3.05/£1.55). In Santo Domingo, the most reliable taxi companies include **Tecni-Taxi** (© **809/567-2010**) and Apollo Taxi (© **809/537-0000**).

WALKING

This is virtually the only way to get around such districts as Zona Colonial, site of the major attractions. Do so during the day and avoid night walks, where you may be the victim of a mugging. Even during the day, you can expect to be hassled by hustlers calling themselves "guides" and offering tours. Many of them are hard to get rid of and will continue to follow you even if you turn down their services.

FAST FACTS: Santo Domingo

American Express The regional office is at Banco Dominicano del Progreso, Av. Kennedy 3 (📞 **809/563-3233**), open Monday to Friday 8:30am to 3pm and Saturday 9am to 1pm.

Currency Exchange All banks will exchange your currency and all maintain ATMs. Two of the most central and convenient are Banco BHD, Avenida 27 de Febrero (📞 **809/243-3232**), and Banco de Reservas, avenidas Duarte and Mella (📞 **809/960-2000**).

Internet Access Internet cafes aren't plentiful. The best and most convenient one is **The Chat Room,** Dr. César Dargan, Esq. 27 (📞 **809/412-7369**), open Monday to Friday 8:30am to 11pm, Saturday 9am to 6pm. The cost is RD$50 (US$1.50/75p) per hour, RD$30 (US90¢/45p) per half hour.

Mail Chances are if you use regular mail in the Dominican Republic, your cards and letters will arrive at their destination long after you've returned home. Many Dominican residents mailing money back to their homeland have their letters stolen and the money removed. If you must use the postal service (and we recommend that you don't), the main office— and the most convenient—is Instituto Postal Dominicano, Parque Colón, in the Zona Colonial (📞 **809/534-5838**), open Monday to Friday 8am to 5pm, Saturday 9am to noon. If you've got to ship something home, try the more reliable **Federal Express,** Avenida de los Proceres, corner of Camino del Oeste (📞 **809/565-3636**), open Monday to Friday 8:30am to 5:30pm and Saturday 8:30am to 12:30pm.

Medical Services The best hospital in Santo Domingo, and the one recommended by the U.S. Embassy, is **Clínica Abreu,** Calle Beller 42 (📞 **809/688-4411**). Most of its English-speaking doctors trained in the United States. It is always open.

Newspapers There are three major dailies. One of the most comprehensive listings of local events, cultural or otherwise, is found in *Hoy*'s "Revista" section. The same data also appears in *Listin Diario*'s "La Vida" section. The afternoon daily, *Ultima Hora,* also carries helpful listings, including movie schedules.

Pharmacies **Carol,** Ricart 24 (📞 **809/562-6767**), and **San Judas Tadeo,** Av. Independencia 57 (📞 **809/685-8165**) are open 24 hours.

Safety   Exercise extreme caution when walking around Santo Domingo at night, and keep your guard up during the day as well. Violent crime against tourists is not commonplace, but muggings are. Avoid the overcrowded barrios at all cost. They are some of the worst slums in the Caribbean, and crime is rampant. One of the worst sections is on the west bank of the Río Ozama just north of Puente Duarte, the bridge. Another section that's riddled with crime is on the east side of Avenida Máximo Gómez north of the Río Isabela. The safest zones are the Zona Colonial or the Malecón, even though these sections are rife with pickpockets and muggers.

Telephone   The area code for the Dominican Republic is **809**. You place calls to or from the Dominican Republic just as you would from any other area code in North America. You can access **AT&T Direct** by dialing ℂ **880/872-2881**. You can reach **MCI** at ℂ **800/999-9000** and **Sprint** at ℂ **800/751-7877**.

Travel Agencies   In addition to American Express (see above), there are a number of travel agencies which can handle your arrangements if you're venturing out of Santo Domingo and into the country. The best ones include **Colonial Tour & Travel**, Calle Arzobispo Meriño 209 (ℂ **809/688-5285**), open Monday to Friday 8:30am to 1:30pm and 2:30 to 5:30pm, Saturday 8:30am to 1:30pm. **Giada Tours & Travel**, inside Hostal Duque de Wellington, Av. Independencia 304 (ℂ **809/686-6994**), also gives good service. It's open Monday to Friday 9am to 5pm and Saturday 9am to noon.

2 Where to Stay

Most hotels in the city (unlike some of the beach resorts) accept only bookings on the European Plan (no meals) and, also unlike the resorts, charge the same rates year-round. If you want nightclubs, action, and lots of restaurant choices, do what most visitors do and stay in a hotel on or near the Malecón, opening onto the Caribbean. If you're a history buff interested mainly in sightseeing, stay in one of the historic old buildings in the Zona Colonial (Colonial Zone), a good area for sightseeing.

Because Santo Domingo can be dangerous at night, some security-conscious guests prefer to stay at one of the larger hotels that combines casino action, nightclubs, a choice of restaurants, and bars all under one roof. After a night of gambling, dining, drinking, or clubbing, all you have to do is take the elevator upstairs.

Note: Nearly all hotels in the Dominican Republic deal in U.S. dollars. Accordingly, our hotel listings reflect the U.S. price rates.

EXPENSIVE

Barceló Lina Hotel ⟨ℛ⟩   Rising nine boxy-looking stories within a traffic-clogged neighborhood in the heart of the capital, and painted in the loudest shade of persimmon-tangerine in the D.R., the Lina is a serviceable and functional but relatively unspectacular hotel that's favored by business travelers. All the units contain refrigerators, and at least a third overlook the Caribbean. Bedrooms are comfortable and many are quite spacious, but the decor is the standard motel style and overall, many could use a comprehensive renovation. The best rooms, on the eighth and ninth floors, have balconies. The tiled bathrooms have spacious marble vanities and shower/tub combinations.

Frankly, most of the fame and high marks generated by this hotel derive from its restaurant, the Lina Restaurant (see "Where to Dine," later in this chapter).

Avs. Máximo Gómez and 27 de Febrero, Santo Domingo, Dominican Republic. ⟨ℂ⟩ **800/942-2461** in the U.S., or 809/563-5000. Fax 809/686-5521. www.barcelolina. com. 217 units. US$95 (£50) double; US$125–US$165 (£66–£87) suite. Extra person US$34 (£18). Rates include breakfast. AE, DC, MC, V. **Amenities:** 2 restaurants; bar; casino; 2 pools; health club; Jacuzzi; sauna; 24-hr. room service; babysitting; laundry service; dry cleaning; snack bar. *In room:* A/C, TV, minibar, hair dryer, iron, safe.

Francés Sofitel ⟨ℛ⟩   A favorite small hotel in the old city, this intimate inn lies within a stone-fronted town house dating from the 16th century. Arches surround an Iberian-style fountain, and columns reach up to the second-floor patios, with palms and tropical plants surrounding the rooms. You'll think you've arrived in Seville. A gracefully winding stone staircase leads to the high-ceilinged and thick-walled bedrooms outfitted in a somber, rather dark colonial style. Accommodations are simple but tasteful, with rugs resting on tile floors; each has a somewhat cramped but tidily kept bathroom with shower and tub. An inn with only 19 rooms, and zealously protected from any architectural changes, it's the smallest Sofitel in the world.

Calle las Mercedes (corner of Calle Arzobispo Meriño), Santo Domingo, Dominican Republic. ⟨ℂ⟩ **809/685-9331.** Fax 809/685-1289. www.sofitel.com. 19 units. US$159 (£84) double. Rates include breakfast. AE, MC, V. **Amenities:** Restaurant; bar; room service; laundry service; dry cleaning. *In room:* A/C, TV, minibar, hair dryer, iron, safe.

Where to Stay in Santo Domingo

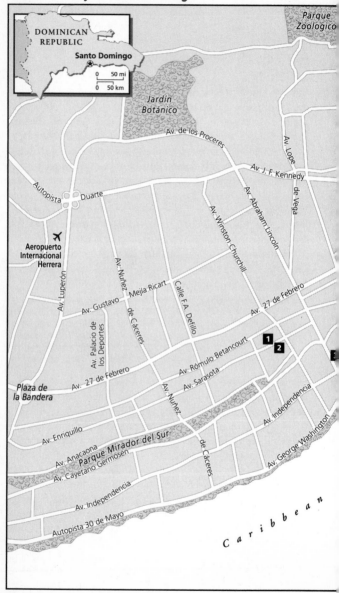

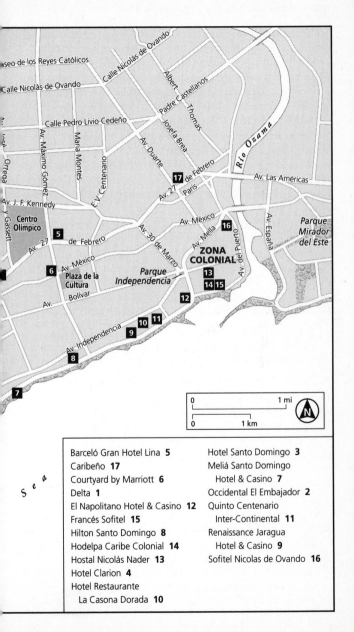

Barceló Gran Hotel Lina **5**
Caribeño **17**
Courtyard by Marriott **6**
Delta **1**
El Napolitano Hotel & Casino **12**
Francés Sofitel **15**
Hilton Santo Domingo **8**
Hodelpa Caribe Colonial **14**
Hostal Nicolás Nader **13**
Hotel Clarion **4**
Hotel Restaurante
  La Casona Dorada **10**

Hotel Santo Domingo **3**
Meliá Santo Domingo
  Hotel & Casino **7**
Occidental El Embajador **2**
Quinto Centenario
  Inter-Continental **11**
Renaissance Jaragua
  Hotel & Casino **9**
Sofitel Nicolás de Ovando **16**

Hilton Santo Domingo ✦✦✦ A soaring, artfully designed tower set directly on the seafront, this is the finest, tallest, and most desirable hotel in Santo Domingo. Its inauguration added the first new major hotel to the landscape of the nation's capital in 15 years, and its location at the corner of the pivotal Máximo Gómez filled what had until then been a gaping dark hole on a key building site in one of the town's showplace neighborhoods. It was configured as part of the Malecón Center, a waterside development that includes three separate towers for condominiums, a 21-story hotel, the newest casino in town, and a small but choice shopping mall. We prefer its ultra-comfortable rooms to any others in town. This hotel is not, and doesn't even try to be, a full-service resort, but if you want to play tennis or golf, the concierge can set it up for you. Rooms, which begin on the eighth floor and go upward from there, are richly furnished and plush, with excellent beds and in most cases, views that stretch far out to sea. Visitors since the inauguration of this hotel have included South African archbishop Desmond Tutu and actors Robert De Niro, Jaime Foxx, Colin Farrell, and Angelina and Brad.

Av. George Washington 500 at the NW corner of Av. Máximo Gómez, Malecón, Santo Domingo, Dominican Republic. © **809/685-0000** or 800/HILTONS. Fax 809/731-4143. www.hiltoncaribbean.com 228 units. US$115–US$215 (£61–£113) double; US$226–US$550 (£119–£289)suite. AE, DC, MC, V. **Amenities:** Restaurant; 2 bars; casino; outdoor swimming pool; room service; laundry service; dry cleaning; workout room. *In room:* A/C, TV, minibar, coffeemaker, iron, hair dryer, safe, Wi-Fi.

Hotel Santo Domingo ✦✦✦ Run by Premier Resorts & Hotels, the Hotel Santo Domingo is tastefully extravagant without having the glitzy overtones of the Jaragua (see below). Those seeking local character in a home-grown hotel should check in here. This waterfront hotel sits on 6 tropical hectares (15 acres), 15 minutes from the downtown area, in the La Feria district.

Oscar de la Renta helped design the interior. Most of the rooms have views of the sea, though some face the garden. Accommodations have bright floral carpets, tasteful Caribbean fabrics, and mirrored closets along with firm double beds. Bathrooms are tiled with tub/shower combos and adequate shelf space. The superior Excel Club rooms offer seaview balconies and other amenities. Excel guests also have access to a private lounge.

The restaurant's cuisine is among the finest hotel food in the capital.

Av. Independencia (at the corner of Av. Abraham Lincoln), Santo Domingo, Dominican Republic. © **800/877-3643** in the U.S., or 809/221-1511. Fax 809/535-0876. www.hotelsantodomingo.com.do. 215 units. Year-round US$140–US$170 (£74–£89) double; US$270 (£142) Excel Club double; US$410 (£216) executive suite. Rates include American breakfast. AE, MC, V. **Amenities:** Restaurant; 2 bars; Olympic-size outdoor pool; 3 lit tennis courts; gym; sauna; business center; salon; room service; babysitting; laundry service; dry cleaning. *In room:* A/C, TV, minibar, beverage maker, hair dryer, safe.

Meliá Santo Domingo ☞ Though still not in the same league as the Renaissance Jaragua, this hotel is much improved following extensive renovations, and now competes successfully for the upmarket traveler. The 12-story building is not very innovative, but is exceedingly comfortable and inviting. The location is about a 35-minute drive from the airport, about a 5-minute taxi ride from the city center, and 1.9km (1¼ miles) from the Colonial Zone. Accommodations range from midsize to spacious, each newly furnished in a tasteful and comfortable style. All the rooms have private marble bathrooms with a combination tub/shower, and most of the units offer a "lookout balcony" with a view of the Caribbean. The public areas include a terrace bar lit by street lamps, a lobby restaurant specializing in lunch and dinner buffets, and a contemporary grill attracting a more upmarket clientele. An evening crowd of patrons pours in for casino action, and there's live Dominican music coming from the bar.

Av. George Washington 365, Santo Domingo, Dominican Republic. ✆ 809/221-6666. Fax 809/687-8150. www.solmelia.com. 245 units. US$155–US$185 (£82–£97) double; US$255–US$305 (£134–£161) suite. Children 11 and under stay free in parent's room. AE, DC, DISC, MC, V. **Amenities:** 2 restaurants; bar; casino; pool; health club; sauna; 24-hr. room service; babysitting; laundry service; dry cleaning. *In room:* A/C, TV, minibar, coffeemaker, hair dryer, iron, safe.

Occidental El Embajador ☞☞ No hotel in Santo Domingo evokes the heyday of the dictator Trujillo in the 1950s more than this plush choice, which manages to rival, but not surpass, the amenities and services of the better Hilton Santo Domingo. Called "the Goat" because of his sexual excesses, Trujillo once maintained a luxury penthouse in this concrete-and-glass deluxe hotel built 15km (9⅓ miles) southwest of the city center. After several renovations, the seven-story structure is as fine today as it ever was.

The hotel is complete with a pool from the golden days of Hollywood and a landscaped drive-up entrance. All guest rooms have been gracefully renewed, with elegant fabrics and marble-lined bathrooms that feature tub/shower combos. For the most part, the rooms are among the most spacious in Santo Domingo, and many have walk-in closets, making living here exceedingly comfortable. Those seeking an ocean view won't be disappointed, as many of the rooms open onto balconies overlooking the sea.

Av. Sarasota 65, Santo Domingo, Dominican Republic. ✆ **809/221-2131.** Fax 809/532-5306. www.occidental-hoteles.com. 278 units. US$95–US$175 (£50–£92) double;

US$250–US$385 (£132–£203) suite. Children 3–11 US$25–US$40 (£13–£21); children 2 and under stay free in parent's room. AE, DC, DISC, MC, V. **Amenities:** 2 restaurants; bar; casino; outdoor pool; tennis court; health club; room service; babysitting; laundry service; dry cleaning. *In room:* A/C, TV, minibar, hair dryer, iron, safe, Wi-Fi.

Quinto Centenario InterContinental &

This hotel was inaugurated in 1992 to mark the 500th anniversary of the landing of Columbus. The hotel doesn't compare favorably with other Inter-Continentals around the world, and it doesn't fare well when compared to such deluxe establishments as the Hilton Santo Domingo. But nonetheless it offers a bright flash of big-city style on an otherwise rather undistinguished stretch of the sea-fronting Malecón. Yet there is much to recommend it, including its location bordering the water. The best public area is the rooftop restaurant opening onto dramatic nighttime vistas of Santo Domingo. The bedrooms are the hotel's best feature, decorated handsomely with Caribbean styling and comfortable, tasteful appointments. They range from midsize to spacious, and come with roomy private bathrooms with tub and shower.

Av. George Washington, NRO 218, Santo Domingo, Dominican Republic. © **809/221-0000.** Fax 809/221-2020. www.ichotelsgroup.com. 196 units. US$115–US$175 (£61–£92) double; US$159–US$229 (£84–£121) triple; US$249 (£131) suite. Children 12 and under stay free in parent's room. AE, DC, DISC, MC, V. **Amenities:** 2 restaurants; 2 bars; outdoor pool; health club; sauna; room service; babysitting; laundry service; dry cleaning; nonsmoking rooms. *In room:* A/C, TV, minibar, coffeemaker, hair dryer, iron, safe.

Renaissance Jaragua Hotel & Casino &&

A Las Vegas–style palace, this 10-story hotel lies on the 6-hectare (15-acre) site of the old Jaragua (Ha-*ra*-gwa) Hotel, which was popular in Trujillo's day. Open since 1988, it's a splashy, pink-colored waterfront palace that doesn't have the dignity and class of the Hotel Santo Domingo. For example, the casino and bars are often rife with prostitutes plying their trade. Located off the Malecón and convenient to the city's major attractions and shops, the hotel consists of two separate buildings: the 10-story Jaragua Tower and the two-level Jaragua Gardens Estate. Jaragua boasts the largest casino in the Caribbean, a 1,000-seat Vegas-style showroom, a cabaret theater, and a dance club. The luxurious rooms, the largest in Santo Domingo, feature multiple phones, refrigerators, and marble bathrooms with large makeup mirrors and tub/shower combinations.

The Jaragua features some of the best hotel dining in the city. You can enjoy tasty Dominican barbecue and some of Santo Domingo's best steaks.

Av. George Washington 367, Santo Domingo, Dominican Republic. ⓒ 800/331-2542 in the U.S. and Canada, or 809/221-2222. Fax 809/686-0528. www.renaissance hotels.com. 300 units. US$109–US$169 (£57–£89) double; US$320 (£168) junior suite; US$500–US$725 (£263–£382) suite. Valet parking US$2 (£1.05). AE, DC, MC, V. **Amenities:** Restaurant; 2 bars; casino; dance club; outdoor pool; tennis center with 4 lit clay courts and pro shop; health club; spa; salon; room service; babysitting; laundry service; dry cleaning; nonsmoking rooms. *In room:* A/C, TV, kitchenettes (in some), minibar, fridge, hair dryer, iron, safe.

Sofitel Nicolas de Ovando ⓡ   In the eyes of nationalists, no other hotel in Santo Domingo elicits such a sense of civic pride. In the heart of the colonial old town, next to the Alcázar de Colón, where Diego, son of Columbus, lived, it originated in 1502 as a private mansion. Between 1999 and 2002, its thick masonry walls, hand-hewn ceiling beams, and a quartet of rhythmically graceful inner courtyards were restored, and the premises were massively enlarged with the construction, immediately next door, of a new wing that was meticulously built to emulate the design of the original core. For historians seeking a security-conscious location within the capital's historic core, this is a good choice, and no one can deny the importance of the place as a linchpin of the city's cluster of A-list historic monuments. However, to some, the place evokes a stiff and somewhat uncomfortable historic monument that never made a graceful transition into a hotel, and it utterly lacks the sense of fun and whimsy of more razzmatazz-y hotels in other parts of the city.

Bedrooms seem underfurnished, with just the hint that they were designed by a government-funded museum board into something resembling the lodgings within a somewhat severe but eminently respectable monastery. And the staff here seems programmed like government-grade bureaucrats instead of workers in the hospitality industry. Frankly, we find it hard to relax within, or to warm up to this museum-hotel. There are, however, areas of great charm, especially in its colonial courtyards, where bar service is available, and its restaurant, where the food, as supervised by the France-based Sofitel chain, is superb. The most expensive accommodations are the suites (actually just very large, high-ceilinged rooms) within the monument's original antique core.

Calle Las Damas, Santo Domingo, Dominican Republic. ⓒ 809/685-9955. Fax 809/686-6590. www.sofitel.com. 104 units. US$160–US$200 (£84–£105) double; US$500 (£263) junior suite; US$650 (£342) suite. AE, DC, MC, V. **Amenities:** Restaurant; 2 bars; dance club; outdoor pool; gym; room service; laundry service; dry cleaning; nonsmoking rooms; rooms for those w/limited mobility. *In room:* A/C, TV, minibar, hair dryer, iron, safe.

MODERATE

Clarion Hotel   Reputable and respected, this 1970s-era hotel contains predictably acceptable middle-bracket lodgings within a 12-story chain-hotel format that was renovated and subsequently maintained in good order by the Clarion chain since they took over its management in 2003. But no other hotel in Santo Domingo, with the possible exception of the Jaragua, relies as heavily as it does on the quality of its nightlife to attract a devoted clientele. And thanks to the presence, on-site, of two hot bars and a restaurant, and the snob appeal of a location that's only about five blocks from the official residence of the President of the Dominican Republic, a goodly percentage of the rooms here are rented to Dominicans who come into the capital from out of town, rent a room, and spend the rest of the weekend partying within one area of the hotel or another.

It probably isn't the most restful venue in town but, in its way, is the most animated, with many fewer U.S. or Canadian clients than you'll find in hotels along, say, the Malecón. There's also a busy neighborhood gym on the premises and a full-service spa and salon, visits to which, either before or after partying, seem to be part of the social rituals associated with this architecturally undistinguished but richly distinctive hotel. This emphasis on good times, body cults, and streaming merengue might either appeal to you or horrify you, depending on your point of view and preferences, but rooms are relatively well maintained, chain-motel efficient, and relatively comfortable. The more frequently talked about of its two bars, "Bottoms," is recommended separately.

Presidente Gonzalez at the corner of Av. Tiradentes, Santo Domingo, Dominican Republic. ✆ **809/541-6226.** Fax 809/549-7743. www.naco.com.do. 175 units. US$105–US$110 (£55–£58) double; US$150 (£79) suite. AE, DC, MC, V. **Amenities:** Restaurant; coffee shop; bar/nightclub; outdoor pool on 3rd-floor terrace; gym; spa; salon; room service; laundry service; dry cleaning. *In room:* A/C, TV, safe, Wi-Fi.

Courtyard by Marriott ✿ *Value*   Set at the top of one of the city's busiest boulevards, about a half-mile uphill from the Malecón, this well-managed, respectable, and fairly priced hotel was a welcome addition to Santo Domingo's hotel scene when it was inaugurated in 2003. Housed in a red-brick building capped with ornamental chimneys that evoke a farmhouse along the Algarve of southern Portugal, its lobby has the kind of grace notes, including deep sofas and touches of wrought iron, that you might have expected within a large and comfortable home in Spain. There's an outdoor pool and a lobby bar, and well-maintained and comfortable bedrooms with uncontroversial decors that are completely appropriate for the many business travelers who make this place their home, sometimes for a week or more. Bathrooms each contain a shower/tub combo and plenty of countertop space.

Av. Máximo Gómez #50A, Santo Domingo, Dominican Republic. ℂ 809/685-1010. Fax 809/685-2003. www.marriott.com. 145 units. US$103–US$139 (£54–£73) double. AE, DC, MC, V. **Amenities:** Restaurant; lobby bar; outdoor pool; room service; laundry service; dry cleaning; on-site mini-market. *In room:* A/C, TV, minibar, safe, Wi-Fi.

El Napolitano Hotel & Casino ℛ *Value*   This comfortable safe haven—and great bargain—is perfect for those who want to stay on the Malecón, right by the water. The hotel has been popular with Dominicans themselves since it opened its seven floors back in the 1970s. The look is traditional in all the bedrooms, which are comfortable but simple. Most bedrooms are midsize and well maintained, each with a modern bathroom with a tub/shower combo. All accommodations open onto the sea, and there's a pool on the second floor. There's plenty to do at night if you like disco or casino action, maybe both. If you prefer crowds, lots of action, and informality, El Napolitano may be for you.

Av. George Washington 101, Santo Domingo, Dominican Republic. ℂ 809/687-1131. Fax 809/686-0255. www.napolitanohotel.com. 72 units. US$108–US$136 (£56–£72) double; US$160 (£84) suite. Children 12 and under stay free in parent's room. AE, DC, DISC, MC, V. **Amenities:** 2 restaurants; bar; casino; disco; outdoor pool; room service; laundry service; dry cleaning. *In room:* A/C, TV, minibar, hair dryer, safe.

Hodelpa Caribe Colonial   This boutique hotel in the Colonial Zone attracts both businesspeople and vacationers to its handsomely decorated precincts. A four-story structure, it is warm and inviting with Art Deco–styled rooms. If you don't mind not being on the water, you'll find the nicely furnished rooms here comfortable. Many of the city's best cafes, restaurants, attractions, and nightlife lie right outside your door. There's a special all-white honeymoon suite and fabric-draped beds are a standard feature. The suites are an especially good deal and have extras like a kitchenette, walk-in closet, balcony with chaise lounges, and bathroom with Jacuzzi. A well-prepared Dominican cuisine is served in the main restaurant, with lots of tropical favorites, and there is also a rooftop sun deck.

Isabel La Católica 159, Zona Colonial, Dominican Republic. ℂ 809/688-7799. Fax 809/685-8128. www.hodelpa.com. 54 units. US$100–US$130 (£53–£68) double; US$190–US$210 (£100–£111) suite. Rates include breakfast. Children 11 and under stay free in parent's room. AE, MC, V. Free parking. **Amenities:** Restaurant; bar; room service; laundry service; dry cleaning. *In room:* A/C, TV, kitchenette, minibar, hair dryer, iron, safe.

Hostal Nicolás Nader 𝒜 *(Finds* This is a small, almost luxurious little hotel from the colonial era and also the former home of a former D.R. president, Ulises Heureaux. This 19th-century building has been sensitively restored. Many people in the area drop in during the day to check out the little art gallery in the courtyard or to patronize the on-site restaurant and bar. The bedrooms range from midsize to spacious, and each is comfortably furnished and comes with a bathroom with a tub/shower combo. The white paint in all the rooms gives the limestone-built mansion a real tropical flavor. You get quite a lot for your money here.

Calle General Luperón 151 at Calle Duarte, Santo Domingo, Dominican Republic. 𝒞 **809/687-6674.** Fax 809/687-7887. www.naderenterprises.com/hostal. 10 units. US$80 (£42) double. Children 8 and under stay free in parent's room. AE, MC, V. **Amenities:** Bar. *In room:* A/C, TV.

Hotel Delta In spite of this hotel's inconvenient location on the west side of town—a 45-minute drive to a good beach—it always seems full of satisfied American clients, attracted to its affordable prices and well-maintained bedrooms. There's an abundance of energy about the place, but the look is rather basic. Okay, it's not the Ritz, but prices aren't as high as the Ritz's, either. Rising eight floors, the Delta is a traditional choice in a building dating from the late 1980s.

Av. Sarasota 53, Santo Domingo, Dominican Republic. 𝒞 **809/535-0800.** Fax 809/535-6448. www.hoteldelta.com.do. 141 units. US$79–US$89 (£42–£47) double; US$107–US$161 (£56–£85) suite. Children 8 and under stay free in parent's room. AE, DC, MC, V. **Amenities:** Restaurant; bar; outdoor pool; room service; babysitting; laundry service; dry cleaning. *In room:* A/C, TV, kitchenette, hair dryer, safe.

INEXPENSIVE

Caribeño Next door to a government building, this nine-floor structure dates from the 1980s but has seen improvements and rejuvenations since. Most of the rooms, painted in lime, range from small to midsize and are simply though comfortably furnished, with tiny bathrooms with a tub/shower combination. Noise might be a factor in some of the rooms, and the place is utterly without style. But few customers complain when it comes time to pay the bill.

Avs. 27 de Febrero and Duarte, Santo Domingo, Dominican Republic. 𝒞 **809/685-3167.** Fax 809/685-3391. hotelcaribeno@hotmail.com. 106 units. US$38 (£20) double; US$40 (£21) triple. Children 11 and under stay free in parent's room. AE,

DC, DISC, MC, V. **Amenities:** Restaurant; bar; outdoor pool; room service; babysitting; laundry service; dry cleaning. *In room:* A/C, TV, minibar, safe.

Hotel Restaurante La Casona Dorada 🏵 *Value*   This 19th-century building was another property that belonged to former president Buenaventura Báez, whose family also owned what is now the Hotel Palacio. A mansion converted to receive paying guests, the hotel lies on tranquil grounds set back from the street at the corner of Calle Osvaldo Báez; it's a 5-minute ride to the Colonial Zone or a 30-minute ride to the beaches. Opened in 1993, the hotel caters to visitors and business clients and is gay-friendly. The small bedrooms are traditionally and comfortably decorated and are well maintained, each with a modern bathroom with tub and shower. The restaurant and bar on-site are popular gathering places even among locals, and the swimming pool is a social mecca, especially in summer.

Av. Independencia 255 at the corner of Osvaldo Báez, Santo Domingo, Dominican Republic. ✆ **809/221-3535.** Fax 809/221-3622. casona.dorada@codetel.net.do. 51 units. US$50 (£26) double. Children US$5 (£2.65) extra. AE, MC, V. **Amenities:** Restaurant; bar; outdoor pool; room service; laundry service; dry cleaning. *In room:* A/C, TV.

3 Where to Dine

Most of Santo Domingo's restaurants stretch along the seaside, bordering Avenida George Washington, popularly known as the Malecón. Some of the best restaurants are in hotels. It's safest to take a taxi when dining out at night.

In most restaurants, casual dress is fine, although shorts are frowned upon at the fancier, more expensive spots. Many Dominicans prefer to dress up when dining out, especially in the capital.

EXPENSIVE
David Crockett 🏵 STEAKHOUSE   The name is corny, suggesting a retro fad of the '50s, but this super-expensive restaurant serves the finest steaks in the Dominican Republic. For those who like red meat, it draws the true carnivore. Huge portions of porterhouse, rib-eye, or even Kobe beef will rest on your plate. Should you want some other meat, the chefs are skilled at turning out a perfectly cooked rack of lamb, aromatic with herbs and infused with garlic. Naturally, the decor is country-and-western style. Serving platters are made of wood, and there are many references to a rustic and simple life on the wide-open range.

Gustavo Meliá Ricart 34. ✆ **809/547-2999.** Main courses RD$880–RD$1,590 (US$27–US$48/£14–£24). AE, MC, V. Daily noon–midnight.

Where to Dine in Santo Domingo

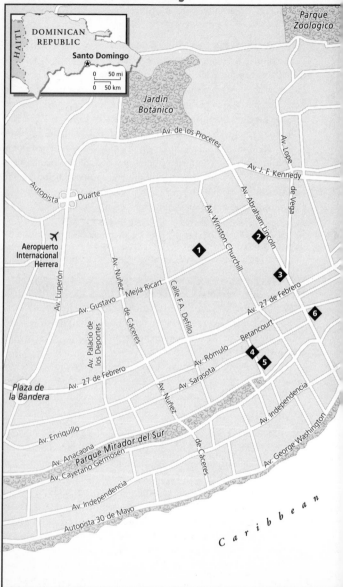

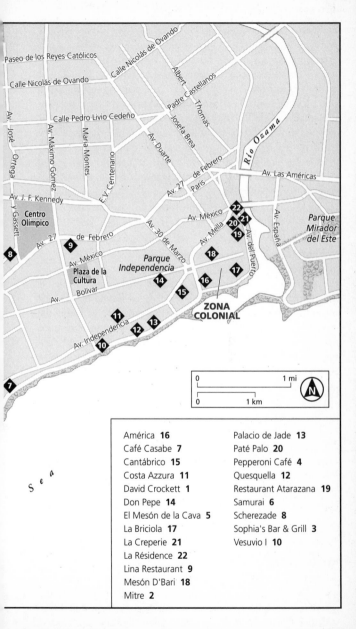

América **16**
Café Casabe **7**
Cantábrico **15**
Costa Azzura **11**
David Crockett **1**
Don Pepe **14**
El Mesón de la Cava **5**
La Briciola **17**
La Creperie **21**
La Résidence **22**
Lina Restaurant **9**
Mesón D'Bari **18**
Mitre **2**

Palacio de Jade **13**
Paté Palo **20**
Pepperoni Café **4**
Quesquella **12**
Restaurant Atarazana **19**
Samurai **6**
Scherezade **8**
Sophia's Bar & Grill **3**
Vesuvio I **10**

El Mesón de la Cava ❀ DOMINICAN/INTERNATIONAL
At first we thought this was a gimmicky club—you descend a perilous iron stairway into an actual cave with stalactites and stalagmites—but the cuisine is among the finest in the capital. The quality ingredients are well prepared and harmonious in flavor. Recorded merengue, Latin jazz, blues, and salsa give the place a festive ambience. Small shrimp are sautéed in a delicate sauce of garlic or white wine, perhaps a mixed seafood or "sexy" conch gratiné. The gazpacho is also an excellent beginning, as is the bubbling *sopa de pescado* (red snapper chowder). Follow it up with the grilled Caribbean rock lobster or the double French lamb chops, which are done to tender perfection.

Mirador del Sur 1. ✆ **809/533-2818.** Reservations required. Main courses RD$350–RD$1,400 (US$11–US$42/£5.40–£22). AE, DC, MC, V. Daily noon–midnight.

Sophia's Bar & Grill ❀❀ *Finds* INTERNATIONAL   Glossy, elegant, upscale, and relatively new on Santo Domingo's dining scene, this is the kind of restaurant where a man might opt to invite his mistress when he first begins cheating on his wife, and to which he might take his wife as an apology after she finds out. Set within the stylish Naco/Piantini District, it contains the kind of *modernista* decor (angular, with tones of midnight blue, black, white, and cherrywood) that might have been inspired by a hip watering hole in Barcelona. There's also a very visible sense of unsmiling security guards lurking in the middle background who show absolutely no sense of humor. Delectable, well-crafted dishes include roasted rack of lamb, slabs of hake crusted with yucca flour and saffron, churrasco-style steaks, Chinese rock shrimp with orange, several different preparations of Chilean sea bass, sushi, risotto with mixed mushrooms, and Thai-style noodles with seafood. There's a dance floor positioned between the dining tables for those romantic moments.

Paseo de los Locutores 9 (between calles Lincoln and Churchill). ✆ **809/620-1001.** Reservations recommended. Burgers and salads RD$310–RD$675 (US$9.40–US$20/£4.75–£10); main courses RD$425–RD$1,100 (US$13–US$33/£6.55–£17). AE, DC, MC, V. Sun–Thurs noon–11:45pm; Fri–Sat noon–1:45am.

MODERATE

América SPANISH/INTERNATIONAL   Two blocks from Parque Independencia, this is one of the most centrally located of all the restaurants in Santo Domingo. The building itself is a dull 1950s structure. The waiters are very attentive, taking care of your needs and advising on specialties or wines as requested. The place is informal, drawing young couples on dates, families, visitors, and locals with its satisfying, filling, and savory cuisine. We like to begin our meal with a bowl of the seafood soup. The fresh fish filet, grilled to your specifications and served with fresh vegetables, is an excellent choice, as is the savory platter of paella studded with shellfish. The tender and well-flavored grilled filet of beef is a perennial local favorite.

Arzobispo Hotel, corner of San Tome 201. ✆ **809/682-7194.**. Main courses RD$350–RD$1,400 (US$11–US$42/£5.40–£22). AE, DC, DISC, MC, V. Daily 11am–midnight.

Cantábrico SPANISH/SEAFOOD Very close to the Colonial Zone, this eatery evokes a Spanish *tasca,* or tavern. Now moving into its third decade, it is an informal crowd-pleaser, drawing many city families as well as visitors. One specialty is *zarzuela,* seafood in a broth seasoned with lots of garlic; another is "El Filete Especial Cantabrico" (beef filet). The chefs also do a most satisfying paella with lots of shrimp, and, like the chefs in the Spanish city of Segovia, they turn out a tender, well-flavored platter of roast suckling pig. Flavorful grilled meats are also a cornerstone of this kitchen.

Av. Independencia 54. ✆ **809/687-5101.** Main courses RD$400–RD$990 (US$12–US$30/£6.15–£15). AE, DC, MC, V. Daily 11am–midnight.

Don Pepe ✿ SPANISH/SEAFOOD Treat yourself to at least one lavish meal here during your stay in Santo Domingo. The seafood, including Caribbean lobster, arrives fresh daily and is displayed extravagantly on ice, awaiting your selection. We usually gravitate to the giant crab, but any of the fresh seafood grilled to your specifications is the way to go here. Begin, perhaps, with a freshly made *caldo Gallego,* a Galician broth with sausages, greens, and potatoes. Plump and sweet red peppers are delectably stuffed with seafood, and the imported salmon arrives with a *salsa verde,* a green sauce made with fresh herbs. To end your meal, dig into the offerings of the dessert tray, an array of smooth flans, delectable cheesecakes, and crème caramel.

Av. Pasteur 41 at Santiago. ✆ **809/686-8481.** Reservations required. Main courses RD$320–RD$1,000 (US$9.70–US$30/£4.90–£15). AE, DC, DISC, MC, V. Mon–Fri 11:30am–3:30pm and 7pm–midnight; Sat–Sun 11:30am–midnight. Closed Dec 24 and 25.

La Résidence ✿ *Finds* CONTINENTAL/CARIBBEAN It isn't particularly animated, but the food is surprisingly lavish at this showcase of the France-based Sofitel chain. The setting is historic (a circa 1502 mansion transformed into a hotel), and if you happen to be within the historic zone, it's an excellent and easy-to-find dining choice. They're one of the few upscale restaurants in town offering spit-roasted lamb (rubbed with spices and served with bacon, garlic, and vinegar sauce) and rabbit (a boned saddle stuffed with bacon and mushrooms). And their grilled tuna, prawns, and salmon (served with leeks and an herb-flavored mousseline sauce) is delicious. Dominican-inspired dishes include roast lobster with wok-fried vegetables, a fricassee of pork chops with local spices, and braised "Dominican-style" red snapper. There's even a frequently changing array of vegetarian dishes.

In the Sofitel Nicolas de Ovando, Calle Las Damas. © **809/685-9955.** Main courses RD$325–RD$890 (US$9.85–US$27/£5–£14). AE, DC, MC, V. Daily 7am–midnight.

Lina Restaurant 🟊🟊 INTERNATIONAL/SPANISH   This is one of the most prestigious restaurants in the Caribbean. Spanish-born Lina Aguado originally came to Santo Domingo as the personal chef of the dictator Trujillo, whom she served until opening her own restaurant. Today, four master chefs, whom Doña Lina entrusted with her secret recipes, rule the kitchen of this modern hotel restaurant. The cuisine is international, with an emphasis on Spanish dishes, and the service is first-rate. Try the paella Valenciana, the finest in the Dominican Republic. We're equally enticed by the sea bass flambé with brandy, and few can resist the mixed seafood medley doused with Pernod (it's cooked casserole-style). Lina's cuisine even wins the approval of some hard-to-please Madrileños we know, who are a bit contemptuous of Spanish food served outside Spain.

In the Barceló Hotel Lina. Avs. Máximo Gómez and 27 de Febrero. © **809/ 563-5000,** ext. 7250. Reservations recommended. Main courses RD$260–RD$1,000 (US$7.90–US$30/£4–£15). AE, DC, DISC, MC, V. Daily noon–4pm and 6:30pm–midnight.

Mitre 🟊🟊 *Finds* INTERNATIONAL   Established in 2006 on a busy street corner in a downtown commercial neighborhood rarely visited by casual tourists, this is one of the most visible of the new crop of hip restaurants popping up throughout Santo Domingo. It evokes a trend-conscious and cutting-edge restaurant you might have expected in Barcelona, thanks partly to a modernistic courtyard through which diners pass on their way into the air-conditioned (and soundproofed from the traffic) interior. If you opt to remain in the courtyard, there will be a lot of things to distract you: Zebra-patterned tilework, Zen-inspired reflecting pools, and a sense of minimalist chic that might be Italian, might be Catalonian, or might be a hybrid kind of hipness imported directly from a point midway between Manhattan and Miami. There's a woodsy-looking wine-and-cigar bar upstairs, where wines cost from RD$170 to RD$220 (US$5.15–US$6.65/£2.60–£3.40) per glass. But the culinary heart and soul of the place is on the street level, where a prominent bar shares space with a sought-after series of tables. The best menu items include carpaccio of *carite* (a Caribbean whitefish); salmon steak teriyaki; braised Chilean sea bass with asparagus and mushrooms; Mongolian-style tenderloin with scallions and snow peas; crisp-grilled octopus, and a selection of sushi, burgers, and pastas.

When the patriarch of the family that owns this place first came from Naples to the Dominican Republic in the late 1940s, the local kitchen help mispronounced the name they gave him ("Mister") as "Mitre," and in 2006, that corruption of the original word was adopted as the name of the new restaurant. By the way, don't overlook the upstairs wine-and-cigar bar as a nightlife option.

Av. Lincoln at the corner of the Calle Gustavo Mejia Ricart. © **809/472-1787.** Reservations recommended. Burgers and pastas RD$275–RD$400 (US$8.35–US$12/£4.25–£6.15); main courses RD$675–RD$900 (US$20–US$27/£10–£14). AE, DC, MC, V. Daily noon–midnight, Fri–Sat till 1am).

Palacio de Jade ✿ CANTONESE/MONGOLIAN   Authentic flavors from faraway China aromatically fill the rooms at this choice restaurant, which is a good change of pace from regular Dominican fare. The chefs specialize in Peking duck, a dish that's almost impossible to duplicate in a home kitchen. The preparations are often minimal but the results are maximal, as exemplified by the chicken with lettuce or the shrimp in a black-bean sauce. Expect spicy, beautifully presented compositions that balance flavor with texture. The only downside is the noise that can emerge from the private karaoke rooms.

José María Heredia 6. © **809/686-3226.** Main courses RD$125–RD$950 (US$3.75–US$29/£2–£15). AE, MC, V. Daily noon–4pm and 7–11pm.

Pepperoni Café ✿ *Finds* FUSION   A real dining discovery, this is a hip, fun rendezvous, with a rustic decor and exotic paintings. The menu boasts beautifully prepared treats based on the use of high-quality ingredients. The pasta might be Thai, with stir-fried vegetables, or else penne with fresh mushrooms, rock shrimp, prosciutto, and Parmesan. A small part of the menu is dedicated to fresh sushi and sashimi. The salads are among the best in town—varied and fresh—including a Southwest chicken salad with grilled poultry, avocado, bacon, and a lime dressing. Starters range from Peking pork spring rolls to a Thai-influenced tuna seviche. Don't miss such house specialties as spicy tuna tartar, Mai Thai Crab (with coconut and curry), or braised short beef ribs with garlic whipped potatoes.

Av. Plaza Universitaria, Sarasota 25. 🕐 **809/508-1330.** Reservations recommended. Main courses RD$325–RD$750 (US$9.85–US$23/£5–£12). AE, DC, MC, V. Sun–Thurs noon–midnight; Fri–Sat noon–1am.

Quesquella 🏵 INTERNATIONAL   The food and service at this deluxe hotel are among the best in the capital, and this dining room is one of the finest places to go. It's also a safe bet if you're strolling along the dangerous Malecón at night. The chefs specialize in imported beef. We've enjoyed the taste, texture, and tenderness of both their T-bone steak and their filet mignon. You could also opt for that 1950s Eisenhower-era steak-and-lobster combination. Many discerning diners prefer their fresh fish grilled with herbs. That retro classic lobster thermidor is still served here with flourish. As one of the chefs said, "If it were a great dish way back when, why change it?"

Av. George Washington 367, Hotel Renaissance Jaragua. 🕐 **809/221-2222.** Main courses RD$780–RD$1,200 (US$24–US$36/£12–£18). AE, DC, DISC, MC, V. Daily 6–11am and noon–midnight.

Restaurant Atarazana INTERNATIONAL/CREOLE   Although it's clear that not much money was spent on the decor, and most of the furnishings look as though they came from someone's outdoor garden patio, the food is so good and affordable it makes dining here worthwhile. Now deep into its fourth decade, this informal restaurant is in a restored colonial building. Lobster is a specialty and is particularly tasty grilled. The various catches of the day can also be grilled to your specification or served in a peppery sauce. One of the chef's finest dishes, and one of our favorites, is sea bass stuffed with shrimp and served in a white-wine sauce with vegetables and rice. Other well-executed dishes include filet of beef stuffed with cheese and served in a savory sauce, and fresh shrimp in a creamy white sauce.

Atarazana 5. 🕐 **809/689-2900.** Reservations recommended. Main courses RD$300–RD$800 (US$9.10–US$24/£4.60–£12). AE, DC, DISC, MC, V. Mon–Sat noon–midnight.

Samurai 🏵 🅺🅸🅳🆂 SUSHI/JAPANESE   A bit unusual in Santo Domingo, this 11-table restaurant is the best sushi bar in town. There's an open view of the kitchen so that you can see what the chefs are up to. Some diners sit Japanese-style on the floor. The service is swift, efficient, and charming. It's rare that you get such an interesting assortment of sushi at such an inexpensive restaurant, but there's a full array here, plus sashimi platters, shabu shabu, and sake to wash everything down. The grilled seafood with rum is perhaps more West Indian than Japanese, but the delightful clam soup will take you on a trip to the Far East. We suggest you finish off with the fried ice cream for dessert.

Av. Abraham Lincoln 902. ⓒ **809/541-0944.** Reservations recommended. Main courses RD$375–RD$850 (US$11–US$26/£5.75–£13). AE, DC, DISC, MC, V. Mon–Sat noon–3pm and 6:30pm–midnight; Sun noon–4pm and 7–11pm. Closed Dec 25 and 31.

Scheherezade INTERNATIONAL/MEDITERRANEAN Arabian nights live again in this mock mosque with faux Moroccan decor, waiters in embroidered vests and fezzes, and the occasional belly dancer. For Santo Domingo, this restaurant is a real change of pace. Since there are two bars, many guests drop in just for drinks. Expect a selection of extremely fresh salads and flaky flatbread. Your best bets are the grilled seafood and lamb. The Italian-style pastas are rather standard. The desserts are truly superb, especially the delightful orange soufflé.

Roberto Pastoria 226. ⓒ **809/227-2323.** Main courses RD$350–RD$1,200 (US$11–US$36/£5.40–£18). AE, DC, DISC, MC, V. Daily noon–midnight.

Vesuvio I ⓡⓡ ITALIAN Along the Malecón, the most famous Italian restaurant in the Dominican Republic draws crowds of visitors and local businesspeople in spite of its fading decor. What to order? That's always a problem, as the Neapolitan owners, the Bonarelli family, have worked since 1954 to enlarge the menu. They have also improved the quality of the cuisine since we first discovered it decades ago. As they claim: "We like to catch it ourselves, cook it from scratch, or even grow it if that's possible." Their homemade soups are excellent. Fresh red snapper, sea bass, and oysters are prepared in enticing ways. Specialties include Dominican crayfish *a la Vesuvio* (topped with garlic and bacon). Other delights are *pappardelle al Bosque* (noodles with porcini mushrooms, rosemary, and garlic) and black tallarini with shrimp *a la crema.*

The owner claims to be the pioneer of pizza in the Dominican Republic. At **Trattoria Vesuvio** next door (ⓒ **809/221-3000**), he makes a unique .9m-long (3-ft.) pizza! There's also **Vesuvio II** at Av. Tiradentes 17 (ⓒ **809/562-6060**).

Av. George Washington 521. © **809/221-3333**. Reservations recommended. Main courses RD$350–RD$850 (US$11–US$26/£5.40–£13). AE, MC, V. Daily 11am–midnight.

INEXPENSIVE

Café Casabe *Value* CREOLE   Within a previously recommended first-class hotel, this is one of the best places in the city for a late-night snack. Many local couples conclude their evenings here devouring the Dominican chicken, which is deep-fried and served in small pieces. Other favorite island recipes include the seafood in Creole sauce; *sancocho,* a typical stew with a variety of meats and yucca; and *mondongo,* tripe cooked with tomatoes and sweet peppers. You might start with a satisfying shrimp soup and follow with a beef stew. Cuban sandwiches, a chef's salad, and everything from filet mignon to fish sticks round out the menu.

Av. George Washington 365, Meliá Santo Domingo. © **809/221-6666**. Main courses RD$495–RD$850 (US$15–US$26/£7.60–£13). AE, DC, DISC, MC, V. Daily 24 hr.

Costa Azurra ITALIAN/INTERNATIONAL   This eatery isn't as formal or fancy as Vesuvio I, but it serves some of the same fine food at slightly cheaper prices. Costa Azurra resembles an Italian trattoria with checkered tablecloths and is patronized by an informal, convivial crowd eating heartily and enjoying both the company and the food. Everything is properly sauced and full of flavor, but it doesn't get much better than the spaghetti marinara. Many dishes have a hint of Creole flavors, making use of such ingredients as fresh tomatoes and sweet peppers. It opens early enough for breakfast if your hotel doesn't serve one. The antipasti, soups, and salads are made fresh daily.

Av. Independencia 1107. © **809/412-7686**. Main courses RD$190–RD$320 (US$5.75–US$9.70/£2.90–£4.90). No credit cards. 9am–9pm daily.

La Briciola *ꞔꞔ* ITALIAN/INTERNATIONAL   This place has a touch of class, offering an elegant setting in two restored colonial palaces from the 16th century. Tables are romantically candlelit at night. In the Colonial Zone, it stands in front of Plazoleta Park. The menu reflects a commitment to prime ingredients and a determination not to let style overrule substance. The dishes here hardly test the creative culinary limits of the chefs but are tried-and-true favorites, beginning with many different pastas and sauces—all made fresh daily. Our favorite is the delectable linguini with "fruits of the sea." Sometimes you're in the mood just for a good steak, and the chefs oblige with a perfectly grilled T-bone cooked to your specifications. This is also a good place at which to order fresh fish. Dominican rice accompanies all the meat and fish courses. A piano bar overlooks a courtyard.

Calle Arzobispo Meriño 152-A. © **809/688-5055.** Reservations required. Main courses RD$300–RD$550 (US$9.10–US$17/£4.60–£8.45). AE, DC, DISC, MC, V. Mon–Sat noon–3pm and 7pm–midnight. Closed Dec 24, 25, 31, and Jan 1.

La Creperie *(Kids* CREPES   The best crepes in all the Dominican Republic are served here. In the Colonial Zone, in the vicinity of the Atarazana, this eatery offers two different types of crepes, both the savory and traditional French variety and some marvelously tasty dessert crepes. Ham and cheese is, of course, the classic, but you can also order many other varieties, including one made with smoked salmon, asparagus points, and a creamy white sauce. Should you not be in the mood for crepes, you can order other dishes as well, including grilled salmon or grilled lobster. Many patrons come here just for the dessert crepes, including a real surprise, a crepe made with homemade orange marmalade. If you want to be completely "illicit," you can order a crepe with grated coconut and chocolate. Their ice creams are to die for, especially the mango.

Atazara 11 © **809/221-4734.** Main courses RD$220–RD$1,000 (US$6.65–US$30/£3.40–£15). AE, DC, DISC, MC, V. Mon, Wed, and Thurs 10:30am–12:30am; Fri–Sun 10:30am–1am. Closed Dec 25 and 31.

Meson D'Bari *(* CREOLE   In the Colonial Zone, in what used to be a private family home, this restaurant has both ambience and good food. Paintings by Dominican artists—the art is for sale—decorate the walls of this handsomely restored building. The chefs use regional and freshly grown produce whenever possible, and dishes are well crafted by the staff. Our favorite main dish is *filete a la criolla,* or filet of beef Creole-style served with tomatoes, onions, and sweet peppers. Beef also appears in a number of other ways, including with a freshly made mushroom sauce. A savory crab stew is one of the best offerings. But savvy diners most often order the grilled fish, based on the catch of the day. The chefs also prepare a daily special that's really local, and may not be to your taste unless you get off on the likes of *chivo guisado* (stewed goat) or other regional fare.

Calle Hostos 302, corner of Salome Ureña. © **809/687-4091.** Main courses RD$295 (US$8.95/£4.55). AE, DC, MC, V. Daily noon–midnight.

Pata é Palo 🏵🏵 INTERNATIONAL   Part of Pata é Palo's charm derives from its location, overlooking Plaza España, the graceful arcades of the Alcazar de Colón, where amiable clusters of Dominican families promenade every night at dusk. During the 1500s, the building was a bistro under the supervision of a mysterious Dutch buccaneer known as Peg-Leg (Pata é Palo), who's credited with establishing the first tavern in the New World.

In the late 1990s, another Dutchman and his four partners transformed the place into an engaging bistro that on weekends is one of the most crowded and popular singles bars in the country. Tables are thick-topped wooden affairs, set either on the plaza outside or within the antique walls of the dark and shadowy interior. The food is some of the best in the capital, and is usually accompanied by live guitar music every Thursday to Sunday from 6 to 10pm. Having dined here many times, we can highly recommend the sautéed shrimp in coconut-curry sauce. On festive occasions, ask for the brochette of mixed meats; the meat has been marinated in fresh spices and herbs and is artfully flambéed at your table. The sea bass with white-wine sauce is a delicious treat, although the fancy Continental dishes such as charbroiled steak with onion sauce and a grilled rack of lamb might be more suited for the cold Alps.

La Atarazana 21, Zona Colonial. ✆ **809/687-8089.** Burgers and salads RD$425–RD$475 (US$13–US$14/£6.55–£7.30); main courses RD$550–RD$1,200 (US$17–US$36/£8.45–£18). AE, MC, V. Mon–Fri 4pm–1:30am; Sat–Sun noon–1:30am.

Exploring Santo Domingo

Santo Domingo—a treasure trove of historic, sometimes crumbling buildings—is undergoing a major government-sponsored restoration. The old town, or Zona Colonial, is still partially enclosed by remnants of its original city wall. The narrow streets, old stone buildings, and forts are like nothing else in the Caribbean, except perhaps Old San Juan. The only thing missing is the clank of the conquistadors' armor.

Old and modern Santo Domingo meet at the **Parque Independencia,** a big city square whose most prominent feature is its **Altar de la Patria,** a national pantheon dedicated to the nation's heroes, Duarte, Sánchez, and Mella, who are all buried here. These men led the country's fight for freedom from Haiti in 1844. As in provincial Spanish cities, the square is a popular family gathering place on Sunday afternoon. At the entrance to the plaza is **El Conde Gate,** named for the count (El Conde) de Penalva, the governor who resisted the forces of Admiral Penn, the leader of a British invasion. It was also the site of the March for Independence in 1844, and holds a special place in the hearts of Dominicans.

In the shadow of the Alcázar de Colón, **La Atarazana** is a fully restored section of one of the New World's finest arsenals. It extends for a city block, holding within it a catacomb of shops, art galleries, boutiques, and some good regional and international restaurants.

Just behind river moorings is the oldest street in the New World, **Calle Las Damas (Street of the Ladies),** named not because it was the red-light district, but for the elegant ladies of the viceregal court who used to promenade here in the evening. It's lined with colonial buildings.

Try to see the **Puerta de la Misericordia** (Calle Palo Hincado just north of Calle Arzobispo Portes). Part of the original city wall, this "Gate of Mercy" was once a refuge for colonists fleeing hurricanes and earthquakes.

You'll see a microcosm of Dominican life as you head east along **Calle El Conde** from Parque Independencia to Columbus Square

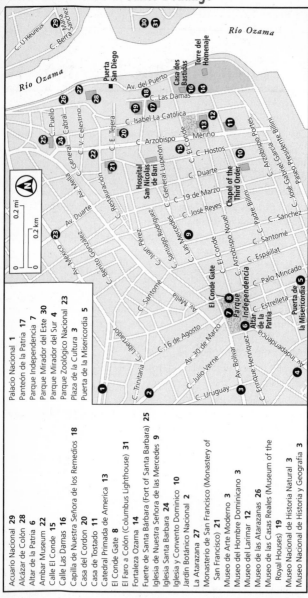

Acuario Nacional **29**
Alcázar de Colón **28**
Altar de la Patria **6**
Ambar Museum **22**
Calle El Conde **15**
Calle Las Damas **16**
Capilla de Nuestra Señora de los Remedios **18**
Casa del Cordon **20**
Casa de Tostado **11**
Catedral Primada de America **13**
El Conde Gate **8**
El Faro a Colon (Columbus Lighthouse) **31**
Fortaleza Ozama **14**
Fuerte de Santa Bárbara (Fort of Santa Barbara) **25**
Iglesia de Nuestra Señora de las Mercedes **9**
Iglesia Santa Bárbara **24**
Iglesia y Convento Dominico **10**
Jardín Botánico Nacional **2**
La Atarazana **27**
Monasterio de San Francisco (Monastery of San Francisco) **21**
Museo de Arte Moderno **3**
Museo del Hombre Dominicano **3**
Museo del Larimar **12**
Museo de las Atarazanas **26**
Museo de las Casas Reales (Museum of the Royal Houses) **19**
Museo Nacional de Historia Natural **3**
Museo Nacional de Historia y Geografía **3**

Palacio Nacional **1**
Panteón de la Patria **17**
Parque Independencia **7**
Parque Mirador del Este **30**
Parque Mirador del Sur **4**
Parque Zoológico Nacional **23**
Plaza de la Cultura **3**
Puerta de la Misericordia **5**

(Plaza de Colón), which has a large bronze statue honoring the discoverer (or to be more accurate, the explorer of an already inhabited land). The statue was created in 1882 by a French sculptor.

As impressive as the old town or Zona Colonial is, monuments are not the total allure of Santo Domingo, as you'll soon discover in this chapter. Following a day of shopping for handicrafts, or perhaps jewelry fashioned from amber or larimar—a semiprecious ocean-blue gemstone found only in a remote mountain in the southwestern region of the country—the sound of merengue will lure you to the bars, dance clubs, and casinos of the capital after dark.

1 Santo Domingo in 1 Day

Most visitors who plan to spend most of their vacation at the beach resorts devote only 1 day for sightseeing in Santo Domingo. To make the most out of that limited time, here are some suggestions.

You can spend an entire morning exploring the **Zona Colonial** ★★★ of the Old City, a 12-block area where Spanish civilization in the New World was launched. Columbus walked these narrow, cobblestoned streets as did Ponce de León, even Cortés. All of the sights below are mentioned later in this chapter, in some cases described more fully. Begin by taking a stroll up:

1. Calle Las Damas, or "Street of the Ladies." The aristocratic ladies of the Spanish empire used to parade up and down this street.

Near the top of the street you can visit:

2. Capilla de Nuestra Señora de los Remedios, which was constructed in the Gothic style in the 16th century.

The major attraction in the Old Town is:

3. Alcázar de Colón, the palace constructed for Columbus's son, Diego, in 1517. You'll need at least an hour to explore it.

After a visit continue north to:

4. Museo de las Atarazanas, a museum filled with treasures rescued from Spanish wrecks. You'll learn much about life aboard the Spanish galleons that used to sail through the West Indies.

Cut south again until you reach:

5. Catedral Primada de América, the oldest cathedral in the Americas, completed in 1540.

After visiting the cathedral, take a taxi to:

6. El Faro a Colón (Columbus Lighthouse) across the river. A chapel in the center of this structure is said to contain the bones of Columbus, although this claim is disputed by the Seville cathedral in Spain.

Santo Domingo in 1 Day

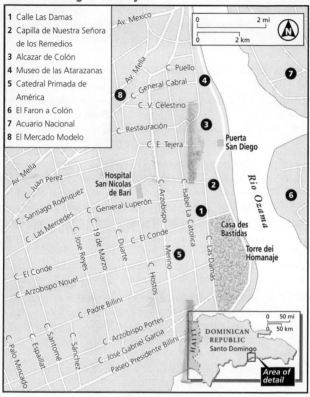

1 Calle Las Damas
2 Capilla de Nuestra Señora de los Remedios
3 Alcazar de Colón
4 Museo de las Atarazanas
5 Catedral Primada de América
6 El Faron a Colón
7 Acuario Nacional
8 El Mercado Modelo

With another hour to spare, visit:

7. Acuario Nacional, the grandest aquarium in the Caribbean.

With the time remaining in the afternoon, climax your day of sightseeing with a visit to:

8. El Mercado Modelo, the national market where you can easily spend an hour or two. It closes at 6pm daily, however.

2 Fortresses & a Cathedral

If you like views more than you do wandering around dusty relics, head for the **Fuerte de Santa Bárbara (Fort of Santa Barbara)** standing at the corner of Juan Parra and Avenida Mella. When it was constructed in the 1570s, it was one of Santo Domingo's principal points of defense. As formidable as it was, it fell to Sir Francis

Drake—locals call him "the pirate"—and his two dozen ships, who took the fort in 1586. Today the place is a complete ruin, but worth a visit for its small garden and little square. The view of Santo Domingo from here is panoramic.

Alcázar de Colón ⭐⭐   The most outstanding structure in the old city is the Alcázar, a palace built for Columbus's son, Diego, and his wife, who was also niece to Ferdinand, king of Spain. Diego became the colony's governor in 1509, and Santo Domingo rose as the hub of Spanish commerce and culture in America. For more than 60 years, this coral limestone structure on the bluffs of the Ozama River was the center of the Spanish court, entertaining such distinguished visitors as Cortés, Ponce de León, and Balboa. The nearly two dozen rooms and open-air loggias are decorated with paintings and period tapestries, as well as 16th-century antiques. A walk downhill from the Alcázar leads to the impressive **Puerto de San Diego,** which dates from 1571 when it was built as the main gate into Santo Domingo. Some of the original wall can be seen by this gate, which once guarded against attacks coming from the river.

Calle La Atarazana (at the foot of Calle Las Damas). ⓒ **809/682-4750,** ext. 232. Admission RD$50 (US$1.50/75p). Mon–Sat 9am–5pm; Sun 9am–4pm.

Catedral Primada de América ⭐⭐   The oldest cathedral in the Americas was begun in 1514 and completed in 1540. With a gold coral limestone facade, the church combines elements of both the Gothic and baroque styles. It also contains a high altar partially chiseled out of silver in the Plateresque style. (Plateresque is a decorative 16th-century Spanish style characterized by elaborate ornamentation in low relief that's suggestive of silver plate.) In 1992, the cathedral was designated as the centerpiece for a celebration of the 500th anniversary of the European colonization of America.

In between calles Arzobispo Meriño and Isabel La Católica (on the south side of Columbus Sq.). ⓒ **809/682-3848.** Admission RD$30 (US90¢/45p). Cathedral Mon–Sat 9am–4:30pm; Mass Sun noon and 5pm, Mon and Wed–Sat 5pm; treasury Mon–Sat 9am–4pm.

El Faro a Colón (Columbus Lighthouse) ⭐   Built in the shape of a cross, the towering 206m-tall (676-ft.) El Faro a Colón monument is both a sightseeing attraction and a cultural center. In the heart of the structure is a chapel containing the Columbus tomb and, some say, his mortal remains. The "bones" of Columbus were allegedly moved here from the nearby Cathedral of Santa María la Menor. (Other locations, including the Cathedral of Seville, also claim to possess the explorer's remains.)

In 2006 it was announced that scientists had confirmed that at least some of the remains of Columbus were buried in the cathedral in Seville (Spain). DNA samples from 500-year-old bone slivers contradict the D.R.'s claim that the explorer was laid to rest in the New World. However, some of his remains could have been buried in Santo Domingo, but not all.

DNA taken form bones buried in Seville was compared to that of Columbus's brother, Diego, who is also buried in Seville. It was an absolute match.

Juan Bautista Mieses, the director of the Columbus Lighthouse, challenged the findings. "The remains never left Dominican territory," he claimed. The D.R. is refusing to allow the remains in Santo Domingo to be tested. "We Christians believe that one does not bother the dead," Mieses said.

The most outstanding and unique feature is the lighting system composed of 149 searchlights and a 70-kilowatt beam that radiates outward for nearly 71km (44 miles). When illuminated, the lights project a gigantic cross in the sky that can be seen as far away as Puerto Rico.

Although the concept of the memorial is 140 years old, the first stones were not laid until 1986, following the design submitted in 1929 by J. L. Gleave, the winner of the worldwide contest held to choose the architect. The monumental lighthouse was inaugurated on October 6, 1992, the day Columbus's "remains" were transferred from the cathedral.

Av. España (on the water side of Los Tres Ojos, near the airport in the Sans Souci district). ✆ **809/591-1492.** Admission RD$65 (US$1.95/£1) adults, RD$5 (US15¢/10p) children 11 and under. Tues–Sun 9am–5:30pm.

Fortaleza Ozama   On the southern side of Old Town's most famous street, this fortress was constructed in 1502, but much was changed and altered over the centuries. It lies on a steep hill over the mouth of the Río Ozama, and, from this point, the Spanish launched conquests of Jamaica, Peru, Mexico, Cuba, and Colombia. Still standing today, it remains the oldest colonial military building in the New World and is now open to the public. Among the walled buildings here stands the Torre del Homenaje (Tower of Homage), evoking a Spanish castle with walls 2m (6½ ft.) thick and a crenellated tower. If you climb to the roof, you'll be rewarded with a 360-degree **view of the city** ★★★.

Other attractions include the excavated ruins of a fort from 1502; the intact wall of Fort Santiago, the first line of defense; and an old arsenal where gunpowder was once stored. In the courtyard beyond the main gate there is a statue of González Oviedo, author of the first *History of the Indies.* He also commanded the fort from 1533 to 1557.

Calle Las Damas. ( ) **809/686-0222.** Admission RD$15 (US45¢/25p). Mon–Sat 9am–7pm; Sun 9am–3pm.

3 The Leading Museums

Amber World Museum   The Dominican Republic is the home of the finest amber in the world. This museum provides a fascinating glimpse into the world of amber. Amber, of course, is hardened tree resin. The resin often trapped and preserved mosquitoes, flies, spiders, ants, and even lizards and frogs, for millennia upon millennia. In addition to displaying amber that preserves animals and insects from long ago, the museum also displays a beautiful collection of amber jewelry and other artifacts. Audiovisual displays show amber being mined and made into jewelry. Amber comes in a variety of colors, ranging from deep red to a light yellow, even a blue or the extremely rare smoky green.

Calle Arzobispo Meriño 452. ( ) **809/686-5700.** Admission RD$50 (US$1.50/75p). Mon–Sat 8:30am–6pm; Sun 9am–2pm.

The Larimar Museum   On the ground floor is an upscale shop selling larimar and amber jewelry at prices that are negotiable. Upstairs is a museum devoted to the rare larimar, a blue pectolite mined only in the Dominican Republic. English- and Spanish-language exhibits explain everything from the original discovery and mining of the stone to how it is used, most often appearing in jewelry. You also learn how nature created larimar, with its distinctive volcanic blue color, and where it is found.

Isabel la Católica 54. ( ) **809/689-6605.** www.larimarmuseum.com. Free admission. Mon–Sat 8:30am–6pm; Sun 9am–1pm.

Museo de las Atarazanas   This is a rarely visited but worthy museum filled with some unexpected treasures, including some of the rescued booty from the 1500s wreck of *Concepción,* the Spanish galleon that was sunk during a hurricane while sailing off the coast of Bahía de Samaná. Divers have spent 4 centuries trying to rescue all the loot that went down to a sea burial, and some of the treasure is exhibited here, including bars of silver, gold coins, ancient china, and shards of pottery. Many other relics rescued from shipwrecks off the Dominican coast are on display, including belt buckles, pipes, brandy bottles, and pewter plates. The building housing the museum was once a customs house and later a storage house.

Calle Colón 4. ( ) **809/682-5834.** Admission RD$50 (US$1.50/75p). Daily 9am–5pm.

Museo de las Casas Reales (Museum of the Royal Houses) ⛅ *Kids*   Through artifacts, tapestries, maps, and re-created halls, including a courtroom, this museum traces Santo Domingo's history from 1492 to 1821. Gilded furniture, arms and armor, and other colonial artifacts make it the most interesting museum of Old Santo Domingo. It contains replicas of the *Niña,* the *Pinta,* and the *Santa Maria,* and one exhibit is said to hold some of Columbus's ashes. In addition to pre-Columbian art, you can see the main artifacts of two galleons sunk in 1724 on their way from Spain to Mexico, along with remnants of another 18th-century Spanish ship, the *Concepción.*

Calle Las Damas (at the corner of Las Mercedes). ⓒ **809/682-4202.** Admission RD$30 (US90¢/45p), children under 12 RD$5 (US15¢/10p). Tues–Sun 9am–5pm.

Plaza de la Cultura ⛅⛅   Once the personal property of the dictator Trujillo, this modern complex of buildings, known as the Plaza de la Cultura, houses four museums. These ultramodern buildings stand in a parklike setting, and you occupy the better part of your day if you choose to visit everything.

Museo de Arte Moderno ⛅   Four floors here are dedicated to 20th-century Dominican art, with the permanent collection on the second and third floors and the temporary exhibits on the first and fourth. Visitors expecting that Dominican art is roughly equivalent to that which Haiti made famous are in for a surprise. Many Dominican artists vie with some of the best modern artists in the world, painting in a variety of styles. Some island artists have gone on to world acclaim, including Cándido Bidó, known for stylized idealizations of *campesino,* or peasant, life. Bidó's works are characterized by exaggerated lips and hollowed-out eyes. All six of the Bidó works on display are on the second floor, including his best known, *El Paseo a las 10am,* depicting a woman in a sun hat with a handful of flowers.

Many island artists were obviously influenced by big names elsewhere—thus, you might encounter an Andy Warhol rip-off or a painting derivative of Diego Rivera's brand of social realism. Other Dominicans, however, produce very original and imaginative art. The greatest art is that of Spanish expat Vela Zanetti, including his *La Vida de los Campesinos* series. Zanetti's work is found in many public buildings, including the United Nations' Security Council chambers in New York.

Avs. Pedro Henríquez Ureña and Máximo Gomes, Plaza de la Cultura. ⓒ **809/685-2153.** Admission RD$50 (US$1.50/75p), students RD$25 (US75¢/40p). Tues–Sun 10am–6pm.

Museo del Hombre Dominicano ★★   If you have to skip all the other museums at the Plaza de la Cultura, try to spare an hour to an hour and a half to explore these exhibits, the finest collection in the Caribbean of the artifacts of the pre-Columbian peoples, including the Taíno Indians. This is, in fact, the most important collection in the world of the Taínos, who greeted Columbus in 1492, little knowing the horrible fate that awaited them, including disease, slavery, and ultimately death at the hands of these strange visitors from another world.

Thousands of magnificently sculpted ceramic, bone, and shell works are on display, along with grinding stones, carved necklaces, axes, and pottery. One section is devoted to the conquest of the West Indies, focusing on the pain suffered by the slaves under the domination of the Spanish. The life of the peasant is brilliantly depicted, including a typical country house that has been reconstructed in the museum. The exhibits are a pastiche of African, Taíno, and Spanish cultures, all of which went to influence Dominican life today. There's a little bit of everything here, even the "throne car" that the pope rode through the streets of Santo Domingo on a 1979 visit. One festive section depicts carnival costumes from around the island.

Av. Pedro Henríquez Ureña, Plaza de la Cultura. © **809/687-3622** or 809/687-3623. Admission for students RD$25 (US75¢/40p), adults RD$50 (US$1.50/75p), children 12 and under free. Tues–Sun 10am–5pm.

Museo Nacional de Historia y Geografía   Near the National Library, this museum displays many personal belongings of Rafael Trujillo, one of the most notorious Caribbean dictators of the 20th century, including items of clothing, military uniforms, even his briefcases and medals he was awarded from such countries as Spain and Argentina, both of which knew a lot about dictators themselves. Many of his personal documents are on exhibit, as well as personal items such as his comb, his razor, and his wallet. Also on display, along with portraits of El Benefactor (as Trujillo liked to call himself), you'll see one of the bullet-riddled cars that was part of the presidential motorcade when Trujillo was assassinated. You also get to look at the pancake makeup kit Trujillo used to hide his Haitian ancestry. There are also exhibits relating the story of the American occupation of the island; artifacts of the conquistadors, the early colonists under Spanish rule; and exhibits depicting the Haitian invasion of the Dominican Republic, as well as other highlights of the nation's history. One wing concentrates on re-creating the legend of General Ulises Heureuax, the D.R.'s most important dictator of the 19th century.

Av. Pedro Henríquez Ureña, Plaza de la Cultura. ✆ 809/686-6668. Admission RD$50 (US$1.50/75p). Tues–Sun 9:30am–4:30pm.

4 Most Historic Churches

The **Monasterio de San Francisco (Monastery of San Francisco)** is a mere ruin, but romantically lit at night. It was built between 1512 and 1544. That any part of it is still standing is a miracle; it was destroyed by earthquakes, pillaged by Sir Francis Drake and his men, and bombarded by French artillery. To get here, go along Calle Hostos and across Calle Emiliano Tejere; continue up the hill, and about midway along you'll see the ruins.

Capilla de Nuestra Señora de los Remedios   You'll recognize this chapel in the Colonial Zone by its attractive triple-arched belfry atop a brick-built facade. The Chapel of Our Lady of the Remedies was constructed in the Gothic style in the 1500s by Francisco de Avila, an alderman. It was not intended for public use but built as a private chapel and family mausoleum for the Ovando and Dávila families, two of the most prominent in the city back then. In time, people of the old town did attend Mass here under a barrel-vaulted ceiling. When city officials pronounced the building dangerous in 1884, it was torn down and rebuilt.

Calle Las Damas corner of Mercedes. ✆ 809/686-8657. Free admission, donations appreciated. Daily 8am–4pm.

Iglesia de Nuestra Señora de las Mercedes   This is one of the most historic churches of Santo Domingo, although the staff overseeing it today aren't the city's brightest bulbs. It may or may not be open at the time of your visit. Constructed back in the 1530s, the Church of Our Lady of Mercy was once sacked by Sir Francis Drake and his "pirates." The building suffered major disasters in the wake of Drake, including hurricanes and earthquakes. Still standing, it is of interest today because of its mahogany altar carved in the shape of a demon serpent. The cloister adjacent to the church is more or less in its original condition. During the Haitian rule of the island, some 6,000 Africans were held here before being shipped off to Puerto Plata and Samaná.

Corner of Las Mercedes y José Reyes. ✆ 809/682-3744. Free admission, donations appreciated. Mon–Fri 4:30–6:30pm; Sat 5–7pm; Sun 8am–8:30pm.

Iglesia Santa Bárbara   Completed in 1574, this is a combination church-and-fortress, the only one of its kind in the country. This impressive whitewashed building honors the saint of the military. The capital crowning the baroque building is ridiculously tiny for such a structure, and its towers are of different height and design, a curious hodgepodge. Two of its three arches were reconstructed without windows, the third framing a massively sturdy door. This architecture followed in the wake of attacks by Sir Francis Drake's men but might also have been to protect the building against hurricanes. There is little of interest inside, so you may be in and out the door in 10 minutes or so.

Isabel la Católica, corner of Gabino Coello. ⓒ **809/682-3307**. Free admission, donations appreciated. Open to the public 5–7pm daily; Sun Mass 7:30am, 9am, and 6pm; Mon–Sat Mass 6pm.

Iglesia y Convento Dominico   Founded in 1510, this is one of the oldest churches and convents in the West Indies. In the Colonial Zone, it lies just south of El Conde. This was the site of the New World's first university, San Tomé de Aquino, before it folded and moved on. Impressive pillars frame the stone facade, and blue Mudéjar tiles, evocative of Spain, run along the top of the portal. Vine ornamentation—which the Spaniards call "Isabelline" style— surrounds the circular window at the core of the church. Saturday and Sunday hours, especially Saturday hours, are severely limited.

Across the plaza, at the corner of avenidas Duarte and Padre Billini, stands **Capilla de la Tercera Orden Domínica,** or the Chapel of the Third Dominican Order. Constructed in 1729, this is the only colonial monument in the city to reach the 21st century intact. Today, it is the office of the archbishop of Santo Domingo. Although you can stop to admire its impressive baroque facade, you're not allowed to peek inside.

Calle Padre Bellini and Av. Duarte. ⓒ **809/682-3780**. Free admission. Open to public during Mass hours Sun 8am, 11am, 7:30pm, Mon–Sat 6pm.

5 Other Attractions & Curiosities

Acuario Nacional 🔆 *Kids*   This is the grandest aquarium in the Caribbean, a project funded during the Balaguer administration that caused great controversy, opponents claiming "the people's money" could be better spent elsewhere, perhaps on public schools, hospitals, and housing. Nonetheless, *el presidente* wanted a grand aquarium and continued to press for funds.

Misspent money or not, the results are spectacular. At one point you can take an underwater corridor under a Plexiglas tank, watching sharks, barracuda, and other ferocious-looking big fish glide by over your head. The exhibits are in Spanish only so you may not know the English names of some of the weirder denizens of the deep. You'll surely recognize a manatee. Lesser known might be the endangered slider turtle, part of a breeding project of the aquarium hoping to save this species from extinction.

Av. España 75. © 809/766-1709. Admission RD$50 (US$1.50/75p) adults, RD$25 (US75¢/40p) children under 11. Tues–Sun 9:30am–5:30pm.

Casa del Cordón ✪ *Finds* Near the Alcázar de Colón, the Cord House was named for the cord of the Franciscan order, which is carved above the door. Francisco de Garay, who came to Hispaniola with Columbus, built the casa from 1503 to 1504, which makes it the oldest stone house in the Western Hemisphere. It once lodged the first Royal Audience of the New World, which performed as the Supreme Court of Justice for the island and the rest of the West Indies. On another occasion, in January 1586, the noble ladies of Santo Domingo gathered here to donate their jewelry as ransom demanded by Sir Francis Drake in return for his promise to leave the city. The restoration of this historical manor was financed by the Banco Popular Dominicano, where its executive offices are found.

Calles Emiliano Tejera and Isabel la Católica. No phone. Free admission. Mon–Fri 9am–5pm.

Casa de Tostado The beautiful Gothic geminate (double) window in the Casa de Tostado is the only one existing today in the New World. The house was first owned by the scribe Francisco Tostado, and then was inherited by his son of the same name, a professor, writer, and poet who, in 1586, was the victim of a shot fired during Drake's bombardment of Santo Domingo. The Casa de Tostado, which at one time was the archbishop's palace, now houses the **Museo de la Familia Dominicana,** which focuses on life in the 19th century in a well-to-do household.

Calle Arzobispo Meriño, corner of Padre Billini. © 809/688-6918. Admission RD$30 (US90¢/45p). Mon–Sat 9am–4pm.

Palacio Nacional You may or may not be granted entrance to the seat of government of the Dominican Republic. Instead of calling on your own, it might be better to have your hotel do it for you. If you do get an invitation extended, show up in the finest garb you brought along. The mammoth palace near the Zona Colonial was built of roseate marble extracted from the Peninsula of Samaná. The architect was an Italian, Guido D'Alessandro, who inaugurated the palace in 1947 in the neoclassical style. It is magnificently furnished with gilt mirrors, crystal chandeliers, and art from some of the nation's most prominent painters. The most dramatic salon is the Room of the Caryatids, with 44 sculpted and clothed women rising like columns in a miniature Hall of Versailles with Baccarat chandeliers and French mirrors. Filled with government offices, the building stretches for nearly a block.

Corner of avs. México and 30 de Marzo. © 809/695-8000. Free admission. By appointment only.

Panteón de la Patria   When this structure was built in 1747, it was a church for the Jesuits. Later it was a warehouse and then a theater before the dictator, Rafael Trujillo, seized it in the days when Santo Domingo was called Ciudad Trujillo. No doubt dreaming of imperial glory, he wanted to make the building a shrine to some of the country's most illustrious citizens, including perhaps a memorial to himself. He did not succeed in his dream. Instead of a monument honoring Trujillo, you get a chapel preserving the ashes of the martyrs of June 14, 1959, who tried in vain to overthrow the dreaded tyrant. In addition, the ashes or remains of many of the nation's most illustrious personages are enshrined here. Trujillo had bodies reinterred. Some figures ended up buried next to their political enemies, as was the case with Pedro Santana, the 19th-century dictator, who rests—perhaps not so peacefully—with a string of *caudillos* who fought bitterly to overthrow each other as *el presidente*. The Spanish dictator, Franco, donated the mammoth central chandelier. Many of the metal crosses, or so the rumor mill has it, were once Nazi swastikas. The rather sterile structure is constructed of mammoth limestone blocks behind a neoclassical facade, its entrance constantly guarded by an armed soldier.

Calle Las Damas, corner of Mercedes. © 809/685-4466. Free admission. Tues–Sun 8am–5pm.

6 Gardens, Parks & a Zoo

Jardín Botánico Nacional   In the northern sector of Santo Domingo, these botanical gardens are the biggest in all of Latin America, containing flowers and lush vegetation from around the island. You can wander at leisure or else take a RD$15 (US45¢/25p) shuttle to get around the park, taking in a wealth of luxuriant planting, including ferns, palms, orchids, and bromeliads. The Japanese

Garden is a special highlight, as are a floor clock and the Great Ravine. If you don't have time to escape to the Dominican countryside, this is your best chance for a preview.

Av. República de Colombia. © **809/385-0860**. Admission RD$10 (30¢/15p) adults, RD$5 (US15¢/10p) children 9 and under. Daily 9am–6pm.

Parque Mirador del Este   This sprawling city park ("Eastern Lookout Park" in English) lies across the Río Ozama from the Zona Colonial. The park's most visible feature is a monument to Christopher Columbus (see "El Faro a Colón," p. 73).

The park is riddled with caves—really, limestone sinkholes—created eons ago. The most famous and most explored of these is **Los Tres Ojos (The Three Eyes),** which can be reached by taking a long staircase carved into the side of this cave. Here, three lagoons are set in these scenic caverns, studded with lots of stalactites and stalagmites. One lagoon is 12m (39 ft.) deep, another 6m (20 ft.) deep. A third lagoon—known as "Ladies Bath"—is only 1.5m (5 ft.) deep. A Dominican Tarzan will sometimes dive off the walls of the cavern into the deepest lagoon. You can explore the caverns on walkways. Admission is RD$20 (US60¢/30p), and visits are possible daily from 9am to 5pm.

Popular with joggers and cyclists, the park is also peopled with some of the most aggressive souvenir hawkers in the Dominican Republic. To see the park's natural attractions, anticipate lots of hassle to buy postcards, jewelry, or whatever.

Along Av. Mirador del Este. Daily 24 hr.

Parque Mirador del Sur   "Southern Lookout Park" (its English name) lies in the southwestern sector of Santo Domingo. The young professional set of the city can be seen here in the early morning in their jogging suits. They also roller-skate and bicycle through the park. Later in the day an older crowd visits the park. After school, it is often filled with mothers and their children. The park was created on a large limestone ridge that is studded with caves, many the size of a football field, although some hardly have room for a mongoose and its offspring. When you get thirsty, you'll find any number of food stands or juice bars. Baseball is the national sport of the Dominican Republic, and you'll note several baseball diamonds scattered about. The park is closed to cars daily from 6 to 9am and 4 to 8pm.

Av. Mirador del Sur. Free admission. Daily 24 hr.

Parque Zoológico Nacional 🐾 *Kids*   This is one of the largest zoos in Latin America, but attracts few visitors as it lies in a hard-to-reach northwest corridor in a poor section of narrow, winding streets. It's best to go by taxi to avoid getting lost. These 128 hectares (316 acres) are home to both native and exotic animals and birds. An aquatic bird lake; a crocodile pond; a snake exhibit; and the huge "African Plain," where fauna from that continent roam, make this a fascinating place to visit. There's also a beautiful pond filled with graceful flamingo and a tiger compound without bars. The zoo has a souvenir shop, snack bar, and rest areas.

Av. Los Arroyos. (*C*) 809/562-3149. Free admission. Tues–Sun 9am–5pm.

ORGANIZED TOURS **Prieto Tours,** Av. Francia 125 ((*C*) **809/ 685-0102**), one of the capital's leading tour operators, offers a 3-hour tour of the **Colonial Zone,** leaving most mornings at 9am and again at 3pm if there's sufficient demand; it costs US$25 (£13). A 6-hour tour visits the Colonial Zone, the **Columbus Lighthouse,** the **Aquarium,** and the city's modern neighborhoods; the US$35 (£18) fee includes lunch and entrance to several well-known museums and monuments. About an hour of the tour is devoted to shopping.

7 Beaches & Other Outdoor Fun

BEACHES The Dominican Republic has some great beaches, but they aren't in Santo Domingo. The principal beach resort near the capital is at **Boca Chica,** less than 3.2km (2 miles) east of the airport and about 31km (19 miles) from the center of Santo Domingo. Here you'll find clear, shallow water, a white-sand beach, and a natural coral reef. The east side of the beach, known as "St. Tropez," is popular with Europeans. In recent years, the backdrop of the beach has become rather tacky, with an array of pizza and fast-food stands, beach cottages, chaise longues, watersports concessions, and plastic beach tables.

Long a favorite of Santo Domingo's city dwellers before its discovery by foreigners, Playa Boca Chica is one of the grand beaches of the Caribbean, very wide with white or golden sands set against a backdrop of coconut palms. The beach is fronted by the shallow Bahía Andrés. Unlike the north coast, with its turbulent waters, this beach is the most tranquil in the country.

The beach is a whirlwind of activity day and night, with an international crowd staking a claim on a "place in the sun." They are not always allowed to rest in peace, as vendors ply the beach hawking fruit or souvenirs. As mariachi bands entertain (wanting a tip, of course), young boys seek out gay tourists (and the occasional woman), and young girls ply their trade with older men desiring sex with a teenager.

Lying only 9m (30 ft.) from the shore is a little uninhabited island covered with shrub that you can wade over to. But once you get here, there's nothing to see.

The general public enters the beach on Avenida Duarte. Near the main entrance here you'll see a number of wooden hovels hawking fried fish and *yani queque,* the pizza-size rounds of flavored batter. If you're seeking less crowded conditions, you can walk west along the beach as the tourist facilities gradually disappear. The drawback here is that the waters this far west are often muddy.

Slightly better maintained is the narrow white-sand beach at **Juan Dolio** or **Playa Esmeralda,** a 20-minute drive east of Boca Chica. Several resorts have recently located here. The beach used to be fairly uncrowded, but with all the hotels now lining it, it's likely to be as crowded as Boca Chica any day of the week.

There are three major beaches spread along the Caribbean Sea, beginning with **Playa Guayacanes** in the west, with **Playa Juan Dolio** in the center, and **Playa Real** in the east. These beaches are often referred to collectively as Playa de Villas del Mar. Our favorite of these is Playa Guayacanes, which is one of the most beautiful beaches in the area and home to a little community of locals called Guayacanes.

⌒Moments *Un, Dos, Tres* Strikes—You're Out

Dominicans were crazy about baseball long before their countryman Sammy Sosa set the United States on fire with his home run race against Mark McGwire. Almost every Major League baseball team has at least one player from the Dominican Republic on its roster these days. Pedro Martinez, Manny Ramirez, and Alfonso Soriano are just a few of the all-star team of players who hail from the Dominican Republic.

If you're here between October and January, you might want to catch a game in the Dominican Republic's Professional Winter League. The **Liga de Beisbol** stadium (© 809/ 567-6371) is in Santo Domingo; check local newspapers for game times, or ask at your hotel. There are also games at the Tetelo Vargas Stadium in San Pedro de Macoris, known to die-hard sports fans as the "land of shortstops" for the multitude of infielders that call this tiny town home.

As you move east from Guayacanes, the sands are better than the water, the latter filled with wide expanses of dead coral, making the swimming less than desirable. Many of the best sandy beaches are maintained zealously by the all-inclusives.

HORSE RACING   Santo Domingo's racetrack, **Galapagos Hipó-dromo V Centenario,** on Avenida Las Américas, km 14.5 (© 809/687-6060), schedules races Tuesday, Thursday, and Saturday at 2pm. You can spend the day here and have lunch at the track's restaurant. Admission is free.

TENNIS   You can often play on the courts at the major resorts if you ask your hotel desk to call in advance for you and make arrangements.

8 Best Shopping Buys

The best buys in Santo Domingo are handcrafted native items, especially amber jewelry. **Amber,** petrified tree resin that has fossilized over millions of years, is the national gem. Look for pieces of amber with objects like insects or spiders trapped inside. Colors range from a bright yellow to black, but most of the gems are golden in hue. Fine-quality amber jewelry, along with lots of plastic fakes, is sold throughout the country.

A semiprecious stone of light blue (sometimes a dark-blue color), **larimar** is the Dominican turquoise. It often makes striking jewelry, and is sometimes mounted with wild boar's teeth.

Ever since the Dominicans presented John F. Kennedy with what became his favorite rocker, visitors have wanted to take home a **rocking chair.** These rockers are often sold unassembled, for easy shipping. Other good buys include Dominican rum, hand-knit articles, macramé, ceramics, and crafts in native mahogany.

BEST SHOPPING AREAS

The street with the densest population of useful shops is **El Conde,** which is known to consumers throughout the capital as a venue that's loaded with middle-bracket, workaday stores selling basic necessities (food, clothing, cleaning supplies), electronic goods, CDs, and luxury items within a street that's peppered with fast-food joints, cafes, and bars, even an outlet for Baskin-Robbins. In the colonial section, **La Atarazana** is more geared for foreign visitors who aren't necessarily maintaining a private home or apartment within the capital, and have no interest in buying soaps, consumer goods, or groceries. La Atarazana has a higher concentration than El Conde of art galleries

> ⟨**Tips**⟩ **You Call That a Bargain?**
>
> Always haggle over the price of handicrafts in the Dominican Republic, particularly in the open-air markets. No stall-keeper expects you to pay the first price asked. Remember the Spanish words for too expensive: *muy caro* (pronounced mwee *cah*-row).

and gift and jewelry stores. Duty-free shops are found within the airport, and in the capital at the **Centro de los Héroes.**

Head first for the National Market, **El Mercado Modelo** ⟨✹✹✹⟩, Avenida Mella, filled with stall after stall (about 100 independent vendors) selling crafts, spices, and produce. The market lies in a battered two-story structure near Calle Santomé, just north of the Colonial Zone, and is open daily from 9am to 6pm. The merchants will be most eager to sell, and you can easily get lost in the crush. Remember to bargain. You'll see a lot of tortoiseshell work here, but exercise caution, since many species, especially the hawksbill turtle, are on the endangered-species list and could be impounded by U.S. Customs if discovered in your luggage. Also for sale here are rockers, mahogany, sandals, baskets, hats, and clay braziers for grilling fish. That's not all. Expect to find everything from musical instruments to love potions, even voodoo objects. *Warning:* Pickpockets, regrettably, are rampant.

Don't overlook the upmarket hotels as shopping venues. In Santo Domingo some of the best shops, at least the highest-quality merchandise, are sold in hotel corridors and arcades. In Santo Domingo, the best shops are found at the **Hilton Santo Domingo** (p. 50), **Meliá Santo Domingo** (p. 51), **Quinto Centenario Inter-Continental** (p. 52), and the **Renaissance Jaragua Hotel & Casino** (p. 52).

SHOPPING A TO Z
AMBER & LARIMAR
Ambar Nacional ⟨✹⟩   This is the most reliable source for stunning amber, as well as coral. This is also the best source for purchasing larimar jewelry. Open Monday to Saturday from 8am to 6pm, Sunday from 8am to noon. Calle Restauración 110. ⟨✆⟩ **809/686-5700.**

The Swiss Mine   In front of the cathedral, this prestigious store is another fine place to purchase amber or larimar jewelry. It is also one of the most convenient outlets. The design work on the jewelry here is the most impressive and imaginative in the city. Prices, it is estimated, are about a third less than what they'd be in such cities as Miami. Open Monday to Saturday from 9am to 6pm; Sunday times are irregular. El Conde 101. ✆ 809/221-1897.

CIGARS

Cigar King   The store is aptly named, as cigars are a big-selling item in Santo Domingo. The best selection of cigars in the colonial city is found here. Its selection of Dominican and Cuban cigars in a temperature-controlled room is wide-ranging. However, those Cuban stogies have to be smoked locally, as they are not allowed into the United States. Open Monday to Saturday from 9am to 6:30pm. Calle Conde 208, Baguero Building. ✆ 809/686-4987.

Santo Domingo Cigar Club   This is another good outlet for all types of tobacco products, featuring both Cuban and Dominican-made cigars. In the lobby of the Renaissance Jaragua Hotel, this is a good place to sit, smoke, and read magazines. Open Monday to Saturday from 9am to 10pm. Av. George Washington 367. ✆ 809/221-1483.

DEPARTMENT STORES

Jumbo   La Sirena (see below) considers Jumbo as its biggest competitor in the mercantile wars over which chain of department stores is preeminent within the D.R. Most of its focus is on middle-to-low-end consumer goods, but prices are low, and the physical settings, as the chain's name implies, are Jumbo-size. Open Monday to Saturday from 8:30am to 8pm, Sunday from 9am to 2pm. In the Mega-Center Mall, Av. San Vincente de Paul s/n. ✆ 809/692-1000.

La Sirena   This is the most comprehensive and best department store in Santo Domingo. Although it exists mainly for the city's residents, visitors are always casing the joint for low prices on any number of items, ranging from cut-rate clothing to innumerable household items. You can also pick up Dominican crafts here inexpensively. In addition to moderately priced merchandise, it also sells upmarket fashions for men and women. Open Monday to Saturday from 8:30am to 8pm, Sunday from 9am to 2pm. Av. Mella 258. ✆ 809/221-3232.

HANDICRAFTS & GIFTS

Columbus Plaza (Decla, S.A.)   Big, noisy, dusty, and guaranteed to give you sensory overload, this is one of the largest supermarket-style gift-and-artifacts stores in the country. The sheer volume of low-end merchandise might overwhelm you at first, but if you are persistent and like to dig deep into piles of stuff, you might pick up some quality items at a low price. It sprawls over three floors of a modern building divided into boutiques specializing in amber, larimar, gold and silver jewelry, cigars, paintings and sculpture, plus craft items. Open Monday to Saturday 9:30am to 6pm, Sunday 11am to 2pm. Calle Arzobispo Meriño 204. ✆ 809/689-0565.

HOME FURNISHINGS

Nuebo ★★   Patronized by some of the capital's most socially conscious, this upmarket and rather expensive outlet sells a carefully chosen assortment of art objects, lamps, and furnishings, including the kind of four-poster beds that tend to be showcased in fashion layouts. In home furnishings, this store is the market leader in Santo Domingo. With some persuasion, anything you buy here can be shipped home for you. Open Monday to Friday 8:30am to 6:30pm, Saturday 8:30am to 6pm. Fantino Falco 36, Naco. ✆ 809/562-3333.

Von   For handcrafted furniture made of mahogany, cedar, or pine, this is your best bet. Designs are original, very contemporary, and not inexpensive. Von will ship whatever you buy directly from its factory to Europe or North America, although you should carefully factor in the shipping costs in your appraisal of the overall cost of whatever deal you make. Open Monday to Friday from 9am to 7pm, Saturday from 10am to 6pm. Calle Virato Fiallo 16, Sánchez Julieta. ✆ 809/566-1433.

PAINTINGS & SCULPTURE

As you're going from gallery to gallery, you might keep an eye out for the works of any of the following artists. Although there are many rising artists, a few have achieved international recognition, including Guillo Pérez (famous for his paintings of oxen), Juan Bautista Gómez ("sensual landscapes"), Adriana Billini Gautreau (known for her remarkable portraits), Luis Desangles (exponent of folkloric art), and Mairano Eckert (depicts workaday Dominican life).

Galería de Arte Nader   In the center of the most historical section of town, you'll find so many Latin paintings here that they're sometimes stacked in rows against the walls. The works of the country's best-known painters and most promising newcomers are displayed here. There is also a lot of tourist junk, shipped in by the truckload from Haiti. In the ancient courtyard in back, you can get a glimpse of how things looked in the Spanish colonies hundreds of years ago. Open Monday to Friday from 9am to 7pm, Saturday from 9am to 1pm. Rafael Augusto Sánchez 22. ✆ 809/544-0878.

Galería El Greco ❧   This is a good showcase for Dominican painters, both newly emerging and more established. As such, it's more selective in its choice of artists than Nader, which seems aimed more at the tourist market. Galería El Greco and Lyle O. Reitzel (see below) are on par with each other in terms of quality art. In business for some 4 decades, this is one of the more reliable galleries in town, and it also features an array of art from neighboring Haiti. Open Monday to Friday from 8am to noon and 2 to 6pm, Saturday from 8am to noon. Av. Tiradentes 16. ✆ **809/562-5921.**

Lyle O. Reitzel Art Contemporáneo ❧   This first-rate gallery displays only the finest work of island artists, with some work by international painters as well. The exhibits tend to focus on well-known artists' work, such as the dark paintings of José García Cordero, a Dominican living in Paris. Open Monday to Friday 9am to 1pm and 4 to 8pm, Saturday 11am to 2pm. Plaza Andalucía II. ✆ **809/227-8361.**

9 Santo Domingo After Dark

CLASSICAL MUSIC & DANCE

Teatro Nacional, Plaza de la Cultura (✆ **809/687-3191**), is the major cultural venue of the Dominican Republic. The 1,700-seat theater is home to opera, ballet, and symphonic performances. The various presentations are announced in the newspapers, and tickets can be purchased at the box office daily from 9:30am to 12:30pm and 3:30 to 6:30pm. Ticket prices vary, depending on the event, but usually range from RD$70 to RD$250 (US$2.10–US$7.60/£1.10–£3.85).

DANCE CLUBS

Local young people flock to the dance clubs in droves around midnight. Even the hotel discos cater to locals as well as tourists. Great dancers abound, so go and watch even if you're not as light on your feet as you wish.

Bachata Rosa   In the Colonial Zone, Bachata Rosa takes its name from a popular song on the island. In fact, Juan Luis Guerra, the Dominican merengue megastar who made the song a hit, is part owner. Currently, this is one of the capital's best dance clubs, with dancing, drinking, and mating games sprawling out over two separate floors. This club draws a heavier concentration of locals than of visitors. There's also a Dominican restaurant on the premises. The food is only standard fare, and you might want to dine elsewhere before heading to this club. At least it'll help you stave off the munchies. Daily 8pm to 4am. La Atarazana 9. ⓒ 809/688-0969.

El Napolitano Disco This place attracts some of the wealthiest of the young Dominicans along with a mixture of visitors who like to dance the night away along the Malecón. Noted by many of its fans as the site of an ocean-fronting terrace whose tables are particularly charming for a romantic date, it's a dress-up place. Music focuses on recorded merengue, salsa, reggae, and other music. An RD$100 (US$3.05/£1.55) cover is imposed Thursday to Saturday. Otherwise the club is free and open daily 6pm to 4am. Av. George Washington 101. ⓒ 809/687-1131.

Fantasy Disco One of the capital's most popular discos, and frequented mostly by already-committed couples, most of whom like to dance, is a dark and shadowy space that's about a block inland from the Malecón. Once you get past the vigilant security staff, you'll find lots of intimate nooks and crannies, a small dance floor, and one of the country's best-chosen medleys of nonstop merengue music. Entrance is free, and beer costs RD$75 to RD$100 (US$2.25–US$3/£1.15–£1.50) a bottle. The place is open daily from 6pm till 4am. Av. Heroes de Luperón 29, La Feria. ⓒ 809/535-5581.

Jet Set ⓡ As one of the capital's most sought-after and most elaborate nightclubs, Jet Set admits couples only, and nobody who is too rowdy. Most of the tables and chairs slope down toward an amphitheater-style dance floor, giving the place the feel of a bullfighting arena. The live orchestras that play here are the best in town. Entrance costs between RD$300 and RD$1,200 (US$9.10–US$36/£4.60–£18), depending on the artist, although if only recorded music is playing on the night of your debut, admission will be free. The Jet Set takes off at 9pm and flies until the early morning. For some reason, local hipsters consider Monday nights here to be as much fun and perhaps just as crowded as a Saturday night would be at another dance club. Centro Comercial El Portal, Av. Independencia. ⓒ 809/533-9707.

La Guácara Taína This is one of the best *discotecas* in the country, drawing equal numbers of locals and visitors. Set in an underground cave within a verdant park, the specialty is merengue, salsa, and other forms of Latin music. There are three bars, two dance floors, and banquettes and chairs nestled into the rocky walls. The cover is RD$300 (US$9.10/£4.60) (includes one drink). Open Tuesday to Sunday from 9pm; closing time varies. Av. Mirador del Sur, in Parque Mirador del Sur. ⓒ 809/533-1051.

ROLLING THE DICE

Santo Domingo has several major casinos. We view gambling here as a very minor attraction and find the odds that you'll haul away any serious money as pretty much against you. Frankly, if gambling is your passion and/or obsession, you'd do better to plan a holiday in Puerto Rico, where casinos are bigger, splashier, and somehow, filled with a greater sense of optimism.

One of the casinos that's cited as big, fun, and splashy enough to keep a semi-addicted gambler amused and entertained is within the **Hispaniola Hotel,** Avenida Independencia (© **809/535-9292**), which is open daily noon to 5am, and which, frankly, is a lot more appealing and a lot better maintained than the hotel that contains it. It's also the site of occasional live concerts by famous bands, where no one objects if you end up dancing in the aisles.

Casino Diamante   This is a relatively stylish and, compared to the Jaragua, a relatively subdued choice. Its bilingual staff will help you play blackjack, craps, baccarat, and keno, among other games. There's also a piano bar. Open daily noon to 6am. In the Meliá Santo Domingo, Av. George Washington 361. © **809/682-2102.**

El Napolitano Casino   While this place is a bit downscale and middle-bracket, catering as it does to a clientele of local clients rather than conspicuous consumers from North America and Europe, the action can sometimes get more frantic than at the more stylish and more upscale Casino Hispaniola. Blackjack, poker, mini-baccarat, and roulette are just some of the games of chance offered here. Open daily 4pm to 6am. Av. George Washington 101. © **809/687-1131.**

The Majestic Casino   Opened in 2005, it is associated with its immediate neighbor, the Hilton Santo Domingo. This is the newest casino in town, managing to be somehow glittery but tasteful at the same time. It's not the most animated casino in the capital, and on quiet nights it can be a bit staid, but you'll quickly get the feeling that it's deep into the process of finding a clientele of its own. Open daily 4pm to 4am. In the Malecón Center, Av. George Washington 500. © **809/687-4853.**

Renaissance Jaragua Hotel & Casino   This is the casino most cited as a venue for big bangs and big bucks, and most razzmatazz. It's appropriately housed in the capital's most glitzy hotel. You can't miss the brightly flashing sign; it's the most dazzling light along the Malecón. You can wager on blackjack, baccarat, roulette, and slot machines in either Dominican pesos or U.S. dollars. Management is relatively indulgent about the many good-looking women who hang out here, most of whom aren't at all shy about creative ways to show an available man a good time. Open daily 4pm to 4am. Av. George Washington 367. ℂ 809/221-2222.

PIANO LOUNGES & BARS

Adrian Tropical   This is the only bar in town that, because of a rental agreement with the government that pre-dated later, more stringent, zoning laws, sits directly astride the Malecón in the heart of town. As such, it's a welcome bright spot for "be-ins" positioned prominently beside a pedestrian walkway that, at night, can sometimes be shadowy and even a bit spooky. Decidedly youth-oriented, it's a wood-and-stone pavilion with seating areas scattered indoors and outdoors on terraces, stairway landings, and mezzanines overlooking the sea. Live music occasionally emanates from strolling musicians, and an unpretentious menu lists a medley of tropical pastas, salads, and grilled meats and fish as accompaniments to bottles of Presidente beer which sell for around RD$75 (US$2.25/£1.15) each. Platters of food cost RD$110 to RD$450 (US$3.35–US$14/£1.70–£6.90) each, but despite the allure of the food, we consider this joint more appropriate for a drink than for a full-fledged meal. Open 24 hours a day. Av. George Washington s/n. ℂ 809/221-1774.

Bottoms   It's dimly lit, it's cramped and claustrophobic, and the dozen or so barstools adjacent to the bar are hotly sought after by several generations of Dominican late-night merengue lovers. Its fans and regulars even claim that it's more famous, and a lot more appealing, than the hotel that contains it, and as such, it's the focal point for dozens of scantily dressed Dominicans who roar through the public areas of this hotel to reach it, especially on weekends. Entrance is free, a bottle of Presidente beer costs about RD$100 (US$3.05/£1.55), and the doors open every night at 6pm. Live music, usually merengue, emanates from a cramped stage most nights after around 10pm, and the rest of the time, recorded music keeps the place jumping. But what do you think the owners intended when they named the place Bottoms? Daily noon to midnight. In the lobby level of the Hotel Clarion, Presidente Gonzalez at the corner of Av. Tiradentes, in the Naco District. ℂ 809/541-6226.

K-Ramba   K-Ramba lies in the Zona Colonial, and is especially popular late at night. Owned by an Austrian expat, the bar features rock 'n' roll, merengue, and sometimes pop. Many visitors are attracted to the area, as it's one of the safer bars at night in this historic district. Snacks and freshly made salads are also served. Open Monday to Saturday 6pm to 3am. Calle Isabel la Católica. ℂ **809/688-3587.**

Marrakesh Bar & Café This cozy and relaxing cocktail bar is set within the precincts of the Hotel Santo Domingo (see chapter 3). Marrakesh serves jumbo-size cocktails to a clientele from the hotel and from the city at large as well. Live music, whose schedule changes frequently, is presented most evenings between 6 and 9pm, and there's never a cover. It's open 4pm to midnight. Av. Abraham Lincoln at Av. Independencia. ℂ **809/221-1511.**

Mesón D'Bari This atmospheric bar is known for its soundtrack of old-time bachata, merengue, and typical music from Cuba known as *son*. In the Colonial Zone, it is a big bar with wooden furniture and floors set on two different levels, the walls decorated with Dominican art. Patrons range in age from their early 20s to their 70s. Open daily noon to midnight. Calle Hostos 302, corner of Salome Urena, Ciudad Colonial. ℂ **809/687-4091.**

Mitre Trend-conscious, fashionable, and separately recommended as a restaurant in "Where to Dine," this place maintains a wine-and-cigar bar upstairs from its dining room that attracts a distinctively hip clientele all its own. Glasses of wine sell for RD$170 (US$5.15/£2.60) or RD$225 (US$6.80/£3.45) each, and if you get hungry, you can order from any of the creatively concocted dishes being served in the restaurant downstairs. In clement weather, you might opt for a seat within the zebra-skin-patterned tilework of the courtyard, where everything about the place evokes a hot spot in, say, Barcelona or Madrid. Daily noon to midnight (till 2am Friday to Saturday). Av. Lincoln at the corner of the Calle Gustavo Mejia Ricart. ℂ **809/472-1787.**

Punto y Corcho This is the city's best wine bar. It can seat 100 patrons, most of whom fall into the 30-to-50 age range. For entertainment, you can hear pop, jazz, and salsa, and sometimes the music is live. The range of wine is one of the most varied in the city, outside of the first-class hotels. Open Monday to Friday 10am to 11pm and Saturday 10am to 6pm. Av. Abraham Lincoln at the corner of Gustavo Mejia Ricart. ℂ **809/683-0533.**

5

Beach Resorts East of Santo Domingo

Once you leave Santo Domingo, heading east along Highway 3, you quickly approach what is virtually the Dominican Republic Riviera centered on the resorts of Boca Chica and Juan Dolio. This is the land where the citizens of Santo Domingo themselves go to cool off in the fiery summer months.

Overcrowded and filled with many cheap, boxy hotels, its beaches riddled with prostitutes of both sexes, Boca Chica and Juan Dolio are not resorts at which we'd like to spend a holiday. Continue east for greater beachfronts and far superior hotels.

The eastward trek continues through San Pedro de Macoris, ringed with sugar plantations, until La Romana and Bayahibe are reached. We prefer this area to either Juan Dolio or Boca Chica, primarily because of its deluxe Casa de Campo (see listing later in this chapter).

At La Romana is found Altos de Chavón, an artists' community built in the style of a 16th-century Mediterranean village. This is the greatest man-made attraction of the Dominican Republic, and is worth a visit even if you have to rush down from Santo Domingo and view the sight in a day before returning to the capital in the evening.

1 La Romana & Bayahibe

114km (71 miles) E of Santo Domingo, 37km (23 miles) E of San Pedro de Macoris

On the southeast coast of the Dominican Republic, La Romana was once a sleepy sugar-cane town that specialized in cattle raising. Visitors didn't come near the place, but when Gulf + Western Industries opened a luxurious tropical paradise resort, the Casa de Campo, about 1.6km (1 mile) east of town, La Romana soon began drawing the jet set. It's the finest resort in the Dominican Republic, and especially popular among golfers.

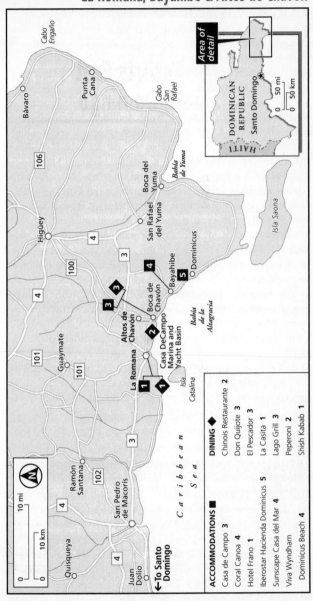

La Romana, Bayahibe & Altos de Chavón

Area of detail

DOMINICAN REPUBLIC

Santo Domingo

HAITI

0   50 mi
0   50 km

Cabo Engaño

Bávaro

Punta Cana

Cabo San Rafael

106

Boca del Yuma

Bahía de Yuma

Isla Saona

Higüey

San Rafael del Yuma

4

3

100

Dominicus

4

Bayahibe

5

3

3

Boca de Chavón

Altos de Chavón

Bahía de la Altagracia

2

Casa DeCampo Marina and Yacht Basin

Guaymate

101

101

101

La Romana

1

1

Isla Catalina

C a r i b b e a n   S e a

3

Ramón Santana

102

San Pedro de Macorís

4

4

Quisqueya

4

Juan Dolio

← To Santo Domingo

0   10 mi
0   10 km

N

ACCOMMODATIONS ■
Casa de Campo **3**
Coral Canoa **4**
Hotel Frano **1**
Iberostar Hacienda Dominicus **5**
Sunscape Casa del Mar **4**
Viva Wyndham
Dominicus Beach **4**

DINING ◆
Chinois Restaurante **2**
Don Quijote **3**
El Pescador **3**
La Casita **1**
Lago Grill **3**
Peperoni **2**
Shish Kabab **1**

Just east of Casa de Campo is Altos de Chavón (see below), a charming and whimsical copy of what might have been a fortified medieval village in Spain, southern France, or Italy. It's the country's leading sightseeing attraction.

Off the coast of La Romana lies **Isla Catalina,** which attracts divers and snorkelers, though there are no facilities. It is mainly uninhabited so bring whatever you need, including fresh water. The tour desks of Casa de Campo or other hotels can arrange excursions, although nothing is organized into a central agency for bookings. Catalina lies only 3.5km (2¼ miles) south of La Romana but 18km (11 miles) west of Bayahibe.

Bayahibe is a relatively new tourist development that's a lot more famous and more heavily patronized with Italian, French, Spanish, and, to a lesser extent, British and Canadian groups than it has been, until now, with American clients. Launched onto the world's consciousness in the early 1990s, it didn't become "important" until around 2000. There's no village center, no monumental architecture, not even a permanent settlement here: only a sea-fronting road with some mega-hotels on the sea-fronting side, each facing a sandy beach.

The location of Bayahibe is 30km (19 miles) directly east of La Romana. **Playa Bayahibe,** its lovely sandy beach, is what put this emerging resort on the tourist map.

You might negotiate with a boat owner at the beach or ask at your hotel if the staff can arrange for a fisherman to the offshore island, **Isla Saona,** which has some good sandy beaches beset by sand flies and some fishermen's cottages.

ESSENTIALS

VISITOR INFORMATION The government maintains **La Romana Tourist Office** at Teniente Amado García 22 (② **809/ 550-6922**), open Monday to Friday 8am to 6pm. The staff is earnest and hardworking, but don't expect to come away with a wealth of information.

GETTING THERE **By Plane** **American Airlines** (② **800/ 433-7300** in the U.S.; www.aa.com) offers one daily flight to the Casa de Campo airport from Miami, with a travel time of about 2½ hours each way. (Yes, it's a slow plane.) **American Eagle** (same phone number) operates at least two (and in busy seasons, at least three) daily nonstop flights to Casa de Campo/La Romana airport from San Juan, Puerto Rico. The flight takes about 45 minutes, and it departs late enough in the day to permit transfers from other flights. **US Airways** (© **800/622-1015**; www.usairways.com) offers direct weekly service, usually on Saturday, from Charlotte, North Carolina.

By Car   You can drive here in about an hour and 20 minutes from the international airport at Santo Domingo, along Las Américas Highway. (Allow another hour if you're in the center of the city.) Of course, everything depends on traffic conditions. (Watch for speed traps—low-paid police officers openly solicit bribes, whether you're speeding or not.)

GETTING AROUND   Most visitors don't rent a car but rely on local transportation, which is very haphazard and operated by independent drivers. You'll find both taxis and *motoconchos* (motorized scooters) at the northeast corner of Parque Central in the heart of La Romana. A typical ride almost anywhere within town costs less than RD$75 (US$2.25/£1.15), with the average taxi ride costing less than RD$150 (US$4.55/£2.30). Prices are always to be negotiated, of course.

You can also rent a car at the airport. Your best bet is **Budget,** La Romana Airport (© **809/813-9111**), open Monday to Saturday 9am to 5pm. A competitor is **Honda Rent a Car,** Calle Santa Rosa 84 (© **809/556-3835**), in La Romana, open Monday to Friday 8am to 6pm, Saturday and Sunday 8am to 4pm.

FAST FACTS

To exchange money, go to **Scotiabank,** a bank at Calle Trinitaría 59 (© **809/556-5151**), open Monday to Friday from 8:30am to 4:30pm. There's an ATM out front. Long-distance calls can be made at **Verizon,** the phone company at Calle Trinitaría 51 (© **809/ 220-7927**), open Monday to Friday 8am to 6pm, Saturday 9am to 1pm. The **La Romana Post Office** (© **809/556-2265**) lies on Calle Francisco del Castillo Marquéz, 2 blocks north of Parque Central. For Internet access, head to the **Casa de Campo** resort (see below). The **business center** here (© **809/523-3333**) is open Monday to Saturday 8am to 7pm, and Sunday 8am to 2pm. Use of a computer costs RD$65 (US$1.95/£1) for 15 minutes or RD$260 (US$7.90/£4) for 1 hour. Within Casa de Campo's Marina and Yacht Basin there's an Internet cafe, **Café Bistro Caribbean Coffee and Tea,** Plaza Portofino (© **809/537-2273**). It charges RD$200 (US$6.05/£3.10) per hour for use of any of four Internet stations, and serves a wide choice of high-octane coffees and teas as well.

WHERE TO STAY
CASA DE CAMPO

Casa de Campo 𝒜𝒜𝒜   Translated as "country house," Casa de Campo, on its own beach, functioned for many years as the most visible, most alluring, and most glamorous resort in the Dominican Republic. And although its preeminence has been challenged by newer, more cutting-edge resorts, it still exerts a powerful hold on the imagination of the country's image of itself as a tourist destination. Casa de Campo originated in the 1960s, when the former Gulf + Western corporation carved up a vast hunk of seafront land, more than 2,800 hectares (6,919 acres) in all, and developed a multifaceted resort with private homes, hotel facilities, condominiums, marina facilities, and much, much more. There's a staggering variety of accommodations you can rent here, lodgings which range from a conventional but very comfortable hotel room to an entire house. Regardless, decors tend to be reasonably consistent throughout: Tiles, craft objects, and mahogany furniture mostly built in the D.R.; mahogany louvered doors; and neutral-toned fabrics, usually white, decorate the interior of both the public areas and the accommodations. And thanks to the vast acreage associated with this place, your lodgings might, according to your preference, be either near the beach or near one of the resort's four golf courses. In addition to the conventional hotel rooms, about 150 of the resort's total of 1,400 private homes are available for rent. Some are clustered in a semiprivate hilltop compound with views overlooking the meadows, the sugar cane, and the fairways down to the distant sea. Regardless, you'll be offered the use of an electric golf cart, priced at US$19 (£10) per day, to putt-putt your way around the premises of this vast resort.

La Romana, Dominican Republic. ℭ **800/877-3643** or 809/523-8698. Fax 809/523-8394. www.casadecampo.com.do. 279 units. Winter US$353–US$385 (£186–£203) double, US$664 (£349) suite; off season US$224–US$250 (£118–£132) double, US$434 (£228) suite. Additional supplement for an all-inclusive plan that includes all meals and drinks within the resort's restaurants, unlimited horseback riding, tennis, non-motorized watersports, and one round of skeet shooting: winter US$176 (£93) adults, US$94 (£49) children; off season US$148 (£78) adults, US$78 (£41) children. Children are defined as anyone ages 4 to 12. AE, DC, MC, V. **Amenities:** 8 restaurants; 5 bars; 2 outdoor pools open to hotel guests (with an additional 20 semiprivate pools scattered across the resort); 4 18-hole golf courses (three of which are available to hotel guests); 13 tennis courts (10 lit); health club; watersports equipment; bikes; children's center (ages 3–12); limited room service; massage; babysitting; laundry service; theater; aerobics; horseback riding; polo. *In room:* A/C, TV, minibar, hair dryer, iron, safe.

LA ROMANA

Hotel Frano *(Value)*   This is for frugal travelers who shun the mega-resorts, preferring more of a guesthouse-type accommodation. The prices are so affordable that many traveling Dominican salesmen often book in here. The midsize bedrooms are simply but tastefully decorated and quite comfortable, each with a small tiled bathroom with tub and shower. The three-story building is from the early '90s and has been kept up-to-date since then. Within the little town of La Romana itself, these are the best guest rooms, though you'll have to travel by taxi to the beach, a 5-minute ride for a good beach.

Calle Padre Abreu 9, La Romana, Dominican Republic. © 809/550-4744. 41 units. US$50 (£26) double. AE, DC, MC, V. Free parking. **Amenities:** Restaurant. *In room:* A/C, TV.

BAYAHIBE

Coral Canoa *(icon)(icon)*   When you come here and see the thatch roof huts, you'll think you've arrived south of Pago Pago. No longer associated with the Hilton Group, which inaugurated it in 1997, it remains stylish and pleasant, with a hardworking staff and a clientele which includes goodly numbers (about 50%) of visitors from Canada and France. The hotel's architecture has a real tropical ambience, with many small villas reproduced in the style of the island's native thatch houses, called *clavos*. Some of the architecture uses such island materials as stone, jute, and canna, along with some symbolic architectural details of the Taíno Indians, the original inhabitants. Bedrooms come in a range of styles, from midsize to spacious, although each has a tiled bathroom with tub/shower combo. Much use is made of rattan, the furnishings placed against creamy walls given added color by the flamboyant fabrics.

Many outdoor enthusiasts like its location on the border of Parque Nacional del Este (see description later this chapter).

One of the resort's outstanding features is its spa, with an array of treatments and classes, everything from yoga to shiatsu massages and hydrotherapy along with beauty treatments. The food is plentiful and fresh, and prepared more or less well without arriving at the sublime. Caribbean and Italian favorite dishes are served, along with a selection of international specialties, including pizza and pastas.

Playa Bayahibe, La Romana, Dominican Republic. © 809/682-2662. Fax 809/688-5799. www.coralhotels.com. 532 units. US$130–US$230 (£68–£121) double; US$195–US$295 (£103–£155) junior suite. Children 2–12 US$60 (£32) extra. Rates are all-inclusive. AE, DC, DISC, MC, V. Free parking. **Amenities:** 4 restaurants; 2 bars; 1 very large lagoon-shaped pool; 3 tennis courts lit for night play; health club; spa; sauna; complete PADI-approved scuba center; children's center; room service;

babysitting; laundry service; dry cleaning; nightly entertainment in the on-site theater. *In room:* A/C, TV, kitchenettes in suites, minibar, beverage maker, hair dryer, safe.

Iberostar Hacienda Dominicus *✦*

Tasteful, plush, manicured, and somewhat more formal in its architecture and layout than many of the hotels nearby, this resort gets high marks for savvy design and classiness. Its public areas are as intriguing as any we saw in Bayahibe, with the exception of the Coral Canoa: Its architectural theme evokes an ochre-painted, tile-roofed hacienda with influences from Spain's 19th-century kings; the Taíno Indians; and some very savvy designers who might have been on a playful session with psychedelics at the time, who articulated the place with lots of undefined but fascinating objects which hang randomly but with great style from the ceilings. Clients from the U.S. tend to come here in midwinter; the rest of the year sees German, French, Canadian, and British clients. This is one of the few hotels in the D.R. which still accept day trippers, charging them US$45 (£24) for a day pass (valid 10:30am–6:30pm) and an equivalent amount for a night pass (valid 6:30pm–2am). Accommodations are comfortable, brightly painted in tones of mostly yellow and blue, and with a vaguely Spanish colonial flair—a bit small, but nonetheless very comfortable. The pool, shaped free-form like a lagoon, is huge. The hotel prefers to accept guests who check in for a minimum of 3 nights.

Playa Bayahibe, La Romana, Dominican Republic. © 809/688-3600. Fax 809/686-8585. www.iberostar.com. 501 units. US$690–US$768 (£363–£404) single for 3 nights; US$820–US$960 (£432–£505) double for 3 nights. Rates are all-inclusive. **Amenities:** 5 restaurants; 4 bars; disco; nightly entertainment; 4 swimming pools (2 for adults, 1 for children, 1 for sporting events); full-service on-site dive shop; wide array of daytime activities; babysitting and day camp facilities; all-inclusive rates include all non-motorized watersports. *In room:* A/C, TV, minibar, hair dryer, safe on request.

Sunscape Casa del Mar *✦ (Kids)*

The golf and tennis facilities here aren't as elaborate as those at Casa de Campo, and there are no polo grounds, but the resort, dating from 1997, is beautifully landscaped, and the beach is palm-fringed. It's a viable choice for those seeking resort facilities but who don't want to pay the high tariffs charged at Casa de Campo.

Accommodations are within a well-designed series of three-story buildings with blue-tiled roofs. Many of them date from 2005 and 2007, reflecting the way the resort has expanded massively since its original construction in the 1980s. Decor inside features lots of tile, varnished hardwood, wicker, and rattan, plus a neatly appointed shower-only bathroom. There's an overall cheerfulness about the place and lots of emphasis on merengue music that helps keep the good times rolling but might be a turn-off for those who prefer a more discreet, less raucous atmosphere. Everything served in all of the resort's restaurants is covered by the all-inclusive price. Da Mario serves Italian food, Chinese is on the menu at Asia, and the Seaside Grill serves beachfront barbecues and grills, Dominican-style. There's also a buffet restaurant and a disco. This is one of the rare all-inclusive resorts that offers a day pass, priced at US$50 (£26) per person per day, allowing up-close-and-personal access to the facilities.

Playa Bayahibe, La Romana, Dominican Republic. (© **866/786-7227** in the U.S., or 809/221-8880. Fax 809/221-2776. www.sunscaperesorts.com. 851 units. Winter US$150–US$167 (£79–£88) per person double, US$184 (£97) per person suite; off season US$60–US$95 (£32–£50) per person double, US$72–US$120 (£38–£63) per person suite. Day pass for nonresidents US$50 (£26) per person. Rates are all-inclusive. AE, MC, V. **Amenities:** 5 restaurants; 6 bars; disco; 2 outdoor pools; 4 tennis courts (each lit for night play); health club; Jacuzzi; sauna; watersports equipment; bikes; children's programs; room service; babysitting; horseback riding. *In room:* A/C, TV, minibar, hair dryer, iron, safe.

Viva Wyndham Dominicus Beach 𝔊 This is a mega-resort that lies 5km (3 miles) east of Bayahibe, opening onto a magnificent golden sandy beach with swimmable surf. Dating from the early '90s, it's like a small village of thatch-roofed buildings of four or fewer floors each, all of them arranged within landscaped gardens, and a network of flagstone pathways. This is a sort of all-purpose resort that's a destination unto itself. Many patrons confess that they hardly leave the premises until the end of their vacation.

The bedrooms are comfortable and medium-size, each featuring decorative accents from the D.R. with a variety of layouts in which to lay your head at night. The least desirable rooms are rated "standard." Since there is so little price difference, it's better to ask for a superior room. Even better might be to request one of the thatch-roof bungalows opening onto the ocean or tropical gardens. Each unit comes with a well-maintained private bathroom with tub and shower.

The food is not "get *Gourmet* magazine on the phone," but it is plentiful and generous, prepared with fresh ingredients. Menus are eclectic, inspired by international recipes, especially those of the Caribbean, Mexico, and Europe, with plenty of American dishes as well. Buffets are big here, and there's also a grill restaurant and a pizzeria. On our latest rounds, we spotted guests still eating at 2:30am.

Although no great competition for Casa de Campo, the resort aggressively features activities around the block, from complimentary land and non-motorized watersports to musical cabaret shows often staged by the staff as performers. During the midsummer months, at least half of the clientele here is Italian, thanks to an arrangement the hotel has with an Italy-based tour operator. If there's any complaint we have with the place, it involves just too much merengue, which is piped into the reception area for hours at a time. And although we adore merengue on a dance floor and after a few drinks, it isn't our cuppa tea early in the morning.

Playa Bayahibe, La Romana, Dominican Republic. ℭ **809/686-5658.** Fax 809/687-8383. www.vivaresorts.com. 530 units. Winter US$190–US$250 (£100–£132) double; off season US$102–US$132 (£54–£69). Rates are all-inclusive. AE, DC, DISC, MC, V. Free parking. **Amenities:** 5 restaurants (1 open 24 hr); 4 bars; disco; nightly entertainment; 3 outdoor pools; 4 tennis courts; health club; spa; Jacuzzi; sauna; watersports equipment; Internet center; babysitting; laundry service; dry cleaning; basketball court; soccer field. *In room:* A/C, satellite-connected TV, hair dryer, iron, safe.

WHERE TO DINE
CASA DE CAMPO

El Pescador ✿✿ SEAFOOD   The best and the freshest seafood in the area is served at one of the lunch-only restaurants inside the Casa de Campo, which is not only the finest place to stay along the southern coast, but serves the grandest cuisine. In an elegant setting, which is adjacent to the resort's isolated Minitas Beach, you can dine inside or out on the alfresco terrace. The atmosphere is informal, but the service is first-rate. The freshest fish, based on the catch of the day, is brought here for the chefs to concoct into a number of delectable dishes, including perfectly grilled fish, the preferred method of cooking for most diners. A justifiably favorite dish is the deep-fry mix of calamari, shrimp, and the catch of the day. For lunch many visitors prefer the fish salad with tropical fruit, or fish sandwiches, which are among the best in the area.

In Casa de Campo. ℭ **809/523-3333.** Reservations recommended. Main courses RD$350–RD$625 (US$11–US$19/£5.40–£9.60). AE, DC, MC, V. Daily noon–4pm.

Lago Grill CARIBBEAN/AMERICAN   With one of the best-stocked morning buffets in the country, Lago Grill is ideal for breakfast or lunch. At the fresh-juice bar, an employee in colonial costume will extract juices in any combination you prefer from 25 different tropical fruits. Then you can select your ingredients for an omelet, and another staff member will whip it up while you wait. All of this happens beneath a soaring replica of a palm-frond-covered Taíno hut that's open on all sides to breezes from the nearby golf course. The lunchtime buffet includes sandwiches, burgers, *sancocho* (the famous Dominican stew), and fresh conch chowder.

There's also an abundant salad bar and an army of uniformed staff rushing around tending to everyone's needs.

In Casa de Campo. ℂ 809/523-3333. Breakfast buffet RD$750 (US$23/£12); lunch buffet RD$1,600 (US$48/£25). AE, DC, MC, V. Mon–Sat 7–11am and noon–3pm; Sun 6:30–11am and noon–4pm.

AT CASA DE CAMPO'S MARINA & YACHT BASIN

Immediately adjacent to one of the most impressive marina facilities along the D.R.'s southern coast, Casa de Campo has carved out a half-moon-shaped piazza that's home to at least six indoor/outdoor restaurants, only some of which are managed by Casa de Campo. The place gets festive at night, evoking a venue along the southern coast of Spain, a large and convivial outdoor living room outfitted with tables, flickering candles, and crisp white napery. Some diners opt to wander around the square picking their preferred dining site. But for the record, here are two of our favorites:

Chinois Restaurante ℱ CHINESE   It's the premier Asian restaurant in the region, with presentation and service rituals that go way, way beyond some of the greasy-spoons purporting to serve Asian cuisine in other parts of the D.R. Some of the best menu items include steamed or fried wontons, egg rolls, sushi, chop suey, chow mein, dragon shrimp, and Beijing-style duck soup, an intriguing change of pace from Dominican cuisine.

At Casa de Campo's Marina and Yacht Basin. ℂ 305/856-5405. Main courses RD$200–RD$500 (US$6.05–US$15/£3.10–£7.70). Tues–Sun noon–3pm and 6–10:30pm.

La Piazzetta ℱℱ ITALIAN/INTERNATIONAL   In our opinion, this is the most appealing and most sophisticated restaurant at Casa de Campo's marina, a bastion of Milanese plush that manages to be both baronial and hip at the same time. Although there's outdoor seating adjacent to a curvy veranda bar, we prefer the air-conditioned interior, where dark mahogany, white napery, gleaming marble, and a hard-to-define sheen of comfort might remind you of a chic restaurant along the harborfront in, say, Portofino. Pizzas emerge from a brick oven whose flames and form evoke something you might have found within the lair of an oracle in ancient Greece. (As you might have guessed, we think this place is cool.) Well-prepared menu items include salads, sushi, pastas, and such specialties as filet of sea bass over risotto, with shrimp and coconut broth; seared salmon over spring risotto with clams; a 12-ounce beefy hunk of Argentina-inspired *churrasco;* and duck breast over strawberry-studded risotto.

At Casa de Campo's Marina and Yacht Basin. ℂ **809/523-2228.** Reservations recommended. Main courses RD$720–RD$1,200 (US$22–US$36/£11–£18). AE, MC, V. Daily noon–11:30pm.

LA ROMANA

Don Quijote ℛ *Finds* INTERNATIONAL/SEAFOOD   Outside Casa de Campo, you get some of your best seafood here. The menu offers few exciting surprises, and the dishes are all very familiar to those who dine here, but each is prepared with fresh, regional ingredients and is deftly handled by a skilled staff. Their seafood paella is the best we've sampled in the area, and we are especially fond of lobster Creole-style. The chicken breast is beautifully sautéed and flavored, and a tender and well-flavored chateaubriand comes with shrimp in a coconut sauce, a combination that's a bit jarring to our palate but which receives praise from the regular diners. If you have no room for dessert, finish off with a strong Dominican coffee.

Calle Diego Avila 42. ℂ **809/556-2827.** Main courses RD$175–RD$275 (US$5.30–US$8.35/£2.70–£4.25). AE, DC, MC, V. Daily 11am–11pm.

La Casita ℛ ITALIAN/ INTERNATIONAL   This is the most elegant and substantial restaurant in downtown La Romana, a stylish and well-managed enclave of chic that's the regular dining choice of some homeowners from nearby Casa de Campo. Established in the late 1980s, and outfitted like a country tavern in the countryside of Italy, it has lined its walls with hand-painted porcelain collected during the owners' travels in Italy and Spain. We'd urge you to seek out the tiny corner bar of this place before or after your meal, where walls are lined with the sophisticated caricatures and cartoons of Dominican artist/architect Roberto Copa, the designer of Altos de Chavón. If you opt for a meal here, you'll be in rather upscale company: Menu items include lobster thermidor, filet of sea bass *meunière;* grilled salmon with white wine and herbs; surf and turf; chicken cordon bleu, and all manner of pastas.

Calle Francisco Richiez 57. ℂ **809/556-5932.** Reservations recommended. Main courses RD$250–RD$1,200 (US$7.50–US$36/£3.75–£18). AE, DC, MC, V. Daily 11am–11pm.

Shish Kabab MIDDLE EASTERN/INTERNATIONAL/ DOMINICAN   Few local residents can even imagine La Romana without the Shish Kabab, a well-managed restaurant with a polite and hardworking staff and a venue that's intricately tied up with the town's politics. At any given moment, you're likely to find well-placed municipal officials here, dining with and lobbying with local constituents. Set within a few blocks of the Parque Central Duarte (La Romana's most central square), it's an informal restaurant, with a Middle Eastern and international cuisine that's a wholehearted change of pace from Dominican fare. Naturally, the chefs specialize in kabobs, but there are many other Middle Eastern specialties as well, notably *baba ghanouj,* with mashed eggplant studded with fresh parsley, fresh garlic, lemon juice, olive oil, and sesame paste. The beef kabobs are tastily grilled. There's even a shish kabob pizza, and skewered grouper is yet another worthy specialty. You can also order substantial platters of meat and fish that include broiled lobster, deep-fried chicken, and/or stuffed grape leaves.

Calle Francisco del Castillo Marquez 32. ⓒ **809/556-2737.** Pizzas RD$320–RD$450 (US$9.70–US$14/£4.90–£6.90); main courses RD$180–RD$390 (US$5.45–US$12/£2.75–£6). AE, DC, MC, V. Tues–Sun 10am–midnight.

HITTING THE BEACH

La Minitas, Casa de Campo's main beach and site of a series of bars and restaurants all its own, is a small but immaculate beach and lagoon that requires a 10-minute shuttle-bus ride from the resort's central core. Transportation is provided by bus, or you can rent an electric golf cart. A bit farther afield (a 30-min. bus ride, but only a 20-min. boat ride), **Playa Bayahibe** is a large, palm-fringed sandy crescent on a point jutting out from the shoreline. Finally, **Playa Catalina** is a fine beach on a deserted island, Isla Catalina, surrounded by turquoise waters; it's just 45 minutes away by motorboat, the only way to reach it. Unfortunately, many other visitors from Casa de Campo have learned of the glories of this latter retreat, so you're not likely to have the sands to yourself.

SPORTS & OTHER OUTDOOR PURSUITS

Any of the hotels recommended within this chapter offer easy and direct access to virtually any land- or water-based sport. Chances are high that if you're staying within any of them, especially any of the all-inclusives such as Casa de Campo or any of the resorts in Bayahibe, you'll arrange your sports through your hotel. But if you're not at one of the all-inclusives and want to get active, your best bet involves contacting Casa de Campo, since it's relatively relaxed about allowing nonresidents onto its premises for use of the beach and sporting equipment. All-inclusive clients staying at Casa de Campo show identification cards proving their resident status. Otherwise, if you want to dine within any of the resort's eight restaurants, you'll pay the cashier directly.

Call Casa de Campo's guest services staff at © **809/523-3333** for more information. Casa del Mar weighs in with a heavy array of outdoor activities ranging from horseback riding to banana boating. Call © **809/221-8880** for more details.

FISHING   You can arrange **freshwater river-fishing trips** through Casa de Campo. Some of the biggest snook ever recorded have been caught around here. A 3-hour tour costs RD$880 (US$27/£14) per person, and includes tackle, bait, and soft drinks. A 4-hour deep-sea fishing trip costs RD$15,500 to RD$20,500 (US$470–US$621/£238–£315) per boat, with 8 hours going for RD$22,250 to RD$30,800 (US$674–US$933/£342–£474). Of course, you never know where the best fishing is from day to day—it's a matter of luck. But the conditions are best between January and June, when anglers in waters 1 to 2 miles off the coast catch marlin and wahoo.

GOLF   *Golf* magazine declared Casa de Campo (© **809/523-3333**, ext. 3187) "the finest golf resort in the world." The **Teeth of the Dog** ✿✿✿ course has been called "a thing of almighty beauty," and it is. The ruggedly natural terrain has 7 holes skirting the ocean. Opened in 1977, **The Links** ✿✿✿ is an inland course modeled after some of the seaside courses of Scotland. In the late 1990s, the resort added a third golf course to its repertoire, **La Romana Country Club,** which tends to be used almost exclusively by residents of the surrounding countryside rather than by guests of Casa de Campo.

The cost for 18 holes of golf is US$160 (£84) at the Links and US$198 (£104) at Teeth of the Dog or the La Romana Country Club. (Some golf privileges may be included in packages to Casa de Campo.) You can also buy a 3-day membership, which lets you play all courses for US$252 (£133) per person (for Casa de Campo guests only). A 7-day membership costs US$502 (£264). You can hire caddies for US$25 (£13); electric golf-cart rentals cost US$20 (£11) per person per round. Each course is open from 7:30am to 5:30pm daily. Call far in advance to reserve a tee time if you're not staying at the resort.

HORSEBACK RIDING   Riding is not particularly adventurous but consists of a tame and scenic ride that goes along the seashore. Trail rides at Casa de Campo or Casa del Mar cost US$25 (£13) per person for 1 hour, US$40 (£21) for 2 hours. The stables shelter 250 horses, although only about 40 of them are available for trail rides. For more information, call **Casa del Campo** at © **809/523-3333**, ext. 5249, or **Casa del Mar** at © **809/221-8880**.

SNORKELING **Casa de Campo** has one of the most complete watersports facilities in the Dominican Republic. You can charter a boat for snorkeling, through clear waters filled with rainbow-hued fish. The area off the coast of La Romana offers some of the island country's finest snorkeling. The resort maintains eight charter vessels, with a minimum of eight people. Full-day snorkeling trips to Isla Catalina cost US$35 (£18) per snorkeler. Rental of fins and masks costs US$5 (£2.65) per day; guests on all-inclusive plans use gear for free. Snorkeling is also included in the all-inclusive rates at **Casa del Mar** (© 809/221-8880).

TENNIS **Casa de Campo**'s 13 clay courts are available from 7am to 9pm (they're lit at night). Charges are US$25 (£13) per court per hour during the day or US$35 (£18) at night. Lessons are US$65 (£34) per hour with a tennis pro, and US$50 (£26) with an assistant pro. Call far in advance to reserve a court if you're not staying at the resort. The four courts at **Casa del Mar** (© 809/221-8880) are reserved for the resort's all-inclusive guests.

PARQUE NACIONAL DEL ESTE ௸

The National Park of the East, its English name, lies in the southeastern part of the island, comprising some 310 sq. km (121 sq. miles) of dry forest, one of the largest such forests in the Caribbean. The park is home to 112 known species of birds, a total of eight endemic to the Dominican Republic including the Hispaniolan lizard-cuckoo, the black-crowned oriole, the black-crowned palm tanager, the limpkin, and the red-legged thrush.

This is a most intriguing park to explore as it is the site of trails, cliffs, caves, mangrove estuaries, sandy beaches, and even Taíno Indian ruins. Traversing the park is hell, however, as no roads lead into its luxuriant interior. The usual method of exploring it is to hire a boat in Bayahibe and travel in a direction that's parallel to the shoreline, checking out the terrain along the water's edge. Often you'll see trails where, if you can convince the pilot to moor his craft for a while, you can hike into the interior.

The road leading into Bayahibe ends at a car park, often filled with tour buses. If you're not part of a group, you can negotiate with one of the captains for a tour of the park, going as far as Peñón Gordo on the park's western coast. A 2-hour trip usually costs RD$600 (US$18/£9.40) per person.

You should not try to visit this untamed park on your own. It's best to use a guide or go on an organized excursion. At one of two park ranger stations you must pay a US$3 (£1.60) entrance fee. The ranger station is at the park's western entrance near Bayahibe. It is from this point that tours are offered along a marked trail leading to a nearby cave filled with bats and owls. This trail is the most visited because it is the most scenic on the island, although there are several wilder trails as well, but one should hire a guide before attempting to explore in the wilderness.

Yet another ranger station is set near the town of Boca del Yuma on the eastern side of the park. Rangers here will guide you along the most scenic trail which runs parallel to the coast.

Although nothing is particularly organized here, if you are an adventurous person you can usually negotiate with one of the local boatmen at the dock to take you to Isla Saona. Speedboats, catamarans, or trimaran take passengers over, but there is no central booking station.

SHOPPING

An artisans market, **El Artístico** (© **809/556-2273**), lies on the northern side of Carretera Romana, Km 3.5, at a point 1km (⅔ mile) east of Yina Bambu Shop (see below). This is set up almost exclusively for tourists and offers a limited selection of arts and crafts. It's mainly for souvenirs, most of which are of dubious quality. The market is open daily from 7:30am to 7pm.

For more substantial shopping, head to **Yina Bambu Shop,** Km 4.5, Carretera Romana (© **809/550-8322**), open daily 7:30am to 7pm. Lying on the south side of the main road into town, this is the best showcase in the area for Dominican handicrafts and furnishings, even amber necklaces and bracelets. The merchandise dims when compared with what's available in the Colonial Zone of Santo Domingo, but you may not be going there to shop.

If you're a true shopper, seeking some quality items, we suggest you head to Altos de Chavón (see below).

Some of the terra-cotta pots and planters manufactured in this part of the D.R. are deeply respected and appreciated by homeowners and gardeners in places as far away as Florida. A purveyor of garden pots and statuary, set about 4.8km (3 miles) west of Higüey, and about 60km (37 miles) west of Casa de Campo, is **El Mundo del Tarro,** Km 4.5, Higüey, Otra Banda (© **809/383-1909**). The raw clay for many of these pots is mined in Mocca, a town in the central D.R. made famous as the home of many generations of political dissidents (including some who participated in the assassination of dictator Trujillo). The clay from Mocca is hauled to workrooms here, near Higüey; crafted into pots and statuary, glazed or not glazed, depending on the pot; and sold. Whereas the store can, after some negotiations, arrange for shipping, you'll probably find that it's a lot easier to simply carry the smaller of your purchases with you. The selection is enormous, and many of the forms were directly inspired by models from Iberia.

LA ROMANA AFTER DARK

The best entertainment is at the hotels, where programs can change weekly or even daily based on their house count (or lack of guests thereof). Since we can't predict where the action is on any given night, you can ask at your hotel to find out what's happening. The best hotels for entertainment include Viva Wyndham Dominicus Beach, Casa de Campo, and Coral Canoa (see below for specifics, including prices).

One popular place is **El Pirata,** Km 12, Carretera San Pedro, Hotel Santana Beach Resort (© **809/412-5342**). Since this is an all-inclusive, you can purchase a night pass for US$25 (£13) entitling you to dinner and drinks. Shows on Wednesday and Friday at 9pm are followed by dancing from 10:30pm to 2am when a DJ plays salsa, merengue, and pop. On-site is a casino, open daily from 8pm to 4am, where the usual games of chance, such as blackjack, are offered.

Within the artists' colony of Altos de Chavón, you'll find a disco, associated with Casa de Campo, that manages to thrive, year after year, self-regenerating, it seems, with every new class of students, and every new group of dance-aholic outsiders. It's **Discoteque Genesis** (© **800/877-3643,** ext. 3165), which is open every Thursday to Sunday from 11pm till at least 2am and often later. Entrance costs RD$100 (US$3.05/£1.55), but on some party nights, the doorman might ask for RD$800 (US$24/£12), which will include access to an open bar throughout the evening. The preferred musical selection is merengue, and whatever Latino nightclubs in Miami might be focusing on at the time.

At the previously recommended Viva Wyndham Dominicus Beach in Bayahibe (© **809/686-5658**), **La Locura,** a dance club, is the scene of much of the local action. DJs play the latest international hits along with a selection of salsa, merengue, and pop. You have to call the management during the day and arrange for a night pass since this is an all-inclusive resort. The cost of RD$600 (US$18/£9.25) entitles you to dinner, drinks, and any entertainment being presented that night. The club is usually open from 11:30pm or 12:30am to about 4am, though it may close earlier on less busy nights.

Many nonguests, willing to purchase night passes, can also go to the previously recommended **Coral Canoa (The Cocuyo Disco),** in Bayahibe (© **809/682-2662**). There are two types of night passes sold here, the regular pass costing RD$1,120 to RD$1,300 (US$34–US$39/£17–£20) for adults. This entitles you to a buffet and "national drinks" of the Dominican Republic, and it's good daily from 6 to 11pm. Night owls might want to purchase the "Disco Pass" for RD$600 to RD$700 (US$18–US$21/£9.25– £11), including admission to the disco and unlimited home-brewed libations. This pass is valid nightly from 11pm to 2am. No live entertainment is presented, but there's usually a hot DJ.

At Casa de Campo (see previous recommendation) **The Pot Bunker Sports Bar** (© **809/523-3333**) is a popular gathering spot at night, especially for male guests, or for anyone who lingered too long at cocktails and suddenly discovered that all the other restaurants at the resort were closed. Major sports events are broadcast live via satellite transmission on large-screen TV sets while visitors cheer their home teams. From 1pm to midnight, a light menu, where platters, including an array of burgers and deep-fried shrimp, cost from RD$300 to RD$650 (US$9.10–US$20/£4.60–£10), is available, although the bar itself, with its table games and pool table, remains open daily from 3pm to midnight.

2 Altos de Chavón: An Artists' Colony

In 1976, a plateau 161km (100 miles) east of Santo Domingo was selected by Charles G. Bluhdorn, then chairman of Gulf + Western Industries, as the site for a remarkable project. Dominican stone-cutters, woodworkers, and ironsmiths began the task that would produce **Altos de Chavón,** a flourishing Caribbean art center set above the canyon of the Río Chavón and the Caribbean Sea. Set within a 10-minute drive from Casa de Campo, with which it is linked, it's a timeless and intelligently crafted accumulation of baroque and rococo style that's architecturally and touristically unique.

A walk down one of the cobblestone paths of Altos de Chavón reveals architecture reminiscent of the era when the Caribbean was being colonized at every turn. Coral block and terra-cotta bricks were fancifully crafted into copies of the architecture you might expect in 18th-century Italy and Spain, all of it arranged into a semi-fortified hilltop village of enormous charm. Various buildings house artists' studios, craft workshops, art galleries, stores, and restaurants.

Set on the town's main square, The **Church of St. Stanislaus** is the village's most central attraction, with its fountain of the four lions, colonnade of obelisks, and panoramic views. Masses are conducted at this church every Saturday and Sunday at 5pm.

Enormous scholarship went into the design for Altos de Chavón. Thanks to elaborate masonry, terra-cotta tiles, and lavish use of wrought-iron window grilles and balustrades, it evokes a movie set for an antique hilltop village in Italy or Spain. Many of its restaurants are recommended within this guidebook, and many visitors, including busloads from cruise ships anchored offshore, wander around buying souvenirs and artwork. But it's much more than just a tourist attraction. Hidden behind the elegant facades are apartments occupied by students at the arts school that's located within the village. The fact that the place is actually lived in, full time, adds enormously to its allure as a living, breathing monument.

The **galleries** (© **809/523-8470**) at Altos de Chavón offer an engaging mix of exhibits. In three distinct spaces—the Principal Gallery, the Rincón Gallery, and the Loggia—the work of well-known and emerging Dominican and international artists is showcased. No one artist is ever showcased or featured for very long, so you'll have to check out the exhibits for yourself. Perhaps you'll discover a new, emerging talent. The gallery has a consignment space where finely crafted silk-screen and other multiple works are available for sale. Exhibits change about every month.

Altos de Chavón's *talleres* are craft ateliers, where local artisans have been trained to produce ceramic, silk-screen, and woven-fiber products. From the clay apothecary jars with carnival devil lids to the colored tapestries of Dominican houses, the rich island folklore is much in evidence. The posters, notecards, and printed T-shirts that come from the silk-screen workshops are among the most sophisticated in the Caribbean. All the products of Altos de Chavón's *talleres* are sold at **La Tienda** (© **809/523-3333,** ext. 5398), the foundation village store.

The Altos de Chavón **Regional Museum of Archaeology** (© **809/523-8554**) houses the objects of Samuel Pion, an amateur archaeologist and collector of treasures from the vanished Taíno tribes, the island's first settlers. The timeless quality of some of the museum's objects makes them seem strangely contemporary in design—one discovers sculptural forms that recall the work of Brancusi or Arp. The museum is open Tuesday to Sunday from 9am to 8pm. Entrance is free.

At the heart of the village's performing-arts complex is the 5,000-seat open-air **amphitheater.** Since its inauguration over a decade ago by Carlos Santana and the late Frank Sinatra, the amphitheater has hosted renowned concerts, symphonies, theater, and festivals, including concerts by Julio Iglesias and Gloria Estefan. The annual Heineken Jazz Festival has brought together such diverse talents as Dizzy Gillespie, Toots Thielemans, Randy Brecker, Shakira, Carlos Ponce, Carlo Vives, and Jon Secada.

The creations at **Everett Designs** (© **809/523-8331**) are so original that many visitors mistake this place for a museum. Each piece of jewelry is handcrafted by Bill Everett in a mini-factory at the rear of the shop.

WHERE TO DINE

El Sombrero MEXICAN   In this thick-walled, colonial-style building, within the upper altitudes of Altos de Chavón, near the village church, jutting timbers and roughly textured plaster evoke a corner of Old Mexico. There's a scattering of rattan furniture and an occasional example of Mexican weaving, but the main draw is the spicy cuisine. Red snapper in garlic sauce is usually very good, as are the beef and chicken fajitas. Most guests dine outside on the covered patio, within earshot of a group of wandering minstrels. Chances are you've had better versions of the standard nachos, enchiladas, tortillas with shrimp, black-bean soup, pork chops, grilled steaks marinated in tequila, and brochettes served here, but a margarita or two will make it a fun night out anyway.

Altos de Chavón. © **809/523-3333.** Reservations recommended. Main courses RD$400–RD$1,000 (US$12–US$30/£6.15–£15). AE, MC, V. Daily 6–11pm.

Giacosa ITALIAN/INTERNATIONAL   This is one of the few restaurants within Altos de Chavón that's not owned and operated by Casa de Campo. As such, its owners and staff tend to try a bit harder. It's a branch of a success story based in Coral Gables, Florida. Within a two-story stone Tuscan-style building whose windows open onto a spectacular view over the Chavón river's chasm, far beneath the balcony on which you'll be standing, you can try Mediterranean dishes like seafood soup with lobster and shrimp; eggplant filled with goat cheese, pine nuts, and prosciutto; black angus filet with wine sauce and truffles; risotto with shrimp and sun-dried tomatoes; or savory imported mussels with olive oil, garlic, white wine, parsley, and fresh tomatoes.

Altos de Chavón. ✆ **809/523-8466.** Reservations recommended. Main courses RD$450–RD$1,450 (US$14–US$44/£6.90–£22). 6-course tasting menu RD$1,700 (US$52/£26). AE, MC, V. Daily noon–midnight.

La Piazzetta ITALIAN   Much of the allure of this place derives from the way its outdoor tables are positioned on a stone terrace that showcases a spectacular view over the river valley of the Chavón, far below. But if you prefer indoor dining, this restaurant offers an air-conditioned replica of an antique stone-sided farm-house, the kind you'd have expected in Tuscany or perhaps Andalusia. You might begin with gnocchi stuffed with three kinds of cheeses, risotto flavored with pumpkin and shrimp, grilled chicken, filet of hake with local greens and sautéed potatoes, and lasagna Bolognese.

In Altos de Chavón, near the church. ✆ **809/523-8698.** Reservations recommended. Main courses RD$400–RD$990 (US$12–US$30/£6.15–£15). AE, DC, MC, V. Daily 6–11pm.

Le Boulanger *Value* INTERNATIONAL/SNACKS   Altos de Chavón has at least a half-dozen restaurants, but this is the only one that caters specifically to a local clientele of mostly art students, many of them full-time residents of the pseudo-antique stone buildings nearby. This is also the only eatery that's packed with business during afternoons, when virtually every other restaurant in the village is closed. There's seating both outside and within the mock-fortified stone interior of this simple restaurant, and a short menu listing salads, sandwiches, pizza, and daily platters. (When we were there, it was chicken salad.) Cocktails include piña coladas and Cuba libres.

In Altos de Chavón. ✆ **809/523-5359.** Reservations not accepted. Ice cream, pizza, sandwiches, and daily platters RD$120–RD$250 (US$3.65–US$7.60/£1.85–£3.85). MC, V. Daily 7:30am–7pm.

6

Punta Cana & Bávaro

On the easternmost tip of the island, 211km (131 miles) east of Santo Domingo, is Punta Cana, the site of major vacation developments, including the Barceló and Meliá properties, with more scheduled to arrive in the near future. Known for its 32km (20 miles) of white-sand beaches and clear waters, Punta Cana and Bávaro are an escapist's retreat. Set against a backdrop of swaying palm trees, these beaches are unrivaled in the Caribbean. Within some of the most arid landscapes in the Caribbean—it rarely rains during daylight hours—Punta Cana and Bávaro have been recognized throughout Europe (especially Spain) and the Americas for their climate.

Both Punta Cana and Bávaro, two resort areas at either end of a long curve of beach lined with coconut palms, are virtually towns within themselves. The beach is so mammoth there is rarely overcrowding, even with masses of visitors every month of the year. Bávaro and Punta Cana combine to form what is nicknamed La Costa del Coco, or the Coconut Coast, land of the all-inclusive resorts. Don't expect a town or city. From Punta Cana in the south all the way to Playa del Macao in the north, there's only one small community, El Cortecito. Everything else is nothing but all-inclusives and beaches.

Capitalizing on cheap land and the virtually insatiable desire of Americans, Canadians, and continentals for sunny holidays during the depths of winter, European hotel chains participated in something akin to a land rush, acquiring large tracts of sugar-cane plantations and pastureland. Today their mega-hotels attract a clientele that's about 70% European or Latin American. Most of the other clients are Canadians and Americans. The hotel designs here range from the not particularly inspired to low-rise mega-complexes designed by the most prominent Spanish architects.

Some of them, particularly the Barceló Bávaro complex (see below), boast some of the most lavish beach and pool facilities in the Caribbean, spectacular gardens, and avant-garde concepts in architecture (focusing on postmodern interplays between indoor and outdoor spaces).

The mailing addresses for most hotels is defined as the dusty and distinctly unmemorable town of Higüey.

If you choose to vacation in Punta Cana, you won't be alone, as increasing numbers of Latino celebrities are already making inroads there, usually renting private villas within private compounds. Julio Iglesias has been a fixture here for a while. And one of the most widely publicized feuds in the Dominican Republic swirled a few years ago around the owners of Casa de Campo and celebrity designer Oscar de la Renta, who abandoned his familiar haunts there for palm-studded new digs at Punta Cana.

Above all, don't expect a particularly North American vacation. The Europeans were here first, and many of them still have a sense of possessiveness about their secret hideaway. For the most part, the ambience is Europe in the tropics, as seen through a Dominican filter. You'll find, for example, more formal dress codes, greater interest in soccer matches than in the big football game, and red wine rather than scotch and soda at dinner. Hotels are aware of the cultural differences between their North American and European guests, and sometimes strain to soften the differences that arise between them.

1 Essentials

VISITOR INFORMATION   Amazingly, with the largest concentration of visitors in the entire Caribbean Basin, and with visitors numbering at least 750,000 a year (no one knows for sure), the Dominican Republic government, in their infinite wisdom, has yet to open a tourist office.

GETTING THERE   In small planes, **American Eagle** (© 800/433-7300 in the U.S.; www.aa.com) offers two to six daily nonstop flights to Punta Cana from San Juan, Puerto Rico; flying time is about an hour. You can also opt for one of American Eagle's two or three (depending on the season) daily flights from San Juan to La Romana and then make the 90-minute drive to Punta Cana.

In addition, **Takeoff Destination Service S.A.,** Plaza Brisas de Bávaro 8 (© 809/552-1133; www.takeoffweb.com), also flies in from Santo Domingo in 55 minutes; frequency of flights depends on demand, with more in the busier winter months. A typical fare—say, from Santo Domingo to Punta Cana's airport—costs US$99 to US$149 (£52–£78) one-way with no discount for flying round-trip. You can also fly from San Juan's airport to Punta Cana.

Lying adjacent to the Punta Cana Resort and Club, the **International Airport of Punta Cana** (© **809/959-2376**) may be the world's first privately owned international airport. Flights, mainly from North America and Europe, wing into this airport at the rate of 100 per week in summer. In winter, the volume of flights increases to approximately 250 per week. Private buses from the all-inclusives wait to shuttle arriving passengers to their respective resorts. When your vacation is over, you're placed in a private van and hauled back to the airport. The location of the airport is about 5km (3 miles) from where the Higüey–Punta Cana main highway reaches the coast.

Motorists driving across the southern tier of the Dominican Republic along Highway 104 reach the rural city of Higüey before continuing to the northeast to the Coconut Coast. Highway 104 runs along the entire length of the Punta Cana/Bávaro resorts before coming to an end at the port city of Miches on the Bahía de Samaná.

THE LAY OF THE LAND

One of the most remarkable real-estate developments in the Caribbean, Punta Cana grew out of the perceived need for a mass-market vacation destination, capable of receiving visitors from Europe and North America, that was near a worthy set of beaches, on land that was cheap, plentiful, and undeveloped. The result is Punta Cana and Bávaro, two resorts completely dependent upon an international airport (which they have), a string of sandy beaches (which they have), and a maze of tarmac-covered roads that wind in a labyrinth through land that used to be (and which to some degree still is) covered with sugar cane.

Don't expect a burgeoning downtown settlement, because until recently, there weren't any sizable communities in the region at all, and certainly nothing with the deep historic appeal and long-established roots of Puerto Plata.

Today, two communities that fill in the gap include the hamlet of Friusa, a dull and dusty settlement with banks, gas stations, repair stations for cars, and refrigeration facilities, but with very little appeal to temporary visitors; and the even smaller but somewhat more charming hamlet of Cortecita. Cortecita originated as a pre-planned community intended to house the workers who built the first of the region's hotels. Today, having adopted some aspects of an independent community in its own right, it's the site of several eateries and bars. And don't expect a coherent set of roads with names, because most of them are unnamed. Look instead for signs with arrows that point the way to the individual hotels, each of which was designed like cities unto themselves. Each resort—especially the all-inclusives—has enough amenities to keep visitors happily sequestered on-site for the duration of their holiday. The result is a necklace of self-contained communities, each with drugstores, food markets, coin-operated laundromats, and all-inclusive food services, draped along the waterfront of the peninsula.

Whereas the policy of self-containment (which is encouraged by the architecture and the closed-off, fenced-in nature of each resort) suits the hoteliers just fine, many small start-up businesses, including restaurants, must rely almost exclusively on local Dominican business for their livelihood, having been cut off from the masses of foreign visitors who remain within their individual hotels. And since the hotels do everything they can to increase their allures in-house, there simply aren't a lot of independently operated Dominican businesses, outside the big resorts, in this community.

Every large resort maintains at least one beachfront kiosk loaded with staff and watersports equipment. They tend to be operated by the same central organization, charge all the same prices, and even move their staff from one kiosk to another, regardless of whose beachfront they're sitting on. And it's entirely likely that the scuba or snorkeling trip you sign up for at the kiosk of your hotel might combine your outing with clients of several other hotels along the same beachfront.

GETTING AROUND   Most **taxi fares,** including those connecting the airport with most of the major hotels, range from RD$800 (US$24/£12) for up to four passengers. Your hotel can summon a cab for you. If you want to tour along the coast, you can **rent a car** on-site at the car-rental desks of all the major resorts.

Guaguas, which tend to be filled, sometimes to overflowing, with local service personnel and construction workers, also run up and down the coastal road during the day, but not at night. Most of these motorized vans charge RD$25 (US75¢/40p) for the average ride within town, and, say, RD$45 (US$1.35/70p) for transit from Punta Cana to Higüey, point of residence for many of the workers who labor in Punta Cana during the day. The price, of course, depends on the distance traveled.

Should you wish, you can also rent a car for the duration of your stay, although most visitors manage to forego this luxury since they are so resort-bound at their all-inclusive. There is little need to get about. If you're interested, **Avis Car Rental,** Carretera Arena Gorda

(© **809/688-1354**), offers a fleet of cars. **Europcar,** Calle Friusa Fiesta (© **809/686-2861**), also rents vehicles. Rates at both companies are subject to wild fluctuations, even in the same season, even from week to week. Just as a general guideline, the same economy car can begin as little as RD$800 (US$24/£12) a day, going up to RD$2,000 (US$61/£31) a day.

FAST FACTS: PUNTA CANA & BAVARO

To call the **police** in an emergency, dial either © **911** or **809/688-8727** for direct access to the tourist police, which have all the power and authority of the mainstream police, but with, at least theoretically, a more defined grasp of how to deal with foreign visitors and a better grasp of foreign (i.e., non-Spanish) languages. For Internet access, go to **Business Center,** Punta Cana Resort and Club, Carretera Punta Cana (© **809/959-2262**), open daily 8am to 9:45pm, charging RD$80 (US$2.40/£1.25) for 15 minutes. The office of **Western Union** is found at Plaza Bávaro (© **809/532-7381**), open Monday to Friday 8am to 10pm, Saturday 8am to 6pm, Sunday 8am to 5pm. Many hotels have offices that will sell you routine drugstore items, and some actually have full pharmacies. Otherwise you'll have to go to the inland city of Higüey 45km (28 miles) to the west, where you'll find that the most central pharmacy is **D'Hidarnis Farmacia,** Av. Trejo 26 (© **809/554-2719**), open Monday to Saturday 8am to 10pm, Sunday 8am to 1pm.

2 Where to Stay & Dine

The rates given below are only for your general guidance. In all candor, we must confess that no one actually pays these so-called rack rates. Guests book into the all-inclusives on some sort of deal, package or otherwise. The prices given below can change within the week, if management, even in the dead of high season (winter), decides that business is slow and they want to lure more business by slashing prices.

In other words, prices along La Costa del Coco, unlike anywhere else in the Caribbean, change from week to week. Charges, incidentally, are always lower when purchased from an agent overseas. If you show up without a reservation seeking a room, you'll be charged about twice as much.

THE ALL-INCLUSIVES

Barceló Bávaro Beach, Golf & Casino Resort ⋪   This huge complex of low-rise luxury hotels opens onto one of the most desirable

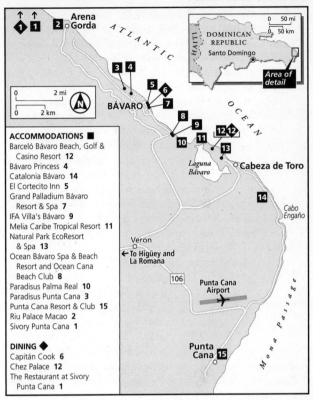

Punta Cana & Bávaro

ACCOMMODATIONS ■

Barceló Bávaro Beach, Golf &
  Casino Resort **12**
Bávaro Princess **4**
Catalonia Bávaro **14**
El Cortecito Inn **5**
Grand Palladium Bávaro
  Resort & Spa **7**
IFA Villa's Bávaro **9**
Melia Caribe Tropical Resort **11**
Natural Park EcoResort
  & Spa **13**
Ocean Bávaro Spa & Beach
  Resort and Ocean Cana
  Beach Club **8**
Paradisus Palma Real **10**
Paradisus Punta Cana **3**
Punta Cana Resort & Club **15**
Riu Palace Macao **2**
Sivory Punta Cana **1**

DINING ◆

Capitán Cook **6**
Chez Palace **12**
The Restaurant at Sivory
  Punta Cana **1**

of the many white-sand beaches along the 32km (20-mile) coast
known as Bávaro Beach. Until it was surpassed by equally ambitious
developments early in the millennium, this was defined, at least for a
while, as the most ambitious resort colony in the Dominican Republic, a project whose scope hadn't been equaled since the early days of
Casa de Campo. It contains what is, by some definitions, the largest
meeting and convention center in Latin America, and a history of
welcoming presidents of several Latin American countries on-site to
address those conventions. There's even a church on the premises for
weddings, and a reputation for good, and in some cases, extremely
good, food. Built in postmodern Spanish style, it occupies almost 12
sq. km (4⅔ sq. miles) of land, including some of the best seafront
property on the island. Developed by the Barceló Group, a group of

Spanish hotel investors, it consists of five separate hotels: Bávaro Beach Hotel, Bávaro Caribe Hotel, Bávaro Golf Hotel, Bávaro Casino Hotel, and the latest contender, the Bávaro Palace Hotel. Arranged within a massive park, and connected via a labyrinth of roadways and bike trails, all but one parallel the beachfront (the Bávaro Casino Hotel faces the golf course). Neither the decor nor the gardens are as well-conceived and stylish as those within, say, the Paradisus group or the Meliá Caribe Tropical Resort (see below), but the effect is nonetheless comfortable and pleasant. Accommodations in all five hotels are roughly equivalent and are outfitted in tropical furniture, with private verandas or terraces, plus an attractively tiled bathroom with tub and shower. (The Bávaro Palace's rooms are bigger and somewhat more comfortable than the others.) Bedrooms have tile floors, Dominican-made furniture, and colorful upholsteries and fabrics. The on-site wedding gazebo, which gets a lot of use, is the stuff of which romantic dreams come true.

Each of the 15 restaurants within this mega-hotel is interconnected by minivan service, and each will cheerfully accept diners from even the most far-flung corners of the compound. The most upscale and "gastronomic" of the lot is Chez Palace, serving French cuisine, some of whose main dishes require that all-inclusive guests pay a reasonable supplement for their meal. Other, slightly less pretentious eateries include Bohío and La Piña for Dominican food; Los Piños for Italian cuisine; the Coral Steakhouse for two-fisted slabs of grilled beef, chicken, and veal; Mexico Lindo for Mexican food; and an absolutely vast buffet setup within the open-to-the-breezes Ambar.

Apdo. Postal 3177, Punta Cana, Higüey, Dominican Republic. © 800/227-2356 in the U.S., or 809/686-5797. Fax 809/656-5859. www.barcelo.com. 1,921 units. Winter US$250 (£132) per person double in Palace, US$190 (£100) per person in any of the other 4 hotels; off season US$154 (£81) per person double in Palace, US$95 (£50) per person double in any of the other 4 hotels. Rates are all-inclusive. Discounts of 45%–65% for children 2–12 staying in parent's room. AE, DC, MC, V. **Amenities:** 12 restaurants; 13 bars; 3 discos; casino; 6 outdoor pools; 18-hole golf course; 9 tennis courts; health club; whirlpools big enough for 30 people; watersports equipment; salon; limited room service; massage; babysitting; laundry service; dry cleaning; aerobics; horseback riding; 3 theaters; nonsmoking rooms; rooms for those w/limited mobility. *In room:* A/C, TV, dataport, minibar, hair dryer, iron, safe.

Bávaro Princess ⊛   This hotel is just too vast for some visitors, but compared to the giant just recommended, it's practically a boutique hotel. Drawing some of its architectural inspiration from Bali, this hotel opens onto a 2km-long (1¼-mile) white-sand private beach. The Spanish-born architect Alvaro Sanz retained most of the palms and mangrove clusters on the property and installed freshwater reservoirs, creating an oasis not only for vacationers, but also for the many species of birds that call the resort home. Clients are mostly from the continent, especially Spain and Italy.

All accommodations lie within 86 low-slung bungalows. The split-level suites contain refrigerators, and each is fitted with comfortable furnishings. The small bathrooms have combo shower/tubs with adequate shelf space.

Playa Arena Gorda, Punta Cana, Higüey, Dominican Republic. © 809/221-2311. Fax 809/686-5427. www.princesshotelsparesorts.com. 935 units. US$170–US$200 (£89–£105) double. Rates are all-inclusive. AE, MC, V. **Amenities:** 7 restaurants; 6 bars; disco; 2 outdoor pools; 4 lit tennis courts; health club; watersports equipment; scooter rental; concierge; car-rental desk; shopping arcade; room service; babysitting; laundry service; dry cleaning; horseback riding. *In room:* A/C, ceiling fans, TV, dataport, minibar, hair dryer, iron/ironing board, safe.

Catalonia Bávaro 🕊 *Kids*   Constructed right at the close of the 20th century, this resort is like a large village of three-story villas, with two dozen rental units per building. It lies in the very heart of Playa Bávaro's resort sprawl. Run by a Spanish chain, and attracting a continental clientele, it is a large U-shaped complex of buildings constructed around a mammoth free-form pool. The beachfront in front of Catalonia is one of the finest strips of white sand along the Coconut Coast. The open-air pavilions sheltering the public areas evoke Bali, with walkways bridging lotus ponds.

Bedrooms are more spacious than many of this resort's competitors, and they come with tiled bathrooms with tub and shower. Standard rooms are junior suites (there are no doubles), and they are as large as suites in most hotels. Rattan furnishings, plus colorful draperies, spreads and fabrics, and local island art create a tropical ambience for doing nothing. When the house count is up, the maids seem overwhelmed.

There are so many restaurants here you're sure to find something you like. When you tire of those endless buffets you can seek out specialty dining such as Italian, French, Japanese, American, or Tex-Mex. Kids are likely to be found at the creperie-ice cream bar. The kids' club is one of the best along the coast. Like the dining options, activities prevail ranging from golf to watersports.

Playa Bávaro, Punta Cana, Dominican Republic. © 809/412-0000. Fax 809/412-0001. www.cataloniabavaro.com. 711 units. US$96–US$176 (£51–£93) double; US$91–US$167 (£48–£88) triple; from US$440 (£232) suite for 2. Rates are all-inclusive. Children 2–12 pay 50% of adult rate. AE, MC, V. Free parking. **Amenities:**

6 restaurants; 4 bars; casino; nightly entertainment; 2 pools (1 for children); 9-hole golf course; 2 tennis courts; health club; spa; sauna; watersports equipment; bikes; babysitting; laundry service; dry cleaning; aerobics; archery; nonsmoking rooms; rooms for those w/limited mobility. *In room:* A/C, TV, minibar, hair dryer, safe.

Grand Palladium Bávaro Resort & Spa 🎇🎇

Right at the front-line action at Playa Bávaro, with some of the best white sandy beachfront on the coast, this is a mega-resort with top-notch facilities. Within the Bávaro grouping, it is more inviting than the Bávaro Princess and the equal of the Barceló Bávaro Beach, Golf & Casino (but not in size). Set within well-landscaped gardens of towering palms, the resort grew up on what had once been a coconut-palm plantation. A special feature is the coral reef right offshore, where diving, sailing, and other watersports are avidly pursued.

There's a wide range of accommodations here, all of them comfortably and tastefully furnished, including two-floor bungalows, four two-floor villas, and standard doubles which give you a choice of a king-size bed or two queens. Built in 1992, the resort receives yearly refurbishing and stays up-to-date. Junior suites, Romance suites, and Superior rooms have been totally renovated.

There are many outdoor pursuits, from water aerobics to windsurfing, but not enough to overwhelm you. The chefs do much to provide you with a variety of foodstuff, everything from a Mediterranean cuisine to Tex-Mex specialties. For the munchies, there is even a late-night pizzeria. Two of the dining rooms are on the beach. The international cuisine buffet is one of the better "showcase" ones.

Playa Bávaro, Punta Cana, Dominican Republic. ✆ **809/221-8149.** Fax 809/221-8150. www.fiestahotelgroup.com. 636 units. US$177–US$240 (£93–£126) double; US$250–US$268 (£132–£141) junior suite. Children 2–12 pay 50% of adult rate. AE, MC, V. Free parking. **Amenities:** 11 restaurants; 17 bars; disco; nightly entertainment; 4 pools; 2 tennis courts; health club; 2 spas (1 on the beach); Jacuzzi; sauna; basketball; mini golf; Internet center; salon; room service; massage; babysitting; laundry service; dry cleaning; basketball; mini golf; pharmacy; photo shop; steam baths; supermarket; 24-hr medical service. *In room:* A/C, TV, minibar, coffeemaker, hair dryer, iron, safe.

Meliá Caribe Tropical Resort 🎇🎇 🅺ids

The Meliá complex is less upscale than the Bávaro complexes, but we prefer its innovative design. A series of bungalows is scattered within a spectacular garden, with palm trees, fountains, and real flamingos. When you tire of the grounds (if ever!), a little train will transport you over to the beach where topless sunbathing is commonplace. The lobby sets a fashionable tone with its lagoons, boardwalks, sculptures, and bubbling fountains. There's even a richly paneled, well-ventilated hideaway outfitted with poker tables, a bar, and an impressive inventory of Dominican cigars where patrons can puff away for hours. The spa is the best in the area, offering special features such as aromatherapy massages.

Accommodations are clustered into four distinct parcels of land, two of them adjacent to the beach and the most dramatic swimming pools in the Dominican Republic. The other two lie about .2km (219 yards) inland, adjacent to the lobby/reception areas and a cluster of dance clubs, cabaret stages, gift shops, and restaurants. Spacious bedrooms are among the best in Punta Cana, with intricately crafted tile and stonework, private terraces or verandas, and roomy bathrooms with tiled showers.

On-site are 11 different **eateries,** including a trio of large-scale dining rooms (Los Atabales, El Turey, and La Alambra) with an ongoing roster of buffets; two **restaurants** with mostly a la carte French food (Le Gourmet and Ma Maison); a Mexican restaurant (Los Panchos) with a mixture of a la carte and buffet service; a pasta and pizza joint (Gondola); a Pan-Asian restaurant (Pagoda); a Japanese sushi bar (Hokkaido); and a seafood restaurant (Capri), which is open only for dinner. Know before you go that during periods when the hotel isn't fully booked, not all of these are likely to be open.

Playa Bávaro, Altagracia, Punta Cana, Dominican Republic. © **800/336-3542** in the U.S., or 809/221-1290. Fax 809/221-6638. www.solmelia.com. 1,144 units. US$343–US$530 (£181–£279) per person. Rates are all-inclusive. AE, DC, MC, V. **Amenities:** 11 restaurants; 20 bars; dance club; casino; 7 outdoor pools; 27-hole golf course; 8 lit tennis courts; health club; 2 spas; children's programs; business center; laundry service; snorkeling; windsurfing; nonsmoking rooms; rooms for those w/limited mobility. *In room:* A/C, ceiling fans, TV, minibar, hair dryer, safe.

Natura Park EcoResort & Spa 🐾🐾 It's "Me Tarzan, you Jane" time. At last a resort comes along that has originality, escaping the peas-in-pod similarity of the Coconut Coast's string of imitative hotel sprawl. Set near a protected island estuary, the resort opens onto one of the coast's premier white sandy beaches. Nature lovers flock to its 32 hectares (79 acres) of park grounds; the setting evokes *The Jungle Book.* It doesn't quite rival Disney, but there's a fantasy aura about the place, where its various rooms are distributed across 13 two-story buildings painted in blinding white and surrounded by an oasis of coconut palms. This unusual vacation retreat burst onto the scene in 1997 and proved an instant hit, with its setting at a lagoon and a mangrove forest.

In general, accommodations are spacious and given homelike touches by the use of area rugs, comfy sitting areas, and king or paired double beds, the setting enhanced by tropical fabrics and the art of island artists.

The tiled bathrooms come with tub and shower and have sliding louvered doors that separate the dressing areas from the toilets. They are politically correct here regarding ecology, offering guests biodegradable soaps and recycling plastic whenever they can.

At the dramatic thatch-roofed main reception building, held up by large beams, you can learn the agenda of the day ranging from watersports to catamaran sailing or dancing lessons. Botanical walks are a big feature. Or else you can indulge yourself and make yourself even more beautiful than you are in the spa, getting health and beauty treatments.

Don't expect to dine in air-conditioned comfort, but in heat-wave conditions. Most dining is at a buffet but you can also enjoy a grill room and a seafood eatery where the quality of the cuisine is top-notch.

Is there a downside to nature's paradise? Yes, we found all the seaweed at the beach a bit disconcerting. Also, we detected a slight anti-American attitude. Yankees are accepted, of course, but, as one waiter privately confided to us, "We're much happier with our clients from Spain or Germany."

Cabeza de Toro, Punta Cana, Dominican Republic. © **809/221-2626.** Fax 809/221-6060. www.blau-hotels.com. 490 units. US$150–US$175 (£79–£92) double. Children 2–12 pay 50% of adult rate. AE, DC, MC, V. Free parking. **Amenities:** 4 restaurants; 4 bars; disco; nightly entertainment; 2 pools; 3 tennis courts; health club; spa; sauna; watersports equipment; bikes; children's center; salon; room service; water aerobics; botanical walks. *In room:* A/C, TV, minibar, coffeemaker, hair dryer, iron, safe.

Ocean Bávaro Spa & Beach Resort and Ocean Cana Beach Club ☆ (Kids)

This two-in-one resort consists of first-class hotels; each is all-inclusive, offering a mass of rooms, spread in front of a beachfront of white sand. Set within a short walk to the south of Cortecito village, the complex has a reputation for consistently housing mass-market planeloads of visitors who fly in for fun in the sun. About half the clientele within this compound come from Italy, with the remainder equally divided among U.S., Canadian, and German nationals. Canals and lagoons cut across the landscaped grounds with a trio of pools, along with habitats for pink flamingos and ducks. Watersports are a strong attraction here, as is the spa with its body treatments, Vichy showers, yoga classes, even tai-chi classes, and lots of other offerings.

Bedrooms are midsize to large, each tastefully decorated in a rather minimalist style with colorful fabrics. Accommodations open onto private balconies or terraces. Bathrooms come with tub and shower, and the larger and more expensive units have their own Jacuzzis. Family units come with two separate bedrooms and two different entrances along with two bathrooms and two closets. Activities range from kayaking to windsurfing, from horseback riding to archery. Unlike most all-inclusives, this resort breaks its kids' programs into ages 4 to 12 and 13 to 17, with different activities planned.

With eight restaurants, there is a wide array of different food choices. Three of the restaurants are a buffet style; the rest are a la carte, featuring both Dominican and international dishes. The cuisine comes off as resort standard, even though fresh ingredients are used whenever possible. As night falls, there's everything from a disco to a beer house to keep you amused, even a live show in La Rumba Theater.

Playa Bávaro, Punta Cana, Dominican Republic. © **888/403-2603** in U.S. and Canada, or 809/221-0714. Fax 809/221-0814. www.oceanhotels.net. 731 units. US$215–US$260 (£113–£137) double. Children 4–12 US$25 (£13) extra. Rates are all-inclusive. AE, DC, MC, V. Free parking. **Amenities:** 9 restaurants; 7 bars; beer house; disco; nightly entertainment; theater; 3 pools; 2 tennis courts; health club; sauna; watersports equipment; bike rentals; children's center; children's playground; salon; massage; babysitting; laundry service; dry cleaning; archery; horseback riding; rooms for those w/limited mobility. *In room:* A/C, TV, safe.

Paradisus Palma Real ★★ (Kids) This is our favorite all-inclusive hotel in Punta Cana, attracting mainly a Spanish clientele. It's one of only four members of the same Spain-based hotels, and the kind of place where the kinks and errors of earlier, less sophisticated hotels have been ironed out and corrected. It's also the beneficiary of one of the most sophisticated designs in Punta Cana, permeated with stylish hints at Iberian antecedents that absolutely reek of the best aspects of creative contemporary design. Its centerpiece is a large courtyard whose proportions replicate those of the Plaza Mayor in Madrid. Scattered artfully are sculptures—are they Taíno, are they by Henry Moore, or perhaps a combination of both?—and fountains, and at night, much of the illumination of the public areas derives from masses of flickering candles that seem to emulate either a medieval church or a pagan temple. Its architecture seems to ripple and undulate from its entrance, past multiple and highly theatrical staircases, and five different restaurants, one of which remains open through the long Caribbean night. The pools are spectacular, as is the beach. A complicated structure of add-on luxuries (spa packages, additional attention from the concierge staff, upgraded children's diversions, etc.) are available, and usually come with occupancy of somewhat upgraded accommodations.

After its inauguration in 2005, the Paradisus Palma Real surpassed the glamour and allure of its slightly older (circa 1996, 542-unit) sibling, the **Paradisus Punta Cana,** which lies about 3.2km (2 miles) away—and charges about 10% less, depending on occupancy.

Rooms were refurbished at least once since its inauguration. Both of the Paradisus hotels are desirable addresses, but frankly, if forced to choose, we'd opt for the Paradisus Palma Real. In both hotels, most rooms have garden views, although some choice units open onto the ocean. Each comes with a tiled bathroom with tub or shower.

One of the reasons to stay at either of these hotels is the food, as the resort offers almost more dining choices than any other along the coast—every cuisine from French to Chinese, from Mexican to Japanese, along with international, Dominican, and American specialties. Grilled fish and barbecues are other notable culinary features. Entertainment is diverse, ranging from a karaoke disco to an aqua bar to bars that often serve Dominican cigars with their drinks. Theme parties are big here, and there are live shows nightly.

Paradisus Palma Real, Playas de Bávaro, Higüey, Dominican Republic. © **809/688-5000.** Fax 809/688-5800. www.solmelia.com. 685 units. US$178–US$950 (£94–£500) double. Children 2–12 pay 50% of adult rate. Rates are all-inclusive. AE, DC, MC, V. Free parking. **Amenities:** 5 restaurants (one open 24 hr.); 6 bars; karaoke disco; casino; nightly entertainment; 2 pools; nearby 18-hole golf course; 3 tennis courts; health club; spa; sauna; watersports equipment; children's center; room service; laundry service; dry cleaning; archery; bike and walking tours; deep-sea fishing; horseback riding. *In room:* A/C, TV, minibar, coffeemaker, hair dryer, iron, safe.

Punta Cana Resort & Club 𝘒𝘒𝘒 *Kids*

This sprawling complex defines what a chic vacation is in the D.R. An oasis of luxury, it opens onto 4.8km (3 miles) of white sandy beaches, all part of a massive 6,070-hectare (15,000-acre) residential community. The hotel itself stands on 42.4 hectares (105 acres) of lush gardens, the creation of Dominican businessman Frank R. Rainieri and Theodore W. Kheel, a New York attorney and labor mediator. Making their vacation homes here are such celebrated personalities as Oscar de la Renta and Julio Iglesias.

The sprawling hotel complex is comprised of three- or four-story buildings, each decorated with tropical flair, with gabled balconies attached. The choice is for a studio, suite, or villa, each with tropical "Dorothy Lamour fabrics," cool tile floors, and carved and painted headboards, along with elegant bathrooms with a tub/shower combo. The villas are also equipped with kitchenettes.

As if this weren't luxury enough, de la Renta designed a pocket of posh within this complex. The Tortuga Bay complex offers 15 luxurious beachfront villas in two-, three-, or four-bedroom villas, with wicker and wood furnishings, and sumptuous amenities ranging from Frette linens to Jacuzzi bathtubs, even private outdoor dining areas, and thoughtful extras that include everything from Fiji water to those chocolate-chip cookies so beloved by Ronald Reagan.

The Six Senses Spa on-site is the finest in the D.R., a center for rejuvenation and beauty treatments, all guided by the country's best therapists, many from countries all over the world. Some of the innovative treatments borrow secrets from China or Thailand. On-site is an 18-hole P. B. Dye championship golf course with 4 holes playing directly along the water. Other features include a 243-hectare (600-acre) private reserve, the Punta Cana Ecological Park, with a treasure of tropical flora and fauna, as well as a PADI dive center and other watersports. At an on-site horse ranch, guests are taken on 1- or 2-hour rides, and at the Punta Cana Marina boats are available for rental, and deep-sea fishing charters can be arranged. There's even a Kids Carousel for ages 4 to 12 as well as a varied program of children's activities including boat rides.

The cuisine at the resort is only surpassed by the restaurants of Sivory Punta Cana. Restaurants range from La Yola, with its grand palapa and glass-bottom floor, a perfect setting for its seafood-based menu, to Bamboo for lighter fare and a de la Renta interior. El Cocoloba serves nouvelle cuisine at the resort's beachfront clubhouse.

Carretera Punta Cana/Bávaro, Punta Cana, Dominican Republic. © **809/959-2262**. Fax 809/959-3951. www.puntacana.com. 420 units. US$100–US$225 (£53–£118) double; US$493–US$750 (£259–£395) 2-bedroom beach casitas for 4 adults; US$703–US$1,100 (£370–£579) 3-bedroom beach casitas for 6 adults. Rates include breakfast and dinner. AE, DC, MC, V. Free parking. **Amenities:** 7 restaurants; 5 bars; nightly entertainment; 2 outdoor pools; golf course; 6 tennis courts; health club; spa; watersports equipment; children's center; room service; babysitting; laundry service; horseback riding; mini-zoo for kids; 24-hr medical center. In room: A/C, TV, kitchenette (in some), minibar, hair dryer, safe.

Riu Palace Macao 🐟🐟   Built in 1994, and continually renovated, this member of the Riu chain attracts mostly German-speaking visitors to its precincts. A casino in its main building, a three-floor colonial-style structure, is one of its chief attractions. We find this the best of the Riu's chain of hotels along the Coconut Coast. The architects wisely planned that this mid-rise hotel fan out along the beach for better views and greater access to the white sands.

Standing in well-landscaped and palm-studded gardens, this is one of the more luxuriously and elegantly decorated of the all-inclusives. As a startling surprise in the tropics, a top-hatted doorman directs you into the reception area. Verde-iron chandeliers and ceiling fans evoking those Bogie and Sydney Greenstreet movies whirl over the granite floors and Asian rugs below.

Rooms are tastefully decorated with rich fabrics and reproductions of classic furnishings, each unit coming with some of the best bathrooms along the coast, complete with tub/shower combos, vanities, and even bidets. Another nice touch is the Dominican rocking chairs on the balconies, the type made famous when JFK was in the White House.

Tropical drinks and endless food flow here from the kitchens and bars. We especially like the on-the-spot cooking stations at both lunch and dinner, where you can order a meal cooked to order even at a buffet. Even better is a specialty restaurant serving Mediterranean cuisine and a grill-steakhouse with some of the best cuts of beef along the coast. Theme buffets are also staged twice a week. Guests here seem more independent than the Club Med types, where everything is planned for them.

Playa Arena Gorda, Punta Cana, Dominican Republic. ② **809/221-7171.** Fax 809/682-1645. www.riu.com. 356 units. US$302–US$422 (£159–£222) double; US$528–US$633 (£278–£333) suite. Children 2–12 pay 50% of adult rate. Rates are all-inclusive. AE, DC, MC, V. Free parking. **Amenities:** 4 restaurants; 4 bars; 2 discos; nightly entertainment; casino; pools (with children's pool); 4 tennis courts; health club; spa center with body and beauty treatments; Jacuzzi; watersports equipment; Internet center; salon; room service; babysitting; laundry service; dry cleaning; pharmacy; photo shop. *In room:* A/C, TV, minibar, hair dryer, iron, safe.

THE NON ALL-INCLUSIVES

The all-inclusives, as we've just previewed, dominate the Coconut Coast. Because of the crazy and ever-changing rate structure, and because of all the deals and the decision of management to suddenly slash prices to get business, you might call any of the all-inclusives a budget deal if you get in on the right price.

This bargain-basement price slashing has severely limited truly charming little inns that might flourish here in a different economy. There are some low-rent dives, including boardinghouses and even private homes for those wanting to escape the curse of the all-inclusive.

Nearly all the hotels along the Punta Cana beachfront want to book you in on an all-inclusive rate—that is, food and drink included in one price. There are a few that do not insist on this requirement (see below).

But even at some of these establishments, you get breakfast and dinner (included), or else you can ask to be quoted a fee that includes meals.

EXPENSIVE

IFA Villas Bávaro ✦ *(Kids)*   This midsize resort from 1998 is one of the most fun-loving along the coast. It's not the most tasteful—certainly not the most elegant—but those who like a party day and night check in here and often don't want to go home. Obviously the focus is on plenty of activities and lots of entertainment.

The balconied rooms are midsize and spread over 23 villa-style houses, each with 10 rental units. Walls are white or cream, with the fabrics and draperies providing the tropical color accents. The food is only ordinary but the settings are amusing, including a margarita snack bar by one of the pools, or food and drinks at the beach club. A more formal dining with wine and excellent service is available as well. Parties, dancing, live shows with carnival themes, and a "Jungle Disco" are just some of the amusements provided.

Playa Bávaro, Punta Cana, Dominican Republic. © **809/221-8555.** Fax 809/221-8556. www.ifahotels.com. 262 units. US$96–US$190 (£51–£100) double. Children 2–12 US$21 (£11) extra. AE, DC, MC, V. Free parking. **Amenities:** 4 restaurants; 5 bars; beach club; nightly entertainment; 3 pools (1 for kids); tennis courts; health club; watersports equipment; bike rentals; salon; room service; massage; babysitting; laundry service; dry cleaning; dance classes. *In room:* A/C, ceiling fan, TV, fridge, hair dryer, safe.

Sivory Punta Cana ✦✦ *(Finds)*   This is the most northerly, and the most upscale, non-all-inclusive hotel in Punta Cana, the quasi-experimental offshoot and personal statement of the heir to a collection of well-respected, mostly urban hotels, the Catalonia group of Barcelona. Clients tend to be from Spain and points along the East Coast of America. There's something posh and minimalist about this place, almost as if a crew of Dominicans learned everything they could during sojourns in New York and Barcelona, and then returned home to dazzle their local competitors with what they had learned abroad. In this case, they've created what might be mistaken for a very upscale Zen-based school for meditation and contemplation, set amid palms, beside a pristine beach, with at least three absolutely spectacular restaurants on-site.

Elegant and ultra-hip touches abound: The cocktail bar features only a series of strong horizontal surfaces, a smiling attendant, and a noteworthy absence of bottles and glasses: Tell the attendant what you want, and it will materialize, pristine and elegantly simple,

The Dominican Republic as "The Next Hawaii"

New forms of tax relief for anyone investing in resort development in the D.R. has diverted floods of money into previously unheard-of regions of the country. At press time for this edition, two of the biggest of these land-development projects were deep into construction, on an awe-inspiring scale that anyone might describe as Pharaonaic.

During the on-site research for this edition, we were guided through advance visions of these developments, each positioned on tens of thousands of acres near the northern and southern fringes, respectively, of the region presently defined as Punta Cana. Both, when completed, will combine the functions of a resort with a full-service residential community, replete with marinas, golf courses, and tennis courts, and every imaginable form of sporting and leisure-class diversion. Both have learned carefully from the earlier mistakes of older, less coherent developments, including Casa de Campo, and both threaten intense competition, perhaps bloody competiton, to less cutting-edge resorts that include Sosúa, Puerto Plata, Bayahibe, and Juan Dolio. Already, long in advance of the opening of these seductive fire-breathing dragons, tremors have been felt as far away as the coasts of overcrowded Florida itself.

We expect these two developments to be at least partially operational during the lifetime of this edition. If you're interested in buying into the visions early, there's always someone on-hand to give well-wishers (and potential investors and/or potential homeowners) a tour, a spiel, and a sometimes mind-blowing insight into where and how money, and lots of it, is being spent.

The more northerly of the two developments is **Roco Ki**, a 10,927-hectare (27,000-acre) marvel whose striking and very

before you. The path between check-in and your ultra-comfortable, ultra-modern accommodations requires passage across a footbridge that spans a Japanese-inspired reflecting pool.

Know before you go that there are only three drawbacks to this place: (1) It's isolated enough, and small enough, to remain meditative and calm even at times when you wish that it wasn't. If you want a go-go nightlife, this is not the place for you. Come with a lover or appealing neo-Taíno architecture looks like something the native Indians might have developed if they'd taken a crash course in Japanese design, then injected their traditional bohíos with steroids and hundreds of millions of dollars' worth of modern building techniques. Westin Hotels has already signed on for the maintenance of the first of what's envisioned as six semi-independent hotel, resort, and/or residential compounds already partially completed.

The more southerly of the two developments is **Cap Cana** which might just be, as its promoters define it, "the most important tourism and real-estate project of the Caribbean." At press time, more than US$200 million had already been invested here: Its developers envision an eventual investment that includes 14,569 hectares (36,000 acres) of what until recently was virtually empty scrubland; a projected total investment of US$1.5 billion; three Jack Niklaus–approved golf courses; the largest marina in the Caribbean; direct access to more than 4.8km (3 miles) of beachfront; as many as five government-rated, five-star hotels managed by some of the most glam hotel operators in North America and Iberia; and a roster of spectacular hotel rooms and private residences which make the gloom and snows of home look very far away indeed.

For additional information on either of these astonishing developments, click on www.CapCana.com and on www.RocoKi.com. Did we mention that both resorts will contain full-service spas, schools for the children of their respective employees, hospitals, and, eventually, many aspects of self-contained cities in their own right?

companion, if you can—either that or a good book, because it's very much a place for contented couples; (2) it takes about an hour to reach the place from the Punta Cana airport; and (3) its swimming pool is not particularly spectacular—but when confronted with that gorgeous beach, its rows of comfortable chaises lounges, and a higher staff-to-guest ratio than virtually any other hotel in Punta Cana (supposedly to bring you drinks or whatever), who cares?

Playa Sivory, Punta Cana, Dominican Republic. © **809/552-0500**. Fax 809/552-8686. www.sivorypuntacana.com. 55 units. US$290–US$750 (£153–£395) junior suite for two; US$400–US$2,400 (£211–£1,263) suite for two. Rates include breakfast. All-inclusive "Sivory Plan" US$150 (£79) per person per day. AE, DC, MC, V. **Amenities:** 3 restaurants; bar; putting green; tennis courts; watersports; full-service spa; personalized concierge; butler; car-rental kiosk; valet; helicopter service; salon; laundry service; dry cleaning. *In-room:* A/C, TV, minibar, safe, Wi-Fi.

INEXPENSIVE

El Cortecito Inn *(Value)*   It's definitely not on the A-list of mega-resorts, but it exerts a strong appeal to independent and frugal travelers who like to keep life (and their vacation hotels) simple. With a goodly percentage of clients from Spain and the D.R., and the remainder from Northern Europe, it's one of the most visible buildings in the hamlet of Cortecito, positioned just across the town's sleepy main street from a bustling stretch of very white beachfront dotted with bohío-style bars and restaurants. This three-level structure offers simply, yet comfortably, furnished bedrooms that each contains a small tiled bathroom with tub/shower combination. The decor, if it could be called that, is very Caribbean and rather minimalist, although the premises are well-maintained. For a lot of your amenities, action, and facilities, you'll have to look outside your hotel, but considering that an entire universe of village life lies just outside the hotel, you probably won't have to go far. The food is home-style and presented in generous portions, much of it like that served in the home of a typical island family.

Av. Meliá Fiesta, Playa Bávaro, Dominican Republic. © **809/552-0639**. Fax 809/552-0641. 75 units. US$70–US$90 (£37–£47) double. Rates include breakfast. AE, MC, V. Free parking. **Amenities:** 2 restaurants; bar; pool. *In room:* A/C, TV, safe.

3 Where to Dine in Punta Cana & Bávaro

Given the wealth of restaurants in the hotels listed above, many guests never leave the premises for meals. But the following are worth a special trip.

Capitán Cook *(★)* SEAFOOD   Positioned between the beachfront and the main street of town, in the center of the hamlet of Cortecito, this is the most enduringly popular local dive in town. Don't expect elaborate food, fancy sauces, or social prestige: In fact, when you approach the outdoor vestibule that prefaces the place, you might think you've entered the forecourt to a garage. The allure here is the ultrafresh seafood that's simply but superbly grilled to order from a chalkboard menu. A battery of outdoor grills lies near the entrance to a dining area whose tables are positioned beneath palm-frond gazebos overlooking a crowded stretch of rather narrow beach. Additional seating is upstairs, within an air-conditioned dining room that resembles a log cabin perched on stilts above Main Street. Some guests don't bother to consult the menu, but order their meal based on whatever is sputtering over coals or displayed on ice as they enter. Platters of grilled fish, freshwater crab, or lobster will be accompanied by lime-flavored butter sauce, salad, and your choice of baked potatoes or french fries. As an alternative, try the paella, spaghetti with shellfish, Creole-style beefsteak, fish brochettes "Captain Cook," and/or a combination platter of grilled shrimp and calamari. Beer is often the accompaniment for anything served here, perhaps preceded by a rum-based cocktail. *Note:* If you phone this place the day of your intended visit, the staff will probably offer to send a motorboat to pick you up at whatever suitable pier lies closest to your hotel, normally without any additional charge. (A US$5/£2.65 tip to the boat attendants, however, would be appreciated.)

Playa El Cortecito, Marina El Cortecito. © 809/552-0645. Reservations recommended for dinner. Main courses RD$250–RD$1,300 (US$7.60–US$39/£3.85–£20). AE, DC, MC, V. Daily noon–midnight.

Chez Palace ☆ *Value* INTERNATIONAL   This is the showcase restaurant of one of the biggest resort complexes in the Dominican Republic. If you're not staying at one of the Barceló hotels, you'll have to make reservations in advance. The decor is cool and stylish, as if it were imported from a chic resort in the south of Spain. A formally dressed staff serves superb dishes that include salmon mousse in a prawn sauce, tartar of tenderloin, grilled red snapper, grouper with mustard sauce, and filet mignon with truffles and foie gras. This excellent set-price menu offers many different choices.

In the Bávaro Palace Hotel, within the Barceló Bávaro Beach, Golf & Casino Resort. © 809/686-5797. Reservations required. Set-price dinner US$25 (£13). AE, DC, MC, V. Daily 7–11pm.

The Restaurants at Sivory Punta Cana ☆☆☆ *Finds* INTERNATIONAL   The amazing thing about this trio of restaurants is how good they are, and that they exist within a relatively tiny boutique hotel set far from the touristic mainstream, along the northern fringe of Punta Cana. Its developers added them to the amenities of the Sivory resort as an added incentive for well-heeled clients looking for a sybaritic and otherwise uncluttered retreat: Basically the resort that contains it includes only 55 supremely comfortable accommodations, a superb stretch of wilderness beachfront, a bar, a (relatively unspectacular) swimming pool, and three absolutely fantastic restaurants, any of which is worth writing home about. In fact, the entire resort can be accurately defined as a beachfront trio of superb restaurants set adjacent to a restful and rather sedate upscale hotel.

The best way to play this would involve informing the staff of your intentions to dine here; slipping into something tropical, fetching, and festive; and paying a taxi driver to take you here and wait to take you back to wherever you happen to be staying in Punta Cana (Sivory itself can arrange this for you). Once you get here, choose which of the three on-site dining venues you like the best. Choices include the Gourmand Restaurant, where you'll quickly surmise that hours were spent training the Dominican staff about how to cook, prepare, and present classic French cuisine in a style they'd approve of in upscale Paris; The Tau Restaurant, where Asian fusion cuisine is served within a Zen-minimalist decor so perfect as to one day be preserved within a museum; and Laveranda Restaurant, a stylish indoor/outdoor venue for international cuisine which, although elegant and restful, seems positively tame when compared to the avant-garde perfectionism of the other two. The wine list, especially in the French restaurant, is awe-inspiring. Even if the sommelier doesn't bring it up, ask for a tour of the wine storage area. It contains 8,000 bottles of sometimes amazingly esoteric wine.

Playa Sivory. ⓒ **809/552-0500.** Reservations recommended. Main courses at all three restaurants US$28–US$35 (£15–£18). AE, DC, MC, V. Daily noon–3pm (Laveranda only) and 7–10pm (in all three restaurants).

4 Beaches & Other Outdoor Pursuits

One of the Caribbean's great beaches stretches along the so-called Costa del Coco, or Coconut Coast, covering more than 32km (20 miles) of brilliant white sand—so there's room for everyone. Flanked by the all-inclusives, the major beaches here include Playa Macao, Playa Cortecito, Playa Bávaro, Playa Punta Cana, and Playa Punta Juanillo. The upmarket all-inclusives have staked out the best beachfront properties, so everything is done for you here, including unlimited access to food and drinks and watersports concessions at each hotel. For facilities, bars, and restaurants, you can use the hotel at which you are a guest.

This beachfront is the stuff of Sunday supplements in travel magazines, with perfect sand and zillions of coconut palms. Under an almost constant blue sky during the day, European, American, and Canadian guests frolic in the gin-clear waters.

A note about drawbacks: Despite the visual beauty of the sands and the swaying palms, there isn't any particularly fabulous snorkeling at Punta Cana. There aren't enough offshore reefs nearby—the kinds that shelter rich deposits of marine life—so if you happen to sign up for a snorkeling or scuba adventure at Punta Cana, chances are high that you'll be escorted to any of several offshore wrecks whose rusting hulks provide the shelter that underwater critters crave.

The beaches at Punta Cana are wide, they're gorgeous, and it's safe to swim offshore throughout the year. An improvised series of barricades runs parallel to some stretches of the coastal road, prohibiting access to the various beaches fronting the hotels. Entrances guarded by security forces prevent nonguests from entering, since once inside you're entitled to unlimited food and drink. We noted that fewer and fewer of the all-inclusives are selling day passes or evening passes to nonresidents. The policy seems to be viewed with increasing disfavor. When such day passes are available, they can cost anywhere from US$40 to US$75 (£21–£39) per person, and are strictly defined as day passes (allowing access from around 9am to around 6pm) and night passes (allowing access from around 6pm till around 1am). The idea, frankly, never caught on, and we estimate that only around 25% of the resorts now offer them. Even then, it's complicated and sometimes unpleasant to talk your way past the security guards at the entrance, even if you're willing to pay.

Activities abound, not only scuba diving but snorkeling, windsurfing, kayaking, water biking, sailing, beach volleyball or soccer, even water polo, along with aqua aerobics and tons of children's activities.

Within Punta Cana, the guest services staff at your hotel can arrange horseback riding for you, but if they can't, consider an equestrian jaunt at the region's biggest stables. These are headquartered at **Rancho RN-23,** Arena Gorda (© **809/747-7356** or 809/747-7538). It supervises as many as 125 horses that are stabled at three separate "ranches," each within a reasonable distance of one another. For RD$1,800 (US$55/£28) an hour, you'll be guided on equestrian tours through groves of coconut palms near the beach and, in most cases, onto the beach itself. We view riding along this scenic beachfront with the wind in your hair as one of the most memorable equestrian experiences in the country. To reach the ranch, you'll follow

How to Spend a Day Outside the All-Inclusive Hotels

The answer for the adventurous would involve a trek to the center of Cortecito Village, where you can pick and choose from at least three beachfront restaurants, each with a radically different style and set of presuppositions. The most glamorous and upscale and "Europeanized" of the lot is **Palma's Sand Beach Club,** Playa Cortecita, Bávaro (© 809/552-1448). It's the most solid, the most elegant, and the most "bourgeois chic" of the lot—the kind of place that patterned itself on (and this is a stretch) an upscale resort in Sardinia, where you might expect a sun-bronzed crowd that's not afraid to sport their jewelry, their suntans, and not a lot else. Presidente beer costs about RD$80 ($2.40/£1.25) each, and main courses cost from US$8 to US$33 (£4.20 to £17).

A second option is the much more ethnic (and separately recommended) **Captain Cook's,** whose raffishness and sense of ethnic Dominican pride makes it much more popular and crowded than Palma's. Of a different texture altogether is the small, cozy, and very friendly **Langosta del Caribe,** immediately next door (© 809/552-1953). It consists of a thatch-roofed bohío on the sands, a staff with a lot of charm, main courses priced at from RD$250 to RD$1,000 (US$7.60–US$30/£3.85–£15), and prideful willingness to divulge the ingredients of their house drink, "Mammajuana." No—it's not hallucinogenic, and it's legal, consisting of rum marinated in pungent mixtures of wood bark, berries, and leaves.

And if you opt for a day with the madding crowds, expect lots of local color, and about a half-dozen artists who execute their opus on plywood or masonite, often with house paints, with enormous amounts of panache and flair. The one we got to know the best is known to locals only as Sijolo. His gallery is the **Sijolo Gallery** (no phone; contact him through the staff at Captain Cook's), consisting of dozens of paintings hanging from clotheslines stretched between palm trees in a lot otherwise peppered with used tires. See if you can tell where influences from Dalí, Picasso, and Velásquez crept in, and bargain hard if you want to acquire one of the charming paintings; most are in the US$50 to US$100 (£26–£53) range.

some clearly marked signs 3km (2 miles) through some of the wildest terrain left in Punta Cana, down winding sandy paths to a series of palm groves, to the site of these stables. Be warned in advance that many potential riders who think that a 2-hour equestrian excursion will be easy often find it more tiring, with more mosquitoes and horseflies, then they might have expected.

The Bávaro Golf Course at **Barceló Bávaro Beach, Golf & Casino Resort,** Bávaro Beach (*©* **809/686-5797**), is the best golf course on this end of the island, and bears the honor of being the golf course whose allure helped open the eastern D.R. to the tourist boom. Greens fees are RD$970 (US$29/£15) for 18 holes, with cart rentals going for RD$1,050 (US$32/£16). Guests of the hotel pay only 50% of greens fees. Open daily from 7am to 5pm.

Punta Cana Golf Club, near the Punta Cana Resort and Club (*©* **809/959-4653**), is the best and most sought-after of the four golf courses now flourishing in Punta Cana. Fronting the sea, it was designed by P. B. Dye of the famous golfing family. Fourteen of its holes open onto panoramic views of the Caribbean Sea, and four play along the ocean itself. Dye is known for crafting each hole to present a unique challenge. For 18 holes, hotel guests pay US$110 (£58), and nonguests are charged US$150 (£79). In summer, greens fees are reduced to US$68 (£34) for hotel guests, US$93 (£47) for nonguests. The clubhouse is spectacular, with interiors by Oscar de la Renta.

MANATI PARK

This animal park, opening in 1997, is the most controversial in the Caribbean. It's your choice if you want to patronize it or not. It features an array of sea lions, parrots, and even a dancing horse show, inspired by the traditional equestrian performances in the Spanish city of Jerez de la Frontera. There's even a crocodile cage, a parade of elegant pink flamingos, and a collection of caged snakes and iguanas. There's also a fenced-in area where brave animal lovers can get close to a colony of iguanas, although we strongly discourage any reader from attempting this, particularly since we've been told that the iguanas tend to attack anything orange and, by extension, anyone wearing clothing that's colored orange. The park is controversial because of its policy of allowing people to swim with dolphins. Marine biologists have claimed that the tank holding the dolphins is too small and that the animals are forced into regular contact with humans. This, it is believed, upsets their natural bacteria levels.

That, in turn, can lead to a breakdown in their immune systems. Already, four "stressed-out" dolphins have died since the park opened. Many countries, including Canada, have requested that the Dominican Republic close this exhibit, calling the park's policy "inhumane." If you must visit, the park is open daily from 9am to 6pm, charging adults US$30 (£16) and children US$15 (£7.90). A swim with the dolphins costs US$75 (£39) with advance booking required. Call ✆ **809/221-9444;** www.manatipark.com.

SHOPPING

We'd not pursue this as a serious activity, although all the mega-resorts feature gift shops for those inevitable souvenirs. If you look beyond your hotel, you'll find an upmarket shopping complex, **Plaza Bávaro,** lying between the Allegro Flamenco Bávaro Resort and Fiesta Palace Beach Resort.

There's another shopping complex, mainly for crafts, on the beach along the northern tier of this shopping complex, reached along a dirt road labeled MERCADO, meaning "market." This leads to a bustling crafts market open daily from 8am to sunset.

PUNTA CANA AFTER DARK

If you're staying at an all-inclusive, your nightly entertainment is already provided. You need not leave the grounds for action. Depending on the night of the week, many hotels present Las Vegas–type revues. As mentioned, many hotels don't like to issue night passes because it is difficult to maintain security and keep track of nonguests. If you don't like the entertainment provided on any given night at your hotel, ask around at the reception desk and see what alternative you might come up with. It's a bit of a hassle. The sprawling Bávaro complex (see below) is your all-around best bet if you want to flee your own hotel at night.

Bávaro Disco, on the grounds of the Barceló Bávaro Beach, Golf & Casino Resort (✆ **809/686-5797**), has emerged as the hottest, most popular, and sexiest disco in Punta Cana, thanks to a superb sound system. The venue is more European than North American, thanks to a heavy concentration of clients from Italy, Spain, and Holland. If you've been tempted to dress provocatively but never had the courage, the permissive and sexually charged ambience at this enormous club will give you the confidence to try. Painted black, with simulated stars overhead and lots of mirrors, the place is open nightly from 11pm to 5am. Entrance is free for guests of the Barceló Hotel complex; nonguests pay RD$1,200 (US$36/£18).

7

The Samaná Peninsula

A real offbeat destination where prices are still affordable, Samaná is an undeveloped 48km-long (30-mile) peninsula located in the northeastern corner of the country. It's about as Casablanca as the Caribbean gets. Hiding out here is an international expatriate enclave of rampant individualists. It also has some of the finest white-sand beaches in the Dominican Republic.

But change is coming quickly to this remote area of the D.R., mainly because of the construction of a spanking-new airport, **El Catey,** thereby eliminating the need for costly, bone-jolting trips from more distant airports within the D.R. for the hundreds of tour groups winging in aboard chartered flights from Canada, France, and the U.S. The location of the airport is a 20-minute drive from the center of Samaná. And sometime during the lifetime of this edition, the opening of a modern highway from Santo Domingo to the Samaná Peninsula will cut driving time from the capital to this remote outpost to, we're told, around 90 minutes.

Unless the new and easier access to the region changes things significantly, don't expect nightlife in this remote area, or even many semblances of urban life. The focus here is on calm, sedate days in the sun beside beautiful beaches, underwater snorkeling and scuba, verdant terrain, and recovery from stress.

The region attracts a denser concentration of visitors from France than virtually any other region of the D.R., and the hamlet of Las Terrenas boasts a thriving colony of French expatriates, the most visible French-speaking community in the country. Las Terrenas, on the peninsula's north coast, is the site of one of the region's most popular beaches. Although the strand strip is narrow, it is filled with white sand set against a backdrop of palms. The beach is never crowded. About the only visitors you'll encounter are at sea: the several thousand humpback whales who swim in from the North Atlantic to birth their calves from late December through March. The main town, **Samaná,** lies on the southern side of the peninsula, overlooking a bay. The north coast of the peninsula is more accessible by boat. The roads are a bit of a joke, better suited for donkeys than cars.

In 1824, the *Turtle Dove,* a sailing vessel, was blown ashore at Samaná. Dozens of American slaves from the Freeman Sisters' underground railroad escaped to these shores. They settled in Samaná, and today, their descendants still live on the island. Although Spanish is the major language, you can still hear some form of 19th-century English, and you'll see villages with names such as Philadelphia or Bethesda.

Samaná Peninsula is one of the fastest-developing tourist regions of the Dominican Republic, but so far the government has yet to open any visitor-information offices here.

GETTING THERE   The Peninsula of La Samaná lies in one of the more remote locations along coastal Dominican Republic, a lush strip of land near the northeastern tip of the country. Many visitors wing their way in because of the difficult approach roads to La Samaná.

It's best to drive southeast along the coast after a stopover on the Amber Coast, perhaps at Puerto Plata or Cabarete. Motorists can head southeast from Cabarete. After you approach the town of Sánchez, Route 5 continues east into the little town of Samaná.

If your ultimate goal is the resort of Las Galeras, continue east from Samaná on Route 5, following the signposts when they cut north into Las Galeras. Should you be going to Las Terrenas on the north coast of Samaná, leave the town of Sánchez (a grungy and somewhat depressing village devoted mostly to commercial fishing) and follow the secondary road northeast to the coast, cutting through some of the interior of the Peninsula of La Samaná.

Driving to Samaná is so difficult you'd anticipate an efficient air service. Not so. Despite the region's new airport, most of the flights coming in there are specially arranged charters. At present, there is no regularly scheduled service to this tourist-trodden peninsula. You have to charter flights aboard **Takeoff Destination Service S.A.** (© **809/522-1333;** www.takeoffweb.com). A small plane can be chartered for RD$5,400 (US$164/£83) for three passengers or else RD$25,000 (US$758/£385) for 15 passengers, all one way. Arrangements to charter a craft should be made at least 2 days in advance. During the life of this edition, air travel to Samaná is likely to change. Although nothing has been announced at the moment, various flights from the United States and Samaná loom in the future. Before going here, check for the latest developments, if any.

If you want to land on the southern coast, the plane will fly you to Aeropuerto Internacional Arroyo Barril, lying a 30-minute drive west of the town of Samaná. The airport for destinations along the north

The Samaná Peninsula

Bahía Escocesa

ATLANTIC OCEAN

Cabo Cabron

Cabo Samaná

Las Terrenas

Portillo El Limón

Cosón El Jamito

El Valle

Las Galeras

La Majagua

Aguas Buenas

Sánchez

Los Róbalos

Majagual Arroyo Barril Pascuala

Samaná

El Francés

Los Cacaos

Río Yuna

Bahía de Samaná

Cayo Levantado

Sabana de la Mar

104

ACCOMMODATIONS ■
Casa del Mar **2**
Coco Plaza Hotel **2**
Gran Bahia Principe Cayacoa **8**
Gran Bahia Principe Cayo Levantado **6**
Gran Bahia Principe El Portillo **3**
Gran Bahia Principe Samaná **5**
Iguana Hotel **2**
Moorea Beach **4**
Plaza Lusitania **4**
Residence Colibri **2**
Serenity House **4**
Tropic Banana **2**
Tropical Lodge **7**
Viva Wyndham Samaná **1**

DINING ◆
Casa Boga **2**
Chez Denise **4**
La Hacienda **7**
El Bambus **7**
El Martinique Resort Restaurant **4**
La Yuca Restaurant y Pizzeria **2**
Rancho Suizo **2**

Area of detail

DOMINICAN REPUBLIC

HAITI

Santo Domingo

0   50 mi
0   50 km

0   10 mi
0   10 km

N

coast is Aeropuerto Internacional El Portillo, which is in the little hamlet 6km (3¾ miles) east of Las Terrenas. Charters leave from the Herrera airport at Santo Domingo or from the Punta Cana airport. Flight time from Herrera takes 30 minutes, or 40 minutes from Punta Cana.

1 Samaná

245km (152 miles) NE of Santo Domingo

The town of Samaná lies on the southern coast, east of the airport at Arroyo Barril and opening onto the scenic Bahía de Samaná. Known for its safe harbor, it was the former stomping ground of some of the Caribbean's most notorious pirates, including such ne'er-do-wells as England's Jack Banister, whose men killed 125

British soldiers when they came to arrest him. Banister escaped, although 40 of his pirates were killed in the melee.

Samaná (more formally known as Santa Bárbara de Samaná), is the main town of the peninsula, fronting a bay of tiny islands, sometimes called Banister Cays in honor of that notorious pirate. Columbus arrived here on January 12, 1493. After battling the Ciguayos Indians, he named the bay Golfo de las Flechas, or "the Gulf of Arrows."

If you stand along the water looking south, the two islets you'll see in the bay are Cayos Linares and Vigia.

In an ill-conceived urban renewal plan under President Balaguer, much of the atmosphere of old Samaná, with its narrow streets and wrought-iron balconies, was destroyed, giving way to ugly concrete buildings and wide asphalt-paved boulevards.

As you arrive in town, expect to be overpowered by hard-to-shake English-speaking local hustlers who will try to sell you virtually anything from a hotel room to themselves. Hipsters from Santo Domingo are quick to tell journalists and casual visitors how boring Samaná is, utterly lacking in the flair and nightlife of the nation's capital. Nonetheless, it's the administrative capital of the region, and most of the peninsula's hotels lie within a 60-minute drive from its boundaries.

Most activity centers along the main road running along the bay front, Avenida La Marina (most often called Malecón, or "sea wall").

VISITOR INFORMATION   As mentioned, there is no local government-sponsored tourist office. However, the somewhat misleadingly named **Samaná Tourist Service,** Av. La Marina 6 (© 809/538-3322; www.samana.net), is a font of information about the area and can take care of most of your travel needs (see below). Hours are Monday to Friday 8:30am to 3pm.

GETTING AROUND

Most visitors walk around Samaná, renting a car only if they prefer to take an independent tour of the peninsula. **Sama Rental Moto,** Av. Malecón 5 (© 809/538-2380), is your best bet, renting economy-size cars beginning at RD$1,750 (US$53/£27) per day. This outfitter also rents bikes for RD$200 (US$6.05/£3.10) daily. Additionally, there are more three-wheeled motorized conveyances (they're known locally as *motoconchas*) than anywhere else in the D.R. Functioning like low-rent versions of taxis, and more readily available, they'll take you virtually anywhere within Samaná for US$5 (£2.60), and virtually anywhere on the Samaná Peninsula for between US$15 and US$20 (£7.90–£11).

FAST FACTS: SAMANA

If you need to make calls (hotels impose huge surcharges), you can go to the main office of the phone company, **Verizon,** Calle Santa Bárbara (© **809/220-7841**), open from Monday to Saturday 8am to 8pm, Sunday 8am to 2pm. They also offer Internet access, charging RD$30 (US90¢/45p) for 30 minutes, RD$50 (US$1.50/75p) for 1 hour. For a pharmacy, go to **Farmacia Bahía,** Francisco del Rosario Sánchez 1 (© **809/538-2236**), open daily 8am to 9pm, or **Farmacia Giselle,** Calle Santa Bárbara 2 (© **809/538-2303**), open Monday to Saturday 8am to 10pm and Sunday 8am to 1pm.

For money exchanges or an ATM, go to **Banco Popular,** Av. Malecón 4 (© **809/538-3666**), open Monday to Friday 8am to 4pm and Saturday 8am to 1pm. The **Samaná Post Office** is at Calle Santa Bárbara (© **809/538-2414**), open Monday to Friday 8:30am to noon and 2 to 5pm, Saturday 8am to noon. Offering emergency medical service 24 hours a day is **Centro Médico San Vicente,** Francisco del Rosario Sánchez 2 (© **809/538-2535**). For Internet access, go to **CompuCenter Samaná,** Calle Lavandier (© **809/538-3146**), open Monday to Friday 9am to 12:30pm and 3 to 6pm. The cost is RD$25 (US75¢/40p) for 30 minutes or RD$50 (US$1.50/75p) for 1 hour. The **Western Union** office is at Francisco del Rosario Sánchez 15 (© **809/538-2195**).

WHERE TO STAY

Gran Bahía Principe Cayacoa ⭐   This serene choice opens onto Samaná Bay and a good beach in an area of lush landscaping. Some of the best views of the southern coast are possible from the windows of this hotel. There are also two panoramic elevators with sea views leading to a large social lounge. During the day guests indulge themselves at the spa or else enjoy a wide range of watersports, including aerobic classes. Even the standard rooms are attractively furnished in modern Caribbean styling, but the junior suites are even better, opening onto water views. Each accommodation comes with a complete bath with tub or shower, and each also opens onto a private terrace or balcony. The main swimming pool boasts an open-air Jacuzzi with hydromassages, plus a large solarium. The food is perhaps the best served at any of the Bahía hotels on Samaná, including a Mediterranean specialty restaurant. Italian dishes are big here. So many honeymooners check in there is a wedding gazebo on-site.

Loma Puerto Escondido, Samaná, Dominican Republic. © 809/538-3131. Fax 809/538-3131. 295 units. US$180–US$195 (£95–£103) double; US$230–US$260 (£121–£137) junior suite. Rates are all-inclusive. AE, DC, MC, V. **Amenities:** 4 restaurants;

3 bars; casino; 2 outdoor pools; spa; salon, watersports; room service; nonsmoking rooms. *In room:* A/C, TV, minibar, hair dryer.

Gran Bahía Principe Cayo Levantado 🏖️🏖️

This hotel chain operates a number of hotels on the peninsula but we prefer this one above all the others because it is on a secluded island off the coast of the town of Samaná. As you wander on this palm-studded island, you may feel like Robinson Crusoe. Everything you might need is here so you never need to leave the island. Guest rooms are spacious for the most part, really junior suites with hydromassage baths. The accommodations open onto a private balcony or terrace. The most desirable units are beach villas opening onto the water with a small porch facing the sea. Honeymooners are drawn here because of the wedding gazebo on the beach. Sometimes the chef stages gala moonlit dinners on the beach. The cuisine is excellent including both seafood and Italian specialty restaurants.

Isla Cayo Levantado, Samaná, Dominican Republic. ⓒ **809/838-3232.** 195 units. US$180–US$210 (£95–£111) double; US$250–US$300 (£132–£158) suite. Rates are all-inclusive. AE, DC, MC, V. **Amenities:** 4 restaurants; 3 bars; disco and pub; 2 outdoor pools; 2 tennis courts; gym; spa; room service; nonsmoking rooms. *In room:* A/C, TV, minibar, hair dryer.

Gran Bahía Samaná 🏖️

Set on a good sandy beach, this hotel has Victorian styling and is one of the stateliest of the Bahía properties. Because it is smaller than most of its siblings, you get more personal service. It offers an active program of watersports, including windsurfing, catamaran sailing, and kayaking. The bedrooms come with a fully equipped private bathroom, and most of them open onto views of the offshore Cayo Levantado island. Many of the beds are in the four-poster plantation style, and bathrooms are fully equipped with shower and tub. Dominican music is often presented at an on-site theater, and there is also a wedding gazebo. We prefer the spa here to those at the other Bahías, because it has a better range of treatments and also a beauty center. If we want to quibble, the cuisine here is not of the high standard of the other hotels.

Ctra. Samaná–Las Galerias, Los Cacaos, Dominican Republic. ⓒ **809/538-3434.** 110 units. US$175–US$195 (£92–£103) double; US$210–US$240 (£111–£126) junior suite. Rates are all-inclusive. AE, DC, MC, V. **Amenities:** 3 restaurants; 1 bar; outdoor pool; 2 tennis courts; gym; spa; watersports; room service; nonsmoking rooms. *In room:* A/C, TV, minibar, hair dryer.

Hotel Tropical Lodge 🏖️ *Finds*

Brigitte and Jean-Philippe Merand operate one of the best inns on the peninsula, and have been in business for some 2 decades. At the end of the Malecón, they are in the center but still set back from the bull's-eye core, with its noise and bustling atmosphere. Their bedrooms are a bit small but still comfortably and tastefully furnished, with small, shower-only bathrooms. The best accommodations open onto a private balcony. The hotel staff will help book you on many jaunts in the area; everything from jeep safaris to horseback riding and waterfall visits, along with sailing, fishing, and biking trips. The kitchen staff is skilled at turning out both Dominican and continental fare, and, for more fast food, there is also a cafeteria and pizzeria. In the tropical garden is a pool with a Jacuzzi constructed on a hill fronting the bustling Malecón.

Av. La Marina, Samaná, Dominican Republic. © **809/538-2480.** Fax 809/538-2068. www.tropical-lodge.com. 17 units. US$40–US$55 (£21–£29) double. Children 2–12 pay 50% of adult rate. Rates include breakfast. AE, MC, V. Free parking. **Amenities:** Restaurant; cafeteria; pizzeria; outdoor pool. *In room:* A/C, ceiling fan, TV.

WHERE TO DINE

El Bambus ❧ DOMINICAN/INTERNATIONAL By the beach, this is one of the best restaurants at this little port. All the tasty main dishes are served with side dishes, including freshly cooked vegetables. A peninsula favorite is the fresh catch of the day, which can be prepared several ways, including grilled. For real Caribbean flair, order it with coconut sauce. Fresh shrimp is garlic-flavored, as are the grilled pork chops. Deep-fried chicken is the favorite dish of the locals. Freshly made salads and such eternal favorites as spaghetti and steaks are also served, along with one of the best arrays of seafood in town.

Av. La Marina 3, Samaná. © **809/538-2495.** Main courses RD$250–RD$400 (US$7.60–US$12/£3.85–£6.15). No credit cards. Daily 7am–11pm.

La Hacienda ❧ *Finds* DOMINICAN/INTERNATIONAL/FRENCH Of the many expat dives along the Malecón, this is a good choice for gourmet international dishes and some expertly prepared French selections such as a shellfish bouillabaisse, the main reason we visit the place. A selection of grilled seafood is set out nightly to entice you. The chefs also prepare octopus, which one satisfied diner recommended to us as "divine." Grilled loin of beefsteak is another favorite, along with fried Dominican chicken.

Av. La Marina 6, Samaná. © **809/538-2383.** Reservations recommended in winter. Main courses RD$200–RD$650 (US$6.05–US$20/£3.10–£10). No credit cards. Daily 5–11:30pm; Aug and Dec–Mar daily 11am–midnight. Closed Wed off season.

BEACHES ALONG THE COAST

The beaches aren't in the town of Samaná itself, except for a stretch of sand at the foot of a steep road leading over to the not particularly inspiring sands of **Bahía Escondido.** To reach the best beaches, you have to go farther afield.

All the beaches either west or east of the town of Samaná can be reached by *guaguas* (small buses or vans) that run to the sands

---

Moments Whale-Watching

For untold millennia, humpback whales have used Bahía de Samaná as a breeding ground and nursery. Even Columbus encountered these mammoth mammals in 1493, as noted in his journal.

After cruising the North Atlantic, where they are often killed, the **whales** 🐋🐋🐋 return to the sanctuary and warm waters of Samaná in December. The colony slowly grows until the end of January, when there are some 4,000 humpbacks in the bay.

It's an awesome sight watching these whales engage in their courting rituals, as the males track down compliant females. It's also enthralling to listen to whale songs—that is, a bizarre melody of chirps and moans. After a 1-year gestation period, babies are born, weighing a ton.

For the best tours, go to the pioneer herself, Kim Beddal, a marine biologist from Canada. Her agency's whale-watching tours are the best and are offered by **Victoria Marine,** Avenida La Marina (📞 809/538-2494; www.whale samana.com), in front of the port at Samaná. Tours, costing US$50 (£26) per person, are available from January 15 to March 20. Tours leave daily at 9am, returning around noon. An unlimited number of rum-based drinks are included free as part of this experience, but because a percentage of clients (and even some of the tour guides) aboard these tours tend to become violently seasick, very few of them are actually consumed.

Samaná Tourist Service, Av. La Marina 6 (📞 809/538-3322; www.samana.net), also offers whale-watching jaunts from January to late March, costing RD$2,000 (US$61/ £31) per person.

frequently throughout the day and can be hailed along the road. A series of good sandy beaches also lies east of Samaná on the road to Las Galeras (see below).

A more approachable beach lies 5km (3 miles) east of Samaná. **Playa Las Flechas** is reached by going along Carretera Las Galeras. Historically, this beach was the site of the first battle between Native Americans and Europeans.

Near the mouth of Bahía de Samaná, **Cayo Levantado** *රර* lies 7km (4⅓ miles) southeast of Samaná. Here in the midst of luxuriant tropical vegetation you will find a trio of lovely beaches of white sand. These beaches are on an island but can be easily reached by public transportation.

You can also travel independently to the island, as various boats leave daily from 8:30 to 11am, with the last return at 4pm. There is no central ferry service, and departures of these boats are from the Samaná Pier Marina. Because the boats are independently owned, fares can vary based on what each boatman charges, but expect to pay a rather pricey fee of around RD$1,000 (US$30/£15) each way per person. Confronted with this price structure, it's actually preferable to pay for participation in a half-day guided tour to the island run by any of the tour operators noted in this chapter. With drinks, round-trip passage, and the services of a local guide included, and with the certainty that your return trip back to Samaná would, indeed, show up, per-person fees for such a tour cost around US$50 (£26).

Cayo Levantado was the original Bacardi Rum island photographed in a famous ad campaign that ran on TV in the '70s. Regrettably, the famous swaying palm featured in the ad was uprooted in a tropical storm. Yet hundreds of its siblings are still here to shade you when you're not racing across the white sands.

Once at Cayo Levantado, should you tire of the beach, you can take one of the trails that crisscross the island; one leads to a promontory on the southern tier of the island, the lookout point opening onto panoramic views. Yet another trail cuts across to the western side of the island, with a beautiful beach on a secluded bay.

PARQUE NACIONAL LOS HAITISES *රර*

On the southern tier of Samaná Peninsula, this sprawling mass is the country's second-most-visited park, covering 202 sq. km (78 sq. miles) and spanning 24km (15 miles) west from Boca de Inferno and Bahía de San Lorenzo to the head of Río Barracote, that river at the western end of Bahía de Samaná. The park can only be visited by boat (see below).

The park, which is actually a mammoth expanse of mangrove swamp, is home to 112 bird species, nearly 100 plant species, a huge variety of marine life, and several Taíno caves once inhabited by the island's original settlers.

The interior of the park is almost impenetrable, the home of a dense rainforest that is eerily punctuated by the ruins of sugar plantations "gone with the wind." On the boat tours offered, you will get to view mangrove rivers with tiny islets and coastal caves that today are the habitat of rainbow-hued tropical birds, such as the jacana or the Hispaniolan parakeet.

The mangroves aren't necessarily green, but red or white in color. You may very well think you're in an aviary with flocks of roseate terns, frigate birds, ruddy ducks, snow-white egrets, narrow-billed todies, white-cheeked pintails, grebes, and the Ridgway's hawk, along with double-breasted cormorants, coots, solenodons, hutias, and the stunning blue heron. Falcons fly overhead.

At least three caves contain pre-Columbian drawings. The best of these is the stunning Cueva San Gabriel because of its stalactites and stalagmites. Some of the most notorious pirates in the Caribbean were said to have hung out in these caves, including Jack Banister and John Rackham.

At the entrance to Cueva de la Línea you'll see a long row of rocks which are the remains of a railroad erected more than 50 years ago as part of a long-abandoned railway to ship sugar cane.

Near the entrance to Cueva Arena is a most unhelpful ranger station, with some bored attendants charging an entrance fee of RD$50 (US$1.50/75p).

Entrance to the park is at a port of entry, Cana Hondo, a small pier. Getting here is not easy, as you must endure a 19km (12-mile) passage along an often rough sea.

Samaná Tourist Service, Av. La Marina 6 (© **809/538-3322**), offers daily tours to Los Haïtises, costing RD$2,000 (US$61/£31) per person and including lunch and drinks. **Victoria Marine,** Avenida La Marina (© **809/538-2494**), runs tours to the park only Wednesday and Friday, leaving at 9:30am with a return at 4:30pm, costing US$50 (£26) per person.

Transporte Marítimo Minadiel, Av. La Marina 3 (© **809/538-2556**), offers combined tours of the park as well as Cayo Levantado (see above). Tours leave around 9:30am daily, returning at 4pm and costing RD$700 (US$21/£11) without food or RD$980 (US$30/£15) with food and drink included. A tour just to the park costs

RD$480 (US$15/£7.40), with a tour to Cayo Levantado going for RD$225 (US$6.80/£3.45). On the Cayo Levantado tour, you can also take a jaunt that includes food and drink for RD$420 (US$13/£6.45).

A final operator, **Colonial Tour and Travel,** Plaza Comercial Tío Billy 13 (© **809/240-6822;** www.colonialtours.com.do), offers combined tours to the Parque and Cayo Levantado on Monday to Friday 9am to 12:30pm and 2:30 to 5pm, costing RD$2,240 (US$68/£34) with meals and drinks or RD$1,960 (US$59/£30) without.

SAMANA AFTER DARK

Given that the region is considered by many Dominicans as hopelessly boring after dark, visitors tend to head for one of the bars or outdoor restaurants along the Malecón and make an evening of it. Many of these are expat joints, and some of them come and go with such frequency that a guidebook can't keep up-to-date with places that change from season to season.

That doesn't matter. All you have to do is stroll along the waterfront and check out the current favorites, which you'll recognize by the blaring merengue and gyrating crowds. There are two or three discos nearby, none of them particularly memorable, that also change their stripes frequently. A Dominican whose opinion we respect has developed a ritual that he follows whenever he's in Samaná and off-duty. He approaches any of the town matriarchs and pays her to cook a fish with coconut *(pescado con coco)* that he insists is best prepared in Samaná, and best when accompanied by rice with a local berry *(arroz con gandules)*. We don't recommend this for newcomers or casual gringos/gringas who aren't familiar with local customs, but if you see either of these dishes on local menus, be alert to the fact that they represent local delicacies.

If you're a woman traveling alone (or one of a group of women), expect a heavy dose of machismo if you patronize many of the waterfront bars. Men traveling alone can anticipate offers from prostitutes, both female and male.

2 Las Galeras

26km (16 miles) NE of Samaná

Lying northeast from the town of Samaná, Las Galeras practically didn't exist until the early '90s. At the end of a scenic road, you approach this quaint, little remote settlement known for its half-mile of white sandy beach, which is what put it on the map in the first place.

Being transported to Las Galeras from La Samaná on a *guagua* in 1 hour is half the fun. Small beaches opening onto a crashing surf from the Bahía de Samaná, coconut plantations, secluded beaches, limestone outcrops, and exotic trees, such as the tamarind, are just some of the sites you'll see as you bump up and down along a bad (but paved) road that rises and falls across the hilly, undulating terrain.

Before foreign visitors discovered it, Las Galeras was a mere fishing village with seemingly hundreds of coconut palms with fronds blowing in the trade winds. Cultural footnote: Thanks to commerce with English-speaking islands of the western Caribbean, including Antigua and Nevis, there's a high percentage of families with English-derived family names like Bell and Smith.

Learning the lay of the land in Las Galeras doesn't require a degree in geography. There's only one main artery, Calle A, running through the little resort. It runs parallel to the beach.

In lieu of a tourist office, many of the local, English-speaking visitors seem friendly and only too willing to help a bewildered visitor. What's the downside to paradise? Las Galeras, in spite of its setting in an area of great natural beauty, is one hell of a hot and humid place, and U.S. and Canadian visitors used to summer air-conditioning might find it tough coming here. The cheaper rentals, and even some of the better hotels and inns, aren't air-conditioned. Locals are used to the heat, but you may not be.

GETTING AROUND Since Las Galeras lies in a luxuriant and remote part of the Dominican Republic, you might consider renting a jeep or a small car if you don't mind potholed roads. The surrounding terrain is Jungle Jim country, and there are many beautiful but secluded beaches within a short distance. Chances are, you might discover an isolated *playa* just for you and yours. **Samaná Rent-a-Motor,** Calle A (✆ **809/538-0208**), offers Hondas for US$45 (£24) per day, with a sometimes much-needed 4WD jeep going for US$65 (£34) per day. You can also rent bikes and motorcycles here. Motorcycles, incidentally, cost US$25 (£13) per day. Open Monday to Friday 9am to 1pm and 3 to 6pm, and Saturday and Sunday 9am to 1pm.

A competitor is **Caribe Fun Rentals,** Calle A (✆ **809/538-0109**), where most car rentals range from RD$1,680 to RD$2,500 (US$51–US$76/£26–£38) per day, depending on the make. It's open Monday to Saturday 9am to noon and 3 to 6:30pm, Sunday 9am to noon.

Both car-rental companies provide area maps offering information about driving in this part of the country, and their employees speak English.

Without a car, you can rely on one of the *motoconchos* that run throughout the area all day. You might see an occasional independently operated taxi or two, but don't count on it.

WHERE TO STAY

Hotel Moorea Beach   This is a well-run and affordable hotel built in a typical whitewashed Dominican style, with balconies, and everything lying under a tiled roof and shaded by coconut palms. Under Greek-German expat management, it is one of the town's favorites. In business since the mid-'90s, the three-story building has vaguely colonial overtones. The midsize bedrooms are simply but comfortably decorated with Dominican wood furnishings, each coming with a small tiled bathroom with shower. Bedrooms are cooled by ceiling fans over a queen-size bed or two doubles. In summer this place can get awfully hot during the day. The hotel lies 148m (486 ft.) from a sandy beach.

Las Galeras, Dominican Republic. ② 809/538-0007. Fax 809/538-0202. www. hotelmoorea.com. 8 units. US$45–US$70 (£24–£37) double; US$65–US$90 (£34–£47) apt. Children 6–12 US$10 (£5.25) extra. Rates include breakfast. AE, MC, V. Free parking. **Amenities:** Pool. *In room:* Fan, safe.

Plaza Lusitania *Value*   This place is a bit rawboned but well maintained and a friendly oasis. It's recommended mainly because it charges prices known to travelers in the 1960s. Launched around the time of the millennium, it is a colonial-style complex of apartments. All are painted white and are midsize, each furnished with local island pieces resting on cool tiled floors. Each also comes equipped with a little kitchenette and a small bathroom with tub and shower. The bedrooms rest on the second floor above a grocery store and restaurant. Amazingly, for such a cheap rental in the area, air-conditioning is mercifully provided. The food is good, solid Dominican fare—nothing more.

Calle Principal, Las Galeras, Dominican Republic. ② 809/538-0093. Fax 809/538-0066. www.plazalusitania.com. 10 units. US$175 (£92) weekly in a double. AE, MC, V. Free parking. **Amenities:** Restaurant. *In room:* A/C, kitchenette.

Serenity House *ఈఈ*   This hotel was built in the early 1990s along the lines of a rambling, two-story Victorian house with a wraparound balcony lying 100m (328 ft.) from the sea. Painted white with a blue-green roof and a large front garden, it sits above a rocky coastline, a 3-minute walk from a relatively uncrowded beach. Each accommodation has a private balcony and a decor that's different from its neighbors—yours might be Chinese, neoclassical gold-and-white, or Laura Ashley romantic. The more expensive rooms are air-conditioned; others have ceiling fans. The beds are most comfortable here, and the bathrooms, which have tub/shower combos, are tidily kept. Conceived for honeymooners, and anyone else who's looking for a place to escape urban life, the site is quiet, isolated, and low-key, with little to do other than swim in the oval-shaped pool, visit the beach, read, and chat with other guests. Many guests order lunch from operators of small charcoal grills set up on the beach (simple platters of pork or fish). The in-house restaurant, however, is the best of the three or four mainstream restaurants in Las Galeras, opening every day for breakfast, lunch, and dinner.

Las Galeras, Dominican Republic. ✆ 809/538-0000. Fax 809/538-0009. 21 units. US$130–US$160 (£68–£84) double with A/C; US$180–US$225 (£95–£118) triple. Children 2–12 pay 50% of adult rate. Rates include breakfast. MC, V. Free parking. **Amenities:** Restaurant; outdoor pool; bikes; kayaks. *In room:* A/C (in some units), fan.

WHERE TO DINE

We gravitate to that array of ramshackle Dominican fish shacks that are found by the entrance to Playa Las Galeras, the local beach. The fish is fresh and caught that day, and eating seafood on the beach is the way to go. On the negative side, when the vendors hear the sound of a foreign voice, they double the price of their food.

Chez Denise FRENCH/INTERNATIONAL   Denise Flahaire, the owner, operates what has been a local favorite with the expat community here for some 2 decades. This is a casual and informal restaurant, but the food coming out of the kitchen is most often delicious. The setting is Caribbean in style, a proper venue for dining on some tasty dishes prepared with fresh ingredients whenever possible. The local catch of the day is hauled in here and often appears on your plate cooked in coconut milk with potatoes and fresh vegetables. Such favorite dishes as beef stew or lasagna also appear with frequency, as does a shellfish-studded paella. The crepes are a specialty.

Carretera Samaná, Las Galeras. ✆ 809/538-0219. Main courses RD$80–RD$350 (US$2.40–US$11/£1.25–£5.40). No credit cards. Mon–Sat 8am–11pm.

El Marinique Resort Restaurant ⓡ *Finds*   One visiting German woman from Düsseldorf helped us discover this place. "I was alone in a foreign country, and they practically adopted me," said Greta H. Keller. We agreed with her assessment of this undiscovered place, finding a choice of different main courses each day, fresh ingredients, flavorful preparation, good service, and generous portions.

Guests check in here for "barefoot vacations," and often come back the next year. In the open-air restaurant, in business for nearly 2 decades, you can feast on the offerings of the day. We recently sampled the fresh catch of the day sautéed in garlic butter, our companion opting for the delectable grilled tuna. For those who want it, the chefs will always throw a T-bone steak on the grill.

Av. Malecón 6, Las Galeras. ℂ 809/538-0262. Reservations required. Main courses RD$150–RD$450 (US$4.55–US$14/£2.30–£6.90). MC, V. Daily 7:30am–7:30pm. Closed Easter–Oct.

BEACHES, SCUBA DIVING & WHALE WATCHING

Condé Nast Traveller called **Playa Rincón** 𝒜𝒜𝒜 "one of the top 10 playas in the Caribbean," and we concur. It's reason enough to go to Las Galeras. In the background appear the cliffs of Cape Cabrón at 600m (1,969 ft.).

If you're a beach buff, this is the one best beach on the peninsula, and you'll often have its sands to yourself. Don't expect much in the way of facilities. It's best to take whatever supplies you need, although vendors come around hawking food and drink. A rocky road leads to it from Las Galeras, taking 40 minutes by jeep along a rough track. A much easier way to go is to take a ferry departing daily from Dive Samaná, Calle las Galeras, and costing RD$100 (US$3.05/£1.55) for the 20-minute ride.

Many families from Santo Domingo come to Playa Rincón to camp out for the night as a base opening onto Bahía Rincón. The beach is tranquil, its waters calm, as it is protected by two large capes at each end. During the day the waters are a bright turquoise. This beach with interruptions stretches along a 7km (4⅓-mile) stretch of diamond-white sands set against the backdrop of a coconut forest.

One daytime thrill from the southern tier of Playa Rincón is to take a 1km (⅔-mile) trail north to Río Frío. The waters of this river are freezing cold even in summer, but locals like to go here to wash off the sand and salt from Playa Rincón. In our view, there's no better place in the Dominican Republic for cooling off on a hot day. Facilities along this beach, other than a fish hut here or there, are very few. There's talk of big development, but right now you can wander like Robinson Crusoe, sometimes walking for 1.6 km (1 mile) before encountering another beach bum.

Coconut Cannons

You've heard of the dessert "death by chocolate." In the Dominican Republic, there's a twist on this: "death by coconut." The whole area is filled with coconut palms, which are remarkable for their beauty but can be lethal. Falling coconuts not only dent the hoods of cars but also shatter the windshields. These plummeting fruits can also be deadly missiles. People are killed every year on the island by coconuts falling from the sky. In a tropical storm, run for cover, as high winds can send a coconut shooting through the air like ammunition blasted from a cannon.

Of course, if you don't want to make that trek to Playa Rincón, all you have to do is walk out your door to discover the sands of **Playa Las Galeras** ⟨★⟩ itself. This half-mile beach of white sands lies in a tranquil and beautiful setting at the eastern end of Samaná Peninsula. Many foreign visitors practically never leave the beach all day, taking lunch at one of the fish huts that line parts of the beach. A small palm-tree island lies out in the bay.

The adjoining beach of **Cala Blanca** is even more spectacular, a picture postcard of Caribbean charm with its tranquil turquoise waters and swaying palms. The offshore reef breaks the waves, so the waters are very gentle here, which makes this beach a particular favorite of families with young children.

Other beaches in the area, also lovely and filled with white sand, are more difficult to reach. To the immediate east is the beautiful beach **Playa Madama,** ridged by crags and rocks and set against a cave-studded backdrop. The water here is excellent for snorkeling, but there are no facilities.

The adjoining **Playa Colorado** is another beautiful stretch of sand set against a backdrop of tropical plants, including coconut palms.

3 Las Terrenas

17km (11 miles) NE of Sánchez, 249km (155 miles) NE of Santo Domingo

On La Samaná's north coast, this former fishing village has grown greatly since its discovery by expats, often from Switzerland and France, in the late '70s. Las Terrenas stands as one of the newest and emerging resorts of the Caribbean.

In an attempt to end urban slums in Santo Domingo, the dictator Trujillo began exporting people here in the 1940s, instructing them to make their living fishing and farming the land.

Of course, it was its beaches (later in this chapter) that put Las Terrenas on the tourist map, and these strips of golden or white sand remain its major attraction. Otherwise, there is very little to see and do here except hang out on the beach, eat seafood dinners at night, and frequent the beachfront merengue dives until the early hours.

Las Terrenas is one of the least formal and least structured resorts in the Dominican Republic.

GETTING AROUND   You don't need a car. *Motoconchos* and taxis will take you where you want to go—even to the airport at El Portillo where most rides there will cost RD$120 (US$3.65/£1.85) per person. Taxis and *motoconchos* are constantly traversing Las Terrenas, and all you have to do is hail one.

FAST FACTS: LAS TERRENAS

In lieu of a government tourist office, you can go to the offices of **Sunshine Services,** Calle del Carmen 151 (© **809/240-6164**), a travel agency. The staff here is very helpful and will provide information about the area and assist you in your travel needs. There's a TOURIST INFORMATION sign posted outside. Of course, this is a profit-making organization, and the English-speaking staff hopes to make some money off you by helping you in your travel arrangements. Hours are Monday to Saturday 9am to noon and 4 to 7pm.

A **Western Union** office is at Calle Principal 165 (© **809/ 240-6551**), open Monday to Saturday 8am to 6pm, Sunday 8am to noon. For the local phone company, head for **Verizon,** Calle Principal s/n (© **809/220-7412**), open daily 8am to 10pm. Internet access is also possible here, costing RD$21 (US65¢/30p) for 30 minutes or RD$42 (US$1.25/65p) for 1 hour.

For a police, fire, or medical emergency, dial © **911.**

The most central pharmacies are **Farmacia de La Plaza,** Calle Principal 6 (© **809/240-5708**), open Monday to Saturday 8am to 7pm, and also **Farmacia R y R,** Ramon Matia Mella 8 (© **809/ 240-6135**), open Monday to Thursday 8am to 7pm, Friday 8am to 6pm, Saturday 7am to 10pm, and Sunday 8am to 10pm.

To exchange money, go to **Banco del Progreso,** Calle Duarte at Plaza El Paseo de la Costanera (© **809/240-6409**), open Monday to Friday 9am to 3:30pm and Saturday 9am to 1pm.

WHERE TO STAY

Casa del Mar ⚘   Katherine Chately, who bought Casa del Mar in 2004, welcomes you to this series of bungalows that lie only 25m (79 ft.) from the golden sands. The little inn offers good value in pleasantly furnished and comfortable bungalow rooms, with terraces and a tropical garden setting. Accommodations are midsize and well organized, each with a tiled bathroom with a shower. In business since 1997, the hotel doesn't have air-conditioning. Mosquito netting protects the beds. A continental breakfast is served, and a restaurant next to the hotel is operated under separate management.

Calle del Portillo 1, Las Terrenas–Samaná, Dominican Republic. ℂ **809/360-2748.** Fax 809/240-6070. 8 units. US$45–US$50 (£24–£26) double. Rates include breakfast. AE, MC, V. Free parking. **Amenities:** Breakfast served in garden setting. *In room:* Fan, safe.

Coco Plaza Hotel ⚘ *(Kids)*   Lying southeast of the center, this hotel opens on a good beach, Playa Las Ballenas. This is a Mediterranean-style building also close to the much-frequented Playa Cacao. Run by Italian expats, the building rents midsize bedrooms that are tastefully and comfortably decorated, each with a tiled bathroom with a tub/shower combination. Families often stay here for two reasons: Management is very family-friendly, and meals can be prepared in the small kitchens in some units (the studios and apartments), cutting down on food costs. The most luxurious way to stay here is to request a spacious penthouse apartment, one of the best accommodations at this resort.

Calle Chicago Boss 2, Las Terrenas–Samaná, Dominican Republic. ℂ **809/240-6172.** 20 units. US$46–US$75 (£24–£39) double; US$60–US$100 (£32–£53) suite; US$70–US$140 (£37–£74) apts. AE, MC, V. Free parking. **Amenities:** Breakfast room. *In room:* A/C, ceiling fan, TV, kitchenette in some, safe.

Gran Bahía Principe El Portillo ⚘ *(Kids)*   On the north coast, this hotel complex outside Las Terrenas is also close to the airport. The hotel opens onto some of the best beaches on the north coast, although their chain sister on Cayo Levantado (see above) has more tranquil waters. Because of an on-site children's club, this hotel attracts more family business whereas Levantado is more suited for honeymooners because of its greater tranquillity. This hotel, however, has some of the best watersports, including kayaking, catamaran sailing, and windsurfing, even diving classes.

The handsomely furnished bedrooms are spacious, with a private terrace or balcony. Bathrooms are fully equipped with both tub and shower. At the hotel theater musical shows are often presented with regional bands. Buffet dining and an Asian restaurant offer standard fare, although the fishermen's specialty restaurant is preferred. Shopping is the best here of all the Bahía Principes. The center is like a miniature shopping village.

Ctra. Las Terrenas–El Limón, km 4, El Portillo, Dominican Republic. ℂ 809/240-6100. Fax 809/240-6104. www.bahia-principe.com. 396 units. US$180–US$210 (£95–£111) double; US$250–US$300 (£132–£158) junior suite. Rates are all-inclusive. AE, DC, MC, V. **Amenities:** 4 restaurants; 4 bars; 2 outdoor pools; 2 tennis courts; gym; watersports; bike rentals; babysitting; laundry service; theater; horseback riding.

Iguana Hotel 🜛 *Kids*   A real discovery, this series of bungalows rented out by French expats lies 720m (2,362 ft.) from a beautiful sandy beach protected by a barrier of coral. A tranquil, secluded hotel, reached by a sandy path, it offers bungalows spread across its grounds that house two to four persons comfortably. As such, this is a good choice for families. Decorations are in a simple Caribbean style, and the bedrooms are small, each with a private bathroom with shower. The bungalows lie in parklike grounds, far removed from the traffic, especially those noisy mopeds.

Playa Las Vallenas, Las Terrenas–Samaná, Dominican Republic. ℂ 809/240-5525. Fax 809/240-6070. www.iguana-hotel.com. 10 units. US$60–US$75 (£32–£39) double; US$105–US$125 (£55–£66) 3–4 persons. Rates include American breakfast. No credit cards. Free parking. **Amenities:** Bar; barbecue grill; babysitting; children's beds; kitchen for clients. *In room:* Fan, safe.

Hotel Residence Playa Colibri 🜛 *Kids*   Launched in 2000, these are a series of fairly elegant apartments for the area, spread across palm-studded grounds in three-story buildings overlooking the beach, one of the best strips of sand at the resort. Close to the center of Las Terrenas, but somewhat protected from the noise, the apartments are modern and spacious, each comfortably appointed with tropical furnishings painted in pastels. Each unit comes with a small tiled bathroom with shower. Families like to stay here because the apartments have fully equipped kitchenettes, each opening onto a balcony with a view, often of the swimming pool and Jacuzzi. The complex takes its name, *colibrí,* from the hummingbirds seen picking nectar from the red hibiscus bushes in the flower beds. Included in the rates are linens and bath towels along with maid service twice a week. On request, a full-time maid can be provided, as can a private cook. On-site is a restaurant and bar run by different people and definitely not recommended.

Calle Francisco Tamayo, Las Terrenas–Samaná, Dominican Republic. ② **809/240-6434.** Fax 809/240-6917. www.playacolibri.com. 45 units. US$53–US$88 (£28–£46) double; US$95–US$190 (£50–£100) for 4. MC, V. Free parking. **Amenities:** Restaurant; bar; outdoor pool; room service; babysitting. *In room:* Fan, kitchenette, safe.

Tropic Banana 🏵 In a tropical park of 2.8 hectares (7 acres), this hotel opens onto a beach of golden sands, lying a 15-minute ride from the Portillo airstrip. It is set against a backdrop of rolling hills and mountains and is a real escapist retreat. Bedrooms are furnished in a light, breezy style with a Caribbean motif, and range from small to midsize, each with a tiny tiled bathroom with shower. Rooms are spread across two buildings on two levels, the hotel dating from the late '70s. The top-floor rooms open onto a private balcony, the lower floor units onto a terrace. A French-run tropical hotel, the inn offers a restaurant serving an excellent French and international cuisine. Every Friday is devoted to sushi prepared from the freshest of the day's catch. The on-site bar is rather exotic and worth a visit on your nighttime prowl. Filled with rattan furnishings, it opens onto a sea view.

Calle Francisco Alberto Camaño, Las Terrenas–Samaná, Dominican Republic. ② **809/240-6110.** www.tropicbanana.com. 21 units. US$70–US$110 (£37–£58) double; US$140–US$170 (£74–£89) triple. Children 2–12 US$10 (£5.25) extra. Rates include breakfast. MC, V. Free parking. **Amenities:** Restaurant; bar; outdoor pool; billiards; library; gift shop; TV room. *In room:* A/C, fan, safe.

Viva Wyndham Samaná 🏵🏵 This was the first government-rated four-star hotel to open on Samaná. Opening onto a white sandy beach, it's still one of the best places to stay on the north shore. The trip along the unpaved road doesn't look too promising, but when you come to the end at this first-class place, and are greeted with a waterfall, the hotel looks like Eden in the tropics. In well-landscaped grounds underneath the sheltering palms, the hotel became an immediate hit when it opened its doors.

Comfortably furnished standard bedrooms open onto private terraces or balconies, most of them with views of the ocean. Each comes with a private bathroom, coated in tile and furnished with shower and tub. The English-speaking hotel staff is helpful in arranging excursions, including everything from whale-watching expeditions to treks through Parque Nacional Los Haïtises (earlier in this chapter).

The food is plentiful, varied, and made, for the most part, with market-fresh ingredients. Dominican-theme dinners are a regular feature, and there is also a pasta and pizzeria dining selection. The location is 12.8km (8 miles) west of the airport at El Portillo and 8km (5 miles) west of the village of Las Terrenas.

Playa Cosón, Las Terrenas–Samaná, Dominican Republic. ⓒ 809/240-5050. Fax 809/ 240-5536. www.wyndham.com. 208 units. Winter US$80 (£42) double, US$85 (£45) suite, US$150 (£79) villa; off season US$70 (£37) double, US$75 (£39) suite, US$95 (£50) villa. Rates are per person daily and all-inclusive. AE, MC, V. **Amenities:** 3 restaurants; 4 bars; disco; outdoor pool; watersports equipment; dive shop; car-rental desk. *In room:* A/C, TV, hair dryer, safe.

WHERE TO DINE

To eat as the islanders do, head west of the mouth of Río Las Terrenas to a series of fishermen's huts under thatch roofs. With a Presidente beer resting beside your plate, dig into the catch of the day, which is most often served fried. If it's raining (highly unlikely), you'll find that a few of these shacks have tables under roofs. Otherwise, you dine outside under the stars.

Casa Boga 🔥 (Finds) BASQUE/SEAFOOD   Launched right before the beginning of the millennium, this restaurant has become an enduring fixture on the local dining scene, lying in front of Paseo de la Costanera. Light and satisfying meals prepared with fresh ingredients put this place on the map, where it is likely to stay. Some of the dishes are Basque-inspired, and many savvy Spanish diners consider that cuisine the finest in their country.

Begin, perhaps, with an inspired tuna carpaccio, and then select from a wide variety of fish, the individual offerings depending on the catch of the day. The fish can be grilled almost to your specifications, and platters are always served with mixed, freshly made salads and fried yucca. Various whitefish can also be sautéed in garlic and onion, and fresh tuna is fried with green peppers and onions. For true Basque flavor, order the fresh mussels in a garlic-laced green sauce made with fresh herbs. The chefs also prepare the resort's best kettle of fish soup.

Playa de Las Terrenas. ⓒ 809/240-6321. Reservations recommended. Main courses RD$340–RD$800 (US$10–US$24/£5.25–£12). MC, V. Mon–Sat 12:30–11pm.

Rancho Suizo 🔥 (Value) STEAKHOUSE   A "Swiss Ranch" sounds like an oxymoron, but this eatery, dating from the late '90s, serves the best cuts and the tenderest steaks along the northern coast of Samaná Peninsula. The reason behind the unusual name is a Swiss expat, named Christian Wiedmer, who formerly owned the restaurant. The new owner, Patrik Muller, who is also Swiss, brings incredibly affordable dining to Las Terrenas, especially if you order one of the fixed-price meals.

Most savvy diners opt for a big platter containing the perfectly cooked T-bone steak with potatoes. More delicate is the entrecôte in a peppery sauce. If you don't want steak, you can order such eternal favorites as spaghetti in a Bolognese sauce made with fresh tomatoes; cheese fondue; barbecue; or raclette.

Carretera Portillo 45. ℂ **809/240-6162.** Main courses RD$180–RD$600 (US$5.45–US$18/£2.75–£9.25). MC, V. Daily 8am–midnight.

BEACHES & OUTDOOR PURSUITS

The aptly named **Playa Bonita** 𝕽𝕽, or "beautiful beach," at Punta Bonita lies only a 10-minute ride by *motoconcho* west from the heart of Las Terrenas. We suggest that you take this ride and not attempt to walk here along a coastal road that is dirty, muddy, and rather steep. Once here, you'll find a kilometer (⅔ mile) of golden sand set against the backdrop of coconut palms and a surf of clean waters. In the distance you can see several palm-studded islets. Humpback whales can be spotted off the coast in season. Playa Bonita is far less discovered than the beach at Las Terrenas, and we prefer it for this reason.

Punta Bonita lies 6km (3¾ miles) west of Las Terrenas and only a 10-minute drive east of the village of Cosón. This is our preferred spot for snorkeling on the north coast of the peninsula, and the usually clear waters contain rainbow-hued fish and beautiful coral formations.

Punta Bonita, beginning west of a lesser beach, Playa Las Ballenas, offers 13km (8 miles) of uninterrupted powdery-white sand. With its tranquil waters, this is a great beach for snorkelers.

Back in Las Terrenas, you can enjoy some good beaches as well, including **Playa Cacao,** although these sands are more crowded, especially in winter. The beachfront at Las Terrenas stretches for 1.9km (1¼ miles) both east and west from the center. The waters are generally tranquil here, suitable for swimming. Projecting out is a coral reef at 98m (322 ft.) that is ideal for some excellent snorkeling.

Scuba divers wanting to explore the northern shore of La Samaná Peninsula head for oné of the peninsula's best dive outfitters, **Stellina Dive Center,** Playa Cacao (ℂ **809/868-4415** or 809/240-6149), the office open daily from 9am to 1pm and 3 to 5pm. The staff here offers diving for all levels from beginner to advanced. A 1-day dive costs RD$850 (US$26/£13) with equipment provided, RD$715 (US$22/£11) without equipment. Night dives go for RD$1,115 (US$34/£17) per person with equipment, RD$850 (US$26/£13) without equipment.

LAS TERRENAS AFTER DARK

The entire waterfront of Las Terrenas becomes festive at night, especially at the **Night Market,** on Friday, Saturday, and Sunday. This is a real happening experience where locals descend on the waterfront to sell Dominican food and liquor (most often rum) from stalls. Hastily assembled island bands play music, and the party goes on until early morning.

The hottest dance club at the resort is **Discoteca Nuevo Mundo,** Calle Duarte 250 (© **809/240-6414**), lying on the main road 197m (646 ft.) south of the local cemetery. Both locals and visitors of all ages frequent this dance club, with its recorded music, mainly merengue, salsa, house, and Latin rock. Three or four times a month they bring in a local or international band to amuse the masses, and on these nights, the joint is packed. Normally there's no cover, but such a charge is likely to be imposed on nights of live performances. It is open Sunday to Friday 9pm to 4:30am and Saturday 9pm to 6am.

8

Puerto Plata & the Amber Coast

Columbus wanted to establish a city at Puerto Plata and name it La Isabela, but a tempest detained him. It wasn't until 1502 that Nicolás de Ovando founded Puerto Plata ("port of silver"). The port became the last stop for ships going back to Europe, their holds laden with treasures taken from the New World.

Puerto Plata appeals to a mass-market crowd that prefers less expensive, all-inclusive resorts. More accommodations of this kind continue to pop up on this coast, and yet many are still booked solid almost year-round. It's estimated that 95% of all visitors to the north coast stay at an all-inclusive, usually in the Playa Dorada complex, and limit their exploration of the coast to a ride from the airport to their resort and back again. An unfortunate byproduct of the all-inclusive trend is that several good restaurants have been forced to close.

Most of the hotels are not actually in Puerto Plata itself but in a tourist zone called Playa Dorada, which consists of about 14 major hotels, a scattering of secluded condominiums and villas, a Robert Trent Jones Jr.–designed golf course, and a riding stable. With the lone exception of Casa Colonial, which is described later in this chapter, each of the hotels within Playa Dorada books their clients in as part of all-inclusive plans. For years, Playa Dorada was the largest all-inclusive resort complex on earth, although other competitors, both within and outside the D.R., have caught up with it. A very short drive to the west from Playa Dorada is Costa Dorada, a smaller plot of carefully landscaped beachfront terrain which contains a scattering of resorts.

Encompassing 299km (186 miles) of prime waterfront property on the north shore of the Dominican Republic, the region around Puerto Plata is known by some as the "Silver Coast." But today more and more people are referring to it as the "Amber Coast" because of the rich deposits of amber found here, and because of the tawny color of the sandy beachfronts.

Recent publicity of such other resorts as Punta Cana have brought that resort's beaches into frequent comparisons to those of Puerto Plata. So here's what we think: Puerto Plata lies on the more verdant, and rainier, north shore of the island; Punta Cana lies on the somewhat drier southeastern tip. Instead of the tranquil Caribbean Sea, the beaches face the Atlantic Ocean, which means that waters can be more turbulent, especially in the winter months. But rainfall in Puerto Plata, when it comes, arrives suddenly, but doesn't last long. And it keeps the landscaping green. Puerto Plata's beaches aren't as wide as some of those in Punta Cana, but recent improvement of the beaches in Puerto Plata has done a lot to even out the equation.

Staff at hotels in Puerto Plata tend to have been born and raised within the region, and they usually retain cultural links to the region and to their families. Staff within hotels in Punta Cana tend to have been recently displaced from other parts of the island, and some of them have complained about feeling sociologically uprooted, now that they might be living in "company housing."

And finally, Puerto Plata maintains an urbanized feel, and an economy based on something in addition to tourism, whereas newer communities (Punta Cana and Samaná) are basically modern communities carved from what was wilderness or scrubland, with none of the feelings of urban life that are so deeply engrained within the Dominican consciousness. Therefore, in the battle presently raging between which resort within the D.R. will reign, we don't by any means underestimate the ongoing allure of the country's Grande Dame of Puerto Plata: In the sweepstakes of what's hot within the D.R., it has a lot going for it, and the race for preeminence is far from over. Incidentally, Americans account for only a quarter of the visitors, the rest coming from Canada or Europe.

You need not confine your visit just to the resorts in and around Puerto Plata and Playa Dorada. To the east lie the emerging resort towns of Sosúa, once a prime center for those seeking sex in the sun, or Cabarete, the windsurfing capital of the Americas.

1 Puerto Plata & Playa Dorada

209km (130 miles) NW of Santo Domingo

The city of Puerto Plata has only a few tourist attractions (albeit considerably more than what's in Punta Cana, its leading rival). Although it's defined as the administrative and cultural centerpiece of the region, it must simply watch as most of the tourist business heads to its eastern and western peripheries, notably to Playa Dorada and Costa Dorada, to the east, and to Cofresi, to the west. Nonetheless, it's a valued symbol of an entity whose value revolves around more than tourism, providing a kind of balance between U.S., Canadian, and European newcomers and an established Dominican infrastructure. Most of the other newly emerging Dominican resort areas, such as Punta Cana, don't have as large or prominent a settlement nearby, and often, labor has had to be imported into relatively new communities from other parts of the country.

Chances are high that you'll be staying outside the city center, but consider a visit to Puerto Plata's restaurants, bars, shops, and its historic colonial-era fort, plus a walk along its oceanfront promenade, El Malecón. Sometimes you can see dolphins frolicking offshore or a humpback whale in winter.

Puerto Plata also contains the Dominican Republic's best shopping outlets for amber and, to a lesser degree, larimar. The town also contains one of the country's only cable cars, from the top of which visitors have dramatic views of the north coast.

Playa Dorada and its immediate neighbor, Costa Dorada, beginning only 1km (⅔ mile) east of Puerto Plata, share between the two of them about 16 hotels, most of them all-inclusive; a gorgeous beach of golden sand; plus an 18-hole golf course, a shopping mall, and a range of ancillary sporting venues, bars, dance clubs, restaurants, at least two casinos, and several additional diversions. They're accessible from Puerto Plata by driving east from Puerto Plata along the coastal road.

Some savvy visitors are bypassing Playa Dorada with its mass appeal and heading about 5km (3miles) east of Puerto Plata to **Playa Cofresi,** site of the newly expanded Ocean World and an all-new blockbuster real-estate and resort development, Sun Village. On Sundays, islanders themselves pour into Playa Cofresi, turning the beach here into a giant house party, with the eating, drinking, picnicking, barbecues, and merengue lasting well into the night.

ESSENTIALS

GETTING THERE   The airport is the **Puerto Plata International Gregorio Luperón Airport,** lying 11km (7 miles) east of Playa Dorada. **American Eagle (©** **800/433-7300** in the U.S. and Canada; www.aa.com) has daily 2-hour flights from San Juan, Puerto Rico, to Puerto Plata. Flights cost from RD$5,600 to RD$11,760 (US$170–US$356/£86–£181) per person round-trip from San Juan to Puerto Plata. American Airlines also flies daily from Miami (2 hr., 10 min) and from New York (3½ hr.). Most of the Puerto Plata resorts are about a 40-minute drive from the airport.

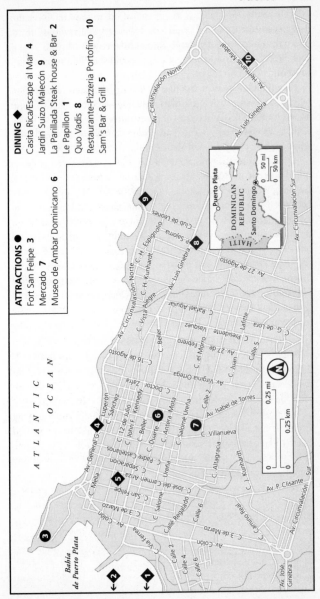

ATTRACTIONS ●
Fort San Felipe **3**
Mercado **7**
Museo de Ambar Dominicano **6**

DINING ◆
Casita Rica/Escape al Mar **4**
Jardin Suizo Malecón **9**
La Parillada Steak house & Bar **2**
Le Papillon **1**
Quo Vadis **8**
Restaurante-Pizzeria Portofino **10**
Sam's Bar & Grill **5**

ATLANTIC OCEAN

Bahía de Puerto Plata

DOMINICAN REPUBLIC
HAITI
Puerto Plata
Santo Domingo

50 mi
50 km

From Santo Domingo, the 3½-hour drive directly north on Autopista Duarte passes through the lush Cibao Valley, home of the tobacco industry and Bermudez rum, and through Santiago de los Caballeros, the second-largest city in the country, 145km (90 miles) north of Santo Domingo.

Takeoff Destination Service S.A. (© **809/552-1333;** www. takeoffweb.com) no longer offers regularly scheduled flights from such Dominican destinations as Santo Domingo or Punta Cana. Today, it's necessary to call and make arrangements for flights, which can be chartered and shared with others to cut costs.

It's a rough ride if you take a bus to reach Puerto Plata, and you might share it with some chickens. **Caribe Express,** corner of José Eugenio Conjas, Plaza Caribe (© **809/586-6796**), offers service between Santo Domingo and Puerto Plata, passing through Santiago en route. Travel time from Santo Domingo to Santiago takes about 2 hours. From here, it will require an additional 90 minutes for ongoing passage to Puerto Plata. Buses run back and forth between the three cities every day between 6am to 7pm (last departures). **Metro Buses,** Calle 16 de Agosto, corner of Calle Beller (© **809/ 586-6062**), also runs buses from Santo Domingo and Santiago to Puerto Plata (or vice versa) daily at the same times. A one-way fare from Santo Domingo to Puerto Plata costs RD$215 (US$7.75/£4).

GETTING AROUND   Avis (© **800/331-1212** in the U.S. and Canada, or 809/586-0214; www.avis.com), **Budget** (© **800/472-3325** in the U.S. and Canada, or 809/586-0413; www.budget. com), and **Hertz** (© **800/654-3131** in the U.S. and Canada, or 809/586-0200; www.hertz.com) all have offices at the airport.

You probably won't need to rent a car, however, if you're staying at one of the all-inclusive resorts. You might just like to get around Puerto Plata by **motor scooter,** although the roads are potholed. You can rent a scooter at the guest services kiosk at just about any large hotel in Puerto Plata.

Minivans are another means of transport, especially if you're traveling outside town. They leave from Puerto Plata's Central Park and will take you all the way to Sosúa. Determine the fare before getting in. Usually a shared ride between Puerto Plata and Sosúa costs RD$45 to RD$60 (US$1.35–US$1.80/70p–90p) per person. Service is daily 6am to 9pm.

If you take a **taxi,** agree with the driver on the fare before your trip starts, as cabs are not metered. You'll find taxis in Central Park in Puerto Plata. At night, it's wise to rent your cab for a round-trip.

If you go in the daytime by taxi to any of the other beach resorts or villages, check on reserving a vehicle for your return trip. A taxi from Puerto Plata to Sosúa will cost around RD$580 (US$18/£8.90) each way (for up to four occupants).

VISITOR INFORMATION   There's an **Office of Tourism** in Central Park (© **809/586-3676**). Hours are Monday to Friday 8am to 3pm.

FAST FACTS   Round-the-clock **drugstore** service is offered by **Farmacia Deleyte,** Calle John F. Kennedy 89 (© **809/586-2583**). Emergency medical service is provided by **Clínica Dr. Brugal,** Calle José del Carmen Ariza 15 (© **809/586-2519**). Medical services are also provided at **Hospital Clínica Dr. José Gregorio Hernández,** Av. 27 de Febrero 21 (© **809/586-1166**), maintaining 24-hour emergency service. The **Clínica Dental** is at Av. Juan Pablo Duarte 80, Galerías Las Bromelias 33 (© **809/971-5689**). To summon the **police** in Puerto Plata, Calle Luis Ginêbra, call © **809/586-2331.** If you need to visit in person, the address is Calle Luis Ginêbra 14. The office of the local **Western Union** is at Playa Plaza Dorada (© **809/320-2501**), open daily from 8am to 9:45pm.

Because so many Canadian visitors descend on Puerto Plata annually, that country has opened a consulate at Virginia e Ortea, Edificio Isabel de Torres (Suite 311-C) at Puerto Plata (© **809/586-5761**), Monday to Friday 9am to 1pm.

The **U.K. Consulate** is at Beller 51 (© **809/586-4244**), open Monday to Friday 8:15am to 12:30pm. The **U.S. Consulate** is at César Nicolas Penson (© **809/221-2171**), open Monday to Friday 7:30am to 4pm.

For Internet access, go to **SR Systems,** Carretera Puerto Plata and Maimon (© **809/320-1603**), where the charge is US$8 (£4.20) for 30 minutes.

For money exchange or banks with ATMs, head for **Banco BHD,** Calle San Felipe (© **809/320-7919**), Monday to Friday 8am to 4pm; or **Banco del Progreso,** Calle Beller 33 (© **809/320-0504**), open Monday to Friday 8:30am to 3pm, Saturday 9am to 1pm.

WHERE TO STAY
PLAYA DORADA
Note: Virtually no one checks in on the rates given below. Travel agents can book people in on some discounted package deal any time of the year, even in the high season of winter.

Casa Colonial ✸✸✸ This is the most sophisticated, most intimate, and most socially prestigious hotel in the Dominican Republic, a relatively recent architectural gem that successfully functions as the crown jewel of a respected local hotel chain, VH. It was the first hotel in the country to join the Small Luxury Hotels of the World marketing group, and as an a la carte boutique hotel, it is distinct and definitely never included within the roster of Puerto Plata's mass-market all-inclusives. It was designed by a member of the family that owns the hotel, Dominican/Italian architect Sarah Garcia. Baronial and aristocratic-looking, it evokes a combination of a Greek Orthodox church and a Palladian-style Renaissance villa, with hints of Andalusia and a definite sense of Spanish colonial chic. Its central core contains two deluxe restaurants, and its annex artfully combines lush gardens and a view of a primal-looking mangrove lagoon immediately adjacent to a stretch of highly desirable beachfront. A pith-helmeted, white-jacketed staff wait courteously amid acres of gleaming white marble. The on-site full-service spa, the Bagua, reeks of haute California hip.

Bedrooms are all-white retreats that are high-ceilinged, large, and in some cases, very large. Other than the Presidential suite, the best accommodations are the lavish oceanfront master suites with private entrances. This is a very adult and appealingly indulgent kind of place, where the presence of children under 12 is not encouraged.

P.O. Box 22, Playa Dorada, Puerto Plata, Dominican Republic. ② **809/571-9727.** Fax 809/320-4017. www.vhhr.com. 50 units. US$260–US$420 (£137–£221) junior suite for 2; US$420–US$670 (£221–£353) specialty suite for 2. Rates are all-inclusive. AE, DC, MC, V. **Amenities:** 2 restaurants; 3 bars; outdoor pool; golf privileges; health club; spa; room service; babysitting; laundry service; nonsmoking rooms; rooms for those w/limited mobility. *In room:* A/C, TV, minibar, beverage maker, hair dryer, iron, safe.

Celuisma Tropical Dorada *Kids* Under a different administration, this had been known as a cost-conscious, low-end resort constructed with less than top-notch materials and plagued with maintenance problems. (Its former name was the Playa Naco Golf & Tennis Resort). In 2005, faced with intense competition from more stylish newcomers, many of its public areas were upgraded, and in 2006, the property was acquired by a Spain-based chain (Celuisma) known for its competent management and lower-middle-end rates. These new factors have redefined this as an older property with an attractive new lease on life.

Rooms are fairly spacious and set within concrete-sided three-story buildings. Each has white walls, flowered fabrics, and a sense of airy, uncluttered (or underfurnished, depending on your point of view) spaciousness that newer hotels with less available land can't match. On-site is a spa plus a low-slung bungalow designed like a log cabin that functions as a children's center. In the past, at least, goodly numbers of guests here hailed from Germany and Canada—under Celuisma, we expect increasing numbers of clients from Spain as well.

The restaurants provide a wide variety of reasonably well-prepared food, at least some of which is presented as a series of buffets. If it's your wish, you can be kept busy with the usual array of activities—horseback riding and watersports. Live music, usually merengue, is presented every evening from 6:30 to 10:30pm. In 2006, management built an all-new Dominican cafe, La Casita Dominicana, adjacent to the beachfront.

Playa Dorada, Puerto Plata, Dominican Republic. © 809/320-6226. Fax 809/320-6225. www.celuisma.com. 414 units. US$90–US$95 (£47–£50) double; US$100 (£53) suite. Children 2–12 US$25 (£13) extra. Rates are per person, double occupancy, and all-inclusive. AE, MC, V. Free parking. **Amenities:** 5 restaurants; 4 bars; dance club; nightly entertainment; 2 outdoor pools (one for children); 18-hole golf course; 4 tennis courts; health club; spa; sauna; watersports equipment; children's center; massage; babysitting; laundry service; dry cleaning; horseback riding; exchange bank; pharmacy. *In room:* A/C, TV, fridge, hair dryer, safe.

Gran Ventana Beach Resort 🏖 (Kids)

This is the largest of three nearly adjacent hotels that are each administered by the VH chain. Of the three, this has the most whimsical and least formal decor, with large numbers of people moving in and out. This is an indulgently fun-loving place that doesn't take itself too seriously. In this rather unsophisticated atmosphere, dress is very informal. It occupies 100 landscaped hectares (247 acres) of ocean-fronting land that's divided into three distinctly defined "pods" or clusters, the quietest and calmest of which is the Beata Wing, which is just a bit removed (but easily accessible, on foot, to the more animated Catalina and Saona clusters). You'll find a higher percentage of children here than at many other of Playa Dorada's resorts, thanks to a Kid's Klub—a glorified day-care center with its own mini-disco for adolescents and lots of good-natured attendants. The resort is composed of a series of three-story buildings, softened with landscaping, that are each trimmed with latticework and vaguely Victorian-inspired fretwork; each unit has mahogany furniture, ceiling fans, a balcony or patio, and, in many cases, views of the sea. Bedrooms are compact but efficiently designed. Bathrooms are a bit small but have up-to-date plumbing with tub/shower combos. The gardens and lawns surrounding the site are dotted with gazebos, flowering shrubs, and tropical plants and palms.

The all-inclusive plan limits a guest to 1 hour per day for each of the following: snorkeling, windsurfing, sailing, horseback riding, kayaks, and scuba diving. It limits dining at the exclusive Octopus (an octagonally shaped "gourmet" dining room with the most elaborate cuisine) to in-house residents who reserve in advance. Some kind of live entertainment is presented here almost every night, and recorded music keeps the good times rolling within more than one of the bars.

Apdo. Postal 22, Playa Dorada, Puerto Plata, Dominican Republic. ⓒ **809/320-2111.** Fax 809/320-2112. www.vhhr.com. 506 units. US$80–US$150 (£42–£79) double; US$115–US$175 (£61–£92) junior suite; US$130–US$270 (£68–£142) suite. Rates are per person, double occupancy, and all-inclusive. AE, DC, MC, V. **Amenities:** 5 restaurants; 7 bars; 3 outdoor pools; tennis court; health club; sauna; watersports equipment; children's center; salon; room service; massage; babysitting; laundry service; dry cleaning; horseback riding; 1 room for those w/limited mobility. *In room:* A/C, TV, minibar, hair dryer, safe.

Holiday Village Golden Beach 🔆 *Kids*

This is the matriarch of Puerto Plata resorts, the first to launch the city as a resort, and the first to snag a desirable plot of flat land immediately adjacent to the beach. It has seen many peaks and valleys since its widely publicized inauguration as a Jack Tar Village in 1983. It was acquired by a joint Canadian/British tour operator, who fills its rooms with ongoing streams of value-conscious holiday-makers who aren't particularly concerned that it isn't cutting-edge. In addition to a woodsy-looking central core, it incorporates 73 villas scattered across 39 hectares (96 acres) of lawns dotted with palms and flowering shrubs. Only a few of them lie directly astride the beach, but pools and the ocean are within a short walk. Clients get the sense that part of the allure of the place involves very close access to an 18-hole golf course that was designed by golf-design guru Robert Trent Jones Jr.

Rooms tend to be midsize, filled with pine furnishings and Dominican paintings, and come with screened windows, purified water, bathrooms with tubs, private balconies, or patios. Sofa beds are installed in the living rooms, and although the decors aren't the most stylish at the resort, they are nonetheless well maintained and comfortable. Because of the resort's large acreage, the "population density" on its grounds is appealingly low. Overall, this is an older property with a rich tradition, lots of scars, and an eagerness to keep up with the competition. The cuisine competes with the best of those served within the Playa Dorada all-inclusives, and there is a trio of specialty restaurants to choose from. The hotel has a kids' club with a crew of child-minders, a pool for kids, and babysitting services.

Playa Dorada, Puerto Plata, Dominican Republic. (C) **809/320-3800.** Fax 809/320-4161. www.FirstChoice.co.uk. 281 units. US$110–US$150 (£58–£79) double. Children 11 and younger stay free in parent's room. Rates are all-inclusive. AE, MC, V. Free parking. **Amenities:** 4 restaurants; 5 bars; disco; casino; nightly entertainment; 3 outdoor pools (including 1 kids' pool); golf course; 3 tennis courts; health club; sauna; watersports equipment; babysitting; laundry service; dry cleaning; horseback riding. *In room:* A/C, ceiling fan, TV, dataport, minibar, hair dryer, safe.

Occidental Gran Flamenco ★ (Kids)

Opening onto a tranquil stretch of Las Papas Beach, this is one of the most consistently reliable hotels in Puerto Plata, exuding Iberian flair and a low-key classiness that some of its competitors lack. Operated by the Spain-based Occidental chain, and radically renovated, it has a tasteful, discreetly elegant lobby outfitted with flowers and reproductions of Taíno statues. Accommodations are set within clusters of three-story buildings with white walls and red terra-cotta roofs. Throughout the accommodations there's a sense of Iberian dignity, with strong contrasts of dark paneling with white walls, and blue-and-white tile work. More expensive rooms, in the Club Miguel Ange, are somewhat larger and have upgraded amenities and round-the-clock access to a concierge. Each bathroom has a tub/shower combo.

Dining options range from hot dogs, burgers, and pizza, to an array of international cuisine including seafood and a sampling of Mediterranean dishes. Our favorite is the grill restaurant, Las Reses.

P.O. Box 547, Complejo Playa Dorada, Puerto Plata, Dominican Republic. (C) **809/320-5084.** Fax 809/320-6319. www.occidental-hoteles.com. 582 units. US$130–US$150 (£68–£79) double. Rates are all-inclusive. AE, MC, V. **Amenities:** 8 restaurants; 6 bars; disco; 2 outdoor pools; golf course; tennis courts; Jacuzzi; watersports equipment; children's center; travel agency; salon; babysitting; laundry service; horseback riding; aerobics. *In room:* A/C, TV, minibar (in suite), safe.

Paradise Beach Resort & Casino ★ (Kids)

Thanks to the fact that it was one of the earliest of the all-inclusive hotels at Playa Dorada, it claimed one of the most central and most desirable stretches of beaches. Today, it's a competent, well-managed, but not particularly fashionable resort, having been surpassed since its original construction with newer competitors nearby. Nonetheless, there's a lot here to recommend, including prices that are at the lower-middle end of the spectrum of Puerto Plata's all-inclusives. Ongoing renovations removed some of its dowdier aspects, and its beachfront was upgraded in 2006 with the pumping in of thousands of tons of sand. Its layout includes a compound of four-story masonry buildings, with white-tile roofs and lattice-laced balconies. Pathways cut through the well-manicured, tropical grounds, and kids have room to romp. Accommodations are neatly furnished with tile floors, twin or queen-size beds, refrigerators (in most cases), and tiled bathrooms with shower/tub combos, and at least half of the units have balconies. Only a few of the units, in most cases suites, have views opening onto the water. It attracts goodly numbers of hip Canadians in winter, and in summer, a lot of Dominican-derived clients presently living in New York City. There's also a spa on-site.

The resort has three restaurants, some of which are buffet-style. The management also hosts poolside barbecues and weekly shows with singing and dancing acts.

Apdo. Postal 337, Playa Dorada, Puerto Plata, Dominican Republic. © 800/752-9236 in the U.S., or 809/320-3663. Fax 809/320-4864. www.amhsamarina.com. 436 units. US$85–US$100 (£45–£53) double; US$175–US$225 (£92–£118) suite. Rates are all-inclusive. AE, MC, V. **Amenities:** 3 restaurants; 4 bars; disco; casino; 2 outdoor pools (one reserved for children); 2 lit tennis courts; spa; whirlpool; watersports equipment; children's center; room service; babysitting; laundry service; dry cleaning; horseback riding; aerobics; scuba available for an additional charge non-smoking rooms. *In room:* A/C, TV.

Victoria Golf & Beach Resort 🏨🏨

It's a 10-minute walk to the beach, but this midsize resort, set on 99 hectares (245 acres), has been a favorite since it opened in 1989. This is the best resort at Playa Dorada that does not directly open onto the beachfront. As such, its designers tried harder with the establishment of landscaping that's a bit more lush and lawns that are a bit better maintained than at some of its competitors. If you don't want to walk to the beach, minivans shuttle back and forth at frequent intervals.

Although this resort originally sported a decorative theme of fretwork and gingerbread inspired by Victorian cottages of the 1890s, all of that changed during a radical reconfiguration in 1998, when talented local architect Sarah Garcia, the daughter of the hotel's owner, ripped away the faux-Victorian frills and reconfigured the design into the kind of modernist and avant-garde angularity and European gray-greens and beiges that you might expect in Milan or Barcelona.

This hotel best appeals to clients who appreciate a venue that isn't particularly raucous, and which consistently shows signs of restrained European elegance in a tropical setting. There is less focus on around-the-clock activities here than in some neighboring resorts, but that may come as a blessing to some guests just wanting some R&R. Our only complaint about this hotel is that the swimming pool isn't as dramatic or as big as some at competing resorts, but in light of this hotel's other virtues, no one seems to mind.

An excellent international cuisine is served here, making use of island-grown produce whenever available. Between June and September, lots of British clients check in here; between December and April, it's the venue for lots of Canadian and American clients.

Playa Dorada, Puerto Plata, Dominican Republic. © 809/320-1200. Fax 809/320-4862. 190 units. US$75–US$145 (£39–£76) double; US$125–US$230 (£66–£121) suite. Children 2–12 sharing their parents' rooms pay US$55 (£29) each. Rates are all-inclusive. AE, DC, DISC, MC, V. Free parking. **Amenities:** 4 restaurants; 4 bars; 2 outdoor pools; 18-hole golf course; 3 tennis courts; health club; sauna; watersports equipment; room service; laundry service. *In room:* A/C, TV, minibar, hair dryer, safe.

COSTA DORADA

Much smaller than Playa Dorada, whose boundaries contain 14 all-inclusive hotels and a golf course, Costa Dorada, at least at press time, contained only two hotels, both of which are recommended below. Costa Dorada lies within a 3-minute drive west from Playa Dorada, within a landscaped compound, a mini version of Playa Dorada, which might expand as newer hotels are added to its infrastructure.

Coral Marien ⚔ *Kids*   This is a stylish and artfully designed compound, which we like almost as much as the Iberostar, which sits immediately next door. Couples seeking privacy at this all-inclusive resort will find it here, but those wanting around-the-clock activities will also be rewarded. Decors inside are stylish and more cutting-edge than what you'll find within some other, older resorts, such as the Paradise Beach in neighboring Playa Dorada. A lagoon-shaped swimming pool and a series of three-story pastel-colored buildings radiate outward from an artful, Taíno-inspired central core, all of it set against a backdrop of sandy beach. A tobacco-leaf theme predominates, including replicas of broad leaves inlaid in ceramic tiles, upholstery fabrics, artwork, and even in the handmade iron headboards in the bedrooms. An on-site theater presents concerts and merengue shows for up to 750 people at a time.

The bedrooms are midsize to spacious; each is well furnished and has a balcony or ground-floor patio. A tropical decor prevails, with terra-cotta tile floors and sand-colored walls. Bathrooms are beautifully maintained with tub/shower combo. Restaurants are colorful enough, and the food is varied enough, so that you shouldn't become bored with the full-board arrangement. All-you-can-eat dinners, Caribbean seafood, barbecue nights, and both Mexican and Dominican specialties are some of the choices awaiting you.

Costa Dorada, Puerto Plata, Dominican Republic. © 877/464-4586 **in the U.S.** or 809/320-1515. Fax 809/320-1414. www.coralmarien.com. 325 units. US$105–US$125 (£55–£66) per person. Rates are all-inclusive. AE, DC, MC, V. **Amenities:** 4 restaurants, including an all-night snack bar; 4 bars; outdoor swimming pool (also children's pool); fitness room; state-of-the-art spa; Jacuzzi; sauna; children's club; babysitting; non-smoking rooms; 1 room for those w/limited mobility. *In room:* A/C, TV, beverage maker, hair dryer, safe.

Iberostar Costa Dorada (F) (Kids)   With easy access to the beach, this hotel is owned and operated by a sophisticated Madrid-based chain, Iberostar. Elegant and striking, it boasts one of the most exciting designs of any hotel in Puerto Plata, with some of the most intricate stone, tile, and mosaic work, and a rambling sophisticated combination of Taíno, Andalusian, and Moorish architecture. Several roofs of this hotel are covered with woven palm fronds, note-worthy for a hotel of this scale, sheltering a design that opens onto views of arcades, hidden courtyards, and fountains. A day or night pass, which entitles you to a meal, a round of drinks, and a view of the unusual design, costs US$40 (£21) per adult (either 6pm to 2am or 10am to 6pm), or half-price per child under age 12.

Rooms are cool and airy, with tilework floors, earth tones, brightly colored upholsteries, wall weavings inspired by Taíno designs, and big windows. Each has a compact, shower-only bath-room, and the staff seems more alert and hip to the expectations of an international clientele.

Costa Dorada, Carretera Luperón, Km 4, Marapicá, Puerto Plata, Dominican Repub-lic. (C) **809/320-1000.** Fax 809/320-2023. www.iberostar.com. 516 units. US$105–US$177 (£55–£93) per person double; US$115–US$187 (£61–£98) per person junior suite. Rates are all-inclusive. AE, MC, V. **Amenities:** 4 restaurants; 5 bars; large pool; kayaks; sailing; windsurfing; children's activities. *In room:* A/C, TV, minibar, hair dryer, iron, safe.

PLAYA COFRESI

Cofresi lies within a 10-minute drive west from the center of Puerto Plata, on the opposite side of the city from the more easterly Costa Dorada and Playa Dorada. Cofresi slumbered under its palm trees for years until the construction of Sun Village and Ocean World, both of which are described within this chapter.

Sun Village Resorts (F)   The development in 2006 of this Cana-dian-owned real-estate and hotel venture radically changed the touristic landscape of the region around Puerto Plata, and might have caused the owners of older, less desirable properties nearby to lose a lot of sleep. It's positioned 4km (2½ miles) west of Puerto Plata's Malecón, on hilly, artfully landscaped terrain that ripples down to a desirable beach (Playa Cofresi). Its virtually self-contained and gleaming infrastructure seems very far indeed from the older order of hotels at Playa Dorada and Costa Dorada, on the opposite side of town. Adding to its allure is the sprawling Ocean World Marina and Casino complex, almost immediately next door, wherein dolphins, sea lions, and pretty girls in sequins are each, respectively, paraded out for razzmatazz and regularly scheduled showtimes. Although the two organizations are not associated with one another in any way, there's lots of traffic between the two, and each benefits, synergistically, from the allure and facilities of the other. It's the most desirable, elegant, and most carefully watched, major development in recent years in Puerto Plata, one which, when completed, will add enormously to the resort's competitiveness and appeal.

The look here manages to combine Taíno with European motifs into a distinguished-looking whole. Some of the buildings are capped with three separate tiers of palm fronds in ways that, from the outside, evoke a Buddhist temple in Tibet. The venue is larger than you might at first have thought, replete with vast circular or octagonal public spaces that segue into other octagonal spaces that in some cases verge on the high-tech. This suits the organizers of the Dominican Film Festival just fine, because the resort has been designated as the organizer of a festival that will surely grow and flourish in years to come. Accommodations are carefully designed, airy, and comfortable, and thanks to their positions on sloping terrain, seem to be within an enormous garden that's intersected with pathways and roadways. If you don't feel like trekking, minivans make frequent runs up and down the hillside to and from the beach. There's a lot to recommend this combination real-estate-and-hotel development. Residential units are being aggressively marketed to investors throughout the U.S. and Canada, and as it gets established, it will almost certainly evolve into an intense new competitor of the existing hotels of Puerto Plata.

1 Paradise Dr., Cofresi Beach, Puerto Plata. (C) 888/446-4695 in the U.S. or 809/970-7538. www.sunvillageresorts.com. 240 units, with an additional 120 scheduled for completion during the lifetime of this edition. US$130–US$170 (£68–£88) per person double. Rates are all-inclusive. AE, DC, MC, V. Amenities: 4 restaurants; 8 bars (2 of them swim-up); night club/disco; nightly live entertainment; golf packages available at either of 2 nearby golf courses; 7 pools; full-service spa; 3 lit tennis courts; motorized watersports including scuba; massage; non-motorized watersports; bicycle rentals; Ping-Pong; horseback riding; billiards; daily activities schedule; daily children's programs (ages 4–12); 24-hour food and beverage service; laundry service; dry cleaning. In room: TV, fan, hair dryer.

WHERE TO DINE
IN & AROUND PUERTO PLATA
Casita Rica/Escape al Mar DOMINICAN/INTERNATIONAL
These two establishments, one a snack bar, the other an upscale dining choice, sit side by side between Puerto Plata's seafront and its

waterfronting boulevard, El Malecón, in the heart of town. As such, they're closely linked to the gossip and goings on of the local community, but somehow manage to emulate the gastronomic style of elegant dining rooms within some of the resort hotels. If you happen to be strolling along the seafront and want a beer, the laid-back but gregarious Casita Rica, an open-air dive a few steps from a wide stretch of beachfront, would be perfect. And if candles and romantic gloss appeal to you at dinner, Escape al Mar has the kind of variety that has successfully sheltered wedding receptions, local charity luncheons, and all ilk of mating games within a classy, napery-strewn setting that evokes seafronting trattorias within popular resorts in Italy or Spain. There's even a bronze statue of Neptune positioned like a guardian on a rocky offshore island, within full view of your table. Menu items include pizzas, fried chicken, burgers, pastas, and a flavorful *casuela de mariscos* that's loaded with fish, saffron, spices, and shellfish. It's wise to wander a bit within the labyrinth of Escape al Mar, finding the spot that most appeals to you. We prefer the areas sheltered from the roar of Malecón traffic by wood-and-glass enclosures.

El Malecón. ℂ **809/261-4990.** Snacks US$6–US$10 (£3.15–£5.25); main courses US$12–US$23 (£6.30–£12). AE, DC, MC, V. Casita Rica daily 7am–midnight; Escape al Mar daily 11am–midnight.

Jardín Suizo Malecón INTERNATIONAL Simple, well-scrubbed, and unpretentious, this restaurant sits directly astride the Malecón's most easterly end and, because of a rather small sign, is a bit difficult to spot. Some things about it might remind you of a trattoria in southern Europe, thanks to tiles, cloth-draped tables set close together, and views out over the seafront promenade. Sliding windows are pulled back to take in views of the ocean. The food is fresh and well prepared, although some of the dishes might be a little heavy for the tropics. You can order such dishes as sliced filet of pork in a mushroom-flavored cream sauce, or three different medallions of meat in a wine sauce. The best item we enjoyed on the menu is the freshly caught fish filet of the day in garlic sauce. Many international dishes are offered as well, including tasty shish kabob, chicken curries, and a thick beef stroganoff.

Av. Circunvalación Norte 13A, at the corner of Calle Paul Harris. ℂ **809/586-9564.** Main courses RD$220–RD$480 (US$6.65–US$15/£3.40–£7.40). AE, DC, MC, V. Mon–Sat 11am–11pm. Closed 3 weeks in July.

La Parrillada Steak House & Bar STEAK/SEAFOOD Come here for some of the best steaks in the area. Both imported and Dominican steaks are served, and they can be cooked pretty much as you desire them. This place often attracts a lively gringo crowd, plus some employees who work at the Playa Dorada complex. The drinks are well priced, and the food is enticing, especially the finest cut served here, the chateaubriand. If you're not a meat aficionado, you can also order such dishes as a savory prawns casserole. You can also order grilled fish based on the catch of the day.

Av. Manolo Tavares, Justo 15. ⓒ **809/261-2211.** Reservations recommended. Main courses RD$315–RD$1,110 (US$9.55–US$34/£4.85–£17). AE, DC, MC, V. Daily 4pm–midnight.

Quo Vadis ITALIAN/INTERNATIONAL   One of the city's newest restaurants was established in 2006 within a gracefully proportioned yellow-and-white Spanish colonial house, nestled within a garden and surrounded by a high wall, in the heart of downtown Puerto Plata. It's a sure bet, especially at night when the candles are flickering, for romantic charm with occasional touches of culinary flair. The polite staff here displays a sense of humor during the preparation and service of dishes that include chicken cordon bleu, pork filets with lemon sauce, sautéed tenderloin of beef with an (optional) mushroom sauce, tripe, and a selection of pastas.

Av. Luis Ginebra 47. ⓒ **809/586-7065.** Reservations recommended. Main courses RD$200–RD$400 (US$6.05–US$12/£3.10–£6.15). AE, MC, V. Wed–Mon noon–midnight.

Restaurante-Pizzería Portofino INTERNATIONAL/ITALIAN   In this guesthouse, the town's best pizzas and pastas are served, along with a selection of well-chosen meat dishes, mostly Italian-inspired, and some fresh fish, usually grilled. It's a safe haven, and its kitchen is well maintained. It has the look of an Italian trattoria with tables draped in checked cloth sitting under a thatched roof. You can expect generous helpings of such dishes as Parmesan breast of chicken, eggplant Parmesan, ravioli, and such regional dishes as *arroz con pollo* (chicken with rice). Chicken breast stuffed with ham and cheese is one of the more delightful offerings. Locals and visitors mingle freely here. It's a casual place to dine.

Av. Hermanas Mirabal. ⓒ **809/261-2423.** Reservations recommended. Main courses RD$80–RD$380 (US$2.40–US$12/£1.25–£5.85). MC, V. Daily 8am–midnight.

Sam's Bar & Grill STEAKHOUSE   The gringo and gringa expats have made Sam's their favorite dive since way back in 1970, when it was first established. In the center of town, only a block and a half from Central Park and the Malecón, it lies in a Victorian building from 1896. Marilyn Monroe photographs and caricatures by local artists form the decor. Here, you can order a plate of meatloaf like your mama made, or the eternal favorite, steak and eggs. The cook does a tasty filet of beefsteak and more ambitious dishes, such as chicken cordon bleu. Come here for the memories, the good times, and, of course, the tasty food. You can start your day with fluffy pancakes, and later enjoy freshly made soups, salads, and sandwiches for lunch along with hot dishes.

Calle José del Carmen Ariza 34, Castilla Hotel. ② 809/586-7267. Main courses RD$180–RD$250 ($5.40–$7.50/£2.70–£3.75). No credit cards. Daily 8am–10pm.

PLAYA DORADA

Hemingway's Café INTERNATIONAL/MEXICAN The rough-hewn character of this place stands in stark contrast to the manicured exterior of the shopping center that contains it. Inside, you'll find a dark and shadowy plank-sheathed bar and grill, dotted with accessories you might have found on a pier in Key West. Critics of this place cite slow service and inattentive waitstaff, and based on a local drinkfest we had here, we concur. But despite its drawbacks, its dark and shadowy interior has witnessed more deal-making and shaky alliances between public and private finance than any other public venue in Puerto Plata. If you opt for a drink or food here, the menu lists pastas, fajitas, quesadillas, meal-size salads, burgers, and generously portioned steaks, while downing one of the "Floridita" cocktails. After around 9pm, a karaoke machine cranks out romantic or rock 'n' roll favorites.

Playa Dorada Plaza. ② 809/320-2230. Sandwiches, salads, and pastas RD$250–RD$300 (US$7.50–US$9.40/£2.70–£4.50); main-course platters RD$330–RD$1,050 (US$10–US$32/£5.10–£16). AE, MC, V. Daily noon–2am.

Lucia/Verandah ✫✫✫ CARIBBEAN/CONTINENTAL/ASIAN FUSION Set within different areas of Puerto Plata's most upscale hotel, these are the two most elegant and sophisticated restaurants along the north shore of the Dominican Republic. Much of their allure derives from chef Rafael Vasquez, whose earthy but elegant culinary style has earned him the justifiable title of the country's most celebrated chef. Both restaurants reek of high-design, boutique-scale, cutting-edge charm, although their respective colors and decors are carefully calibrated for view in streaming sunlight (La Verandah) or within the shadows of the evening (Lucia). La Verandah, beside the beach, is a study in angular lines and cool tones of aqua and turquoise; Lucia, with its acres of white linen, evokes the high-ceilinged, candle-lit, intensely Europeanized dining room of a land baron on a colonial plantation. Señor Vasquez's menu might include, depending on his mood on the night of your visit, grilled red snapper with grilled pineapple, coconut-flavored Creole sauce, yucca fritters, and basmati rice; slices of lobster tail prepared tempura-style and served with avocados; and one of the most sophisticated duck dishes we've ever seen in the Caribbean: an adaptation of a classic French dish wherein sautéed breast of duck, a crispy leg of duck "en confit," and fresh foie gras are served with a reduction of brandy, honey, hoisin, apple-cider vinegar, pine nuts, and chives. Delectable desserts include mango tacos with pistachio ice cream. An even more decadent dessert choice is known as a "volcano." Combining in sculptural elegance a deep-fried pyramid of semi-melted chocolate with ice cream, it tastes even better than it looks.

In the Casa Colonial, Playa Dorada. Verandah main courses US$8–US$24 (£4.20–£13); Lucia main courses US$12–US$35 (£6.30–£18). AE, DC, MC, V. Verandah daily 11:30am–5pm; Lucia daily 6pm–midnight.

AT PLAYA COFRESI

Chris & Mady's ® (Finds) SEAFOOD/INTERNATIONAL   This eatery is reason enough to drive over to Playa Cofresi if you aren't staying here. Since 1995, a Canadian man and his island wife have been attracting customers here for some of the best and freshest seafood along this part of the north shore. The price of freshly caught lobster changes daily based on market quotations, but it is among the most affordable in the area. We also like to come here to feast on Dominican crayfish (called *langostinos*). Guests sit at wood tables under a thatch roof, feasting on fettuccine with shrimp, Cajun-style chicken breast deep-fried and served with a zesty tomato sauce, or fat shrimp cooked and flavored only with fresh garlic and olive oil. If you're stopping in for lunch, you'll find freshly made salads and sandwiches, along with regular hot food. A number of Dominican beef and chicken dishes are also served.

Playa Cofresi. (© 809/970-7502. Reservations recommended only Dec–Apr. Main courses RD$225–RD$400 (US$6.80–US$12/£3.45–£6.15). AE, MC, V. Daily 8am–11pm.

Cofresi Bar & Grill DOMINICAN/AMERICAN   This restaurant occupies an orderly, well-maintained building, originally built as a private home, on a hillside immediately uphill from Ocean World, with which it is not associated in any way. It's of most distinct appeal to residents of the nearby Sun Village resort, who sometimes appreciate the chance to roam outside the boundaries of their all-inclusive plans for the experience of a local eatery whose food is well recommended. There are tables within the building's big-windowed, air-conditioned interior or beneath the roof of the open-to-the-breezes gazebo-inspired dining pavilion on the lawn of a hillock a few steps uphill. Menu items are straightforward, and with an emphasis on steaks and seafood. Examples include rib-eye steak, filets of pork, surf and turf, and *sopa de mariscos* (spicy shellfish stew). If you're not hungry, or if you just want to soak up some unpretentious local color, no one will mind if you drop into this place just for a beer. There's occasional live music presented on Friday and Saturday after around 9pm.

In front of Ocean World. ℂ **809/970-7366.** Main courses RD$95–RD$640 (US$2.90–US$19/£1.45–£9.85). AE, DC, MC, V. Daily 9am–2am.

Le Papillon CARIBBEAN/CONTINENTAL   This is an unusual but charming restaurant set on a hillside in a residential neighborhood about 5km (3 miles) southwest of Puerto Plata. The expatriate German owner, Thomas Ackermann, manages to combine aspects of the Black Forest with merengue music. The best way to start a meal here is with a *caipirinha* (a Brazilian cocktail) at the bar beneath the cane-frond ceiling. Later, within an open-sided pavilion overlooking a forest, you'll be presented with a menu that's divided into categories that feature different preparations of pork, chicken, beef, seafood, rabbit, and even vegetarian offerings. Enduring favorites include fettuccine with lobster; "pirate" kabobs with shrimp, tenderloin of beef, and vegetables; an especially worthy chicken stuffed with shrimp and served with saffron sauce; and a four-fisted version of chateaubriand that's only prepared for two. Some savvy locals have complained that this restaurant can get just a bit pricier than it should, but in light of its cultural oddities, it's probably worth it.

Villas Cofresi, Playa Cofresi. ℂ **809/970-7640.** Reservations recommended. Main courses US$14–US$23 (£7.35–£12). AE, MC, V. Tues–Sun 6–10:30pm. From the center of Puerto Plata, drive 5km (3 miles) south, following the signs to Santiago. Turn left at the signs to Villas Cofresi.

Teddy's BARBECUE   Canadian-owned and operated, and permeated with a distinct sense of expatriate perceptions and values, this is the restaurant most likely to be visited by all-inclusive clients at the nearby Sun Village Resort. It's one of a chain of barbecue joints operated by Ontario-based Ted Reader, who *GQ* magazine described as "a crazy Canuck Barbecue kingpin" whose barbecue is virtually a household word north of the U.S. border. Part of the reason for this restaurant's popularity, other than its good barbecue, derives from a location directly astride Cofresi Playa, midway between Sun Village and its neighbor, Ocean World, within an easy beachfronting walk from either. Another reason is based on ribs and deep-spiced meats that spend a full 12 hours in a smoker prior to being served as part of an urbanized, big-city version of what comes out of lesser smokehouses. In the words of its staff, "We provide an absolute taste of North America that's an attractive alternative to a week of all-inclusive buffets. Come and get sticky with us." Menu items include grilled grouper, wrapped in banana leaves, served with French-cut fries; "pork sliders" (three mini-sandwiches prepared with smoked pork and barbecue sauce); burgers and chicken club sandwiches; Teddy's lettuce-wrapped nachos; and an array of over-size salads. And then there are those "mamajuana smoked ribs" that anyone who's familiar with St. Louis–style barbecue will recognize as just a wee bit different from the original. (Coconut shells and scented, legally available herbs known locally as "mamajuana" are added to the wood chips.) Despite the availability of a rainbow of party-colored drinks, the libation of choice here is Presidente beer.

Playa Cofresi. ✆ 809/970-7672. Main courses US$15–US$30 (£7.90–£16). AE, DC, MC, V. Daily noon–midnight.

BEACHES & WATERSPORTS

It was the beaches of the Dominican Republic's north coast that originally put the country on the world's tourist map, and in 2006, the Dominican government pumped hundreds of thousands of tons of sand from deeper offshore waters onto Playa Dorada's beaches, restoring them to wide, expansive stretches of pale amber-colored sands. The beaches, as along the nation's north shore, are collectively known as the "Amber Coast" because of their color and because of the rich deposits of amber that have been discovered here.

Playa Dorada has one of the highest concentrations of hotels on the north coast, so the beaches here, though carefully maintained and very clean, can get crowded during peak season, both with visitors and locals. During midwinter, rain that's swept in upon the winds of the Atlantic might fall unexpectedly, but only for very brief interludes. Many concession stands along the beach rent watersports equipment.

Don't expect Robinson Crusoe–style isolation at Playa Dorada; you'll rarely, if ever, be alone on a stretch of beach in Puerto Plata, since the waterfronting sands are shared with residents at all of the all-inclusives. But if you enjoy beige sand that's rarely too hot to walk on, and a seemingly never-ending array of watersports kiosks and chaises longues, as well as an occasional loudspeaker projecting merengue music, you'll be happy here.

Lying 5km (3 miles) west of Puerto Plata is a gorgeous beach, **Playa Cofresi,** set against a backdrop of all-inclusive hotels and some vacation villas that started to be built here in the 1990s.

Although you can find plenty of space on this beach on weekdays, it comes alive on Sunday when several hundred local Dominican families descend from the hinterlands for fun, food, and sun.

Another good choice in the area, **Playa Luperón** lies about an 80-minute drive to the west of Puerto Plata. This is a wide beach of powdery white sand, set amid palm trees that provide wonderful shade when the noonday sun grows too fierce. It's more ideal for windsurfing, scuba diving, and snorkeling than for general swimming. Various watersports concessions can be found here, along with several snack bars. Since this is a long drive, we wouldn't bother to go here just for the beach. But if you're eager to go windsurfing and scuba diving, it's worth the jaunt.

Your watersports options in Puerto Plata are numerous. Most of the kiosks on the beach here are ultimately run by the same company, and prices don't vary among them. If there isn't one close to your hotel, try **Playa NACO Centro de Deportes Acuáticos** (© 809/320-2567), a rustic clapboard-sided hut on the beachfront of the Dorada NACO Hotel. Prices are as follows: banana-boat rides, RD$280 (US$8.50/£4.30) for a 10- to 12-minute ride; water-skiing, RD$560 (US$17/£8.60) for a 10- to 15-minute ride; sea kayak and Sunfish sailboat rental, RD$560 (US$17/£8.60) per hour; sailboards, RD$560 (US$17/£8.60) a day; and paragliding, RD$1,400 (US$42/£22) for a 10-minute ride.

There are watersports kiosks about every 100m (328 ft.) along the beach, any of which will rent you snorkeling gear and tell you the best spots for seeing fish. Puerto Plata isn't great for snorkeling, but you can take a boat trip to some decent sites.

SPORTS

GOLF   Robert Trent Jones Jr. designed the 18-hole **Playa Dorada** championship golf course (© 809/320-3472), which surrounds the resorts and runs along the coast. Even nongolfers can stop at the clubhouse for a drink or a snack and enjoy the views. Greens fees are US$75 (£39) for 18 holes, US$50 (£26) for 9 holes; a caddy costs US$15 (£7.90). It's best to make arrangements at the activities desk of your hotel.

The 4,888-yard (4,470m) **Playa Grande Golf Course** at Playa Grande, Km 9, Carretera Rio San Juan–Cabrera (© 800/858-2258 **in the U.S.** or 809/582-0860), continues to generate a lot of excitement. Some pros have already hailed it as one of the best courses in the Caribbean. Its design consultant was Robert Trent Jones Jr. Ten of its holes border the Atlantic, and many of these are also set atop dramatic cliffs overlooking the turbulent waters of Playa Grande Beach. Greens fees are US$90 (£47) for 18 holes or US$50 (£26) for 9 holes in winter. In the off season fees are lowered to US$60 (£32) for 18 holes or US$35 (£18) for 9 holes.

TENNIS Nearly all the major resort hotels have tennis courts.

SEEING THE SIGHTS

Ocean World *AA*, Calle Principale 3 at Cofresi (© **809/291-1111;** www.oceanworld.net), is the largest entertainment complex in the country, lying 5km (3 miles) west of Puerto Plata. It combines a plush casino and a world-class marina with such mass-market venues as a kiddie park and an aquarium for marine life. There is a series of watery "pens" and habitats for the care, feeding, and display of dolphins, sea lions, sharks, stingrays, piranhas, and other denizens of the Amazon rainforest. A number of close encounters with these nautical creatures, especially dolphins, is offered, but these encounters are not cheap, ranging from US$70 to US$250 (£37–£132) per person, depending on your age and the length of exposure you opt for. Supervision of man and beast is carefully monitored by trainers, and reservations are recommended. For those 13 and up, charges are US$55 (£29), lowered to US$40 (£21) for ages 4 to 12. Free for those 3 and under.

Fort San Felipe, the oldest fort in the New World, is a popular attraction (© **809/261-6043**). Philip II of Spain ordered its construction in 1564, a task that took 33 years to complete. Built with 2m-thick (6½-ft.) walls, the fort was virtually impenetrable, and the moat surrounding it was treacherous—the Spaniards sharpened swords and embedded them in coral below the surface of the water. The doors of the fort are only 1m (3¼ ft.) high, another deterrent to swift passage. During Trujillo's rule, Fort San Felipe was used as a prison. Standing at the end of the Malecón, the fort was restored in the early 1970s. Admission is RD$20 (US60¢/30p), free for children under 12. It's open daily 9am to 4:45pm.

Isabel de Torres (© **809/970-0501**), an observation tower that was heavily fortified during the reign of Trujillo, affords a panoramic view of the Amber Coast from a point near the top, 780m (2,559 ft.) above sea level. You reach the observation point by *teleférico* (cable car), a 10-minute ascent. Once here, you're also treated to 3 hectares (7½ acres) of botanical gardens. The round-trip costs RD$200 (US$6.05/£3.10) for adults, RD$100 (US$3.05/£1.55) for children age 12 and under. The aerial ride runs Thursday to Tuesday 8:30am to 5pm. There's often a long wait in line for the cable car, and at certain times it's closed for repairs, so check at your hotel before you head out.

You can see a collection of rare amber specimens at the **Museo de Ambar Dominicano (Museum of Dominican Amber),** Calle Duarte 61 (© **809/586-2848**), near Puerto Plata's Central Park. It's open Monday to Friday 8am to 6pm, Saturday 9am to 5pm. Guided tours in English are offered. Admission is RD$40 (US$1.20/60p) or RD$7 (US20¢/10p) for children.

Rum drinkers might want to head out for the **Brugal Rum Bottling Plant,** Carretera Luperón, Km 3.5 (© **809/586-2531;** www.brugal.com.do), on the outskirts of Puerto Plata, 1km (⅔ mile) from Puerto Plata. Admission is free, and it is open Monday to Friday 8:30am to 4pm. Some 350,000 bottles—maybe a lot more—of rum are filled and boxed annually for shipment. On a guided tour, visitors are taken through the plant to see how rum is bottled. At the end of the tour, you're treated to a fruit daiquiri and can purchase Brugal hats and other gifts or souvenirs if you wish.

One of the most visited attractions in the Dominican Republic is **Parque Nacional La Isabela** (© **809/472-4204**), open daily from 9am to 5:30pm, charging US$3.50 (£1.85) for admission. In spite of its fame, there isn't a lot to see once you're here. Nevertheless, this park contains what's left of Columbus's second settlement on Hispaniola.

At the park, excavations have revealed the outlines of what may have been the explorer's house, the church where the first Mass in the New World was conducted, and an observation tower where Columbus used to gaze at the stars.

The buildings were constructed of mud and limestone. The settlement established by the sailor of Genoa was ill-fated, one-third of the population falling sick within 4 or 5 days.

The ruins of La Isabela are reached along a paved road lying 15km (9⅓ miles) west of the town of Luperón. It was declared a national park in 1998. The government has messed with the site and added more to the ruins, so its original remains have been tainted. A little museum displays artifacts believed to have been owned by these early settlers from Europe.

Getting to the park isn't easy. The most direct route is to go by one of the *guaguas* leaving from the center of Puerto Plata heading for Imbert. At Imbert you must take yet another minivan to Luperón. From here, *motoconchos* go to La Isabela. All this takes 2 hours or so. Alternatively, you can drive here by rented car, or ask at one of the tour operators (see above) if any tours to La Isabela are being organized during the time of your stay.

SHOPPING

The neoclassical house sheltering the Museum of Dominican Amber (see above) also contains the densest collection of **boutiques** in Puerto Plata. Many of the paintings here are from neighboring Haiti, but the amber, larimar, and mahogany wood carvings are local.

Although the marketplace at Puerto Plata hardly resembles the greater one at Santo Domingo in the Zona Colonial, the **Mercado** at Puerto Plata merits a visit. It lies at the corner of Avenida Isabel de Torres and Calle 2, and is open Monday to Saturday 8am to 5pm (it starts winding down after 3pm, however). Everything is sold here, from both Dominican and Haitian art (loads of it) to handicrafts, along with the inevitable T-shirts, as well as luscious fruits and vegetables. It's a photo op.

Plaza Turisol Complex, the largest shopping center on the north coast, has about 80 different outlets. You may want to make this your first stop so you can get an idea of the merchandise available in Puerto Plata. This complex also has the most upscale and tasteful merchandise. You might want to stop in here if you don't have time to visit all the shopping centers. It's about 5 minutes from Puerto Plata and Playa Dorada, on the main road heading east. Nearby is a smaller shopping center, **Playa Dorada Plaza,** with about 80 shops, selling handicrafts, clothing, souvenirs, and gifts. Both it and the Plaza Turisol are open daily from 9am to 9pm. The **Amber Shop,** in the Playa Dorada Plaza (© **809/320-2215**), is associated with the Amber Museum. This shop sells the best collection of Dominican amber in town, artfully displayed on racks and on shelves. It features necklaces, pendants, bracelets, and rings crafted from amber ranging in color from oil-clear yellow to dark blue. A competitor, **Galería de Ambar,** Calle 12 de Julio (© **809/586-2101**), is both a museum and shop. On the ground floor, both amber and larimar are sold along with Dominican and Haitian arts and crafts and with bottles of rum. Upstairs, a museum displays rare samples of Dominican amber, often with prehistoric insects imbedded inside. It is open Monday to Friday 8:30am to 6pm, Saturday 9am to 5:30pm, charging an admission of US$1 (55p). **Tobacco Shop,** in the Playa Dorada Plaza (© **809/320-2216**), is the best shop selling cigars around Puerto Plata. Don't overlook the benefits of cigars rolled in the Dominican Republic from tobacco grown with Cuban seeds. They're a lot less expensive than most of the Cubans, and many of them are surprisingly good. Plus, you can take them into the U.S.

Plaza Isabela, in Playa Dorada about 455m (1,493 ft.) from the entrance to the Playa Dorada Hotel complex, is a collection of small specialty shops constructed in Victorian gingerbread style, although much of its inventory has a Spanish inspiration or flair. Here you'll find the main branch of the Dominican Republic's premier jeweler, **Harrison's** (© **809/586-3933**), a specialist in platinum work. Madonna, Michael Jackson, and Keith Richards have all been spotted wearing Harrison's jewelry. The store has a special clearance area; tours are available. Another branch is in the Centro Comercial Playa Dorada (© **809/320-2219**) in the Playa Dorada Hotel complex.

Back in Puerto Plata, you can also patronize **Cuevas y Hermanos Fabricantes de Cigarros,** Tan Tan Café, Malecón 6 (© **809/837-8866**), open Tuesday to Sunday 1pm to midnight. This is the best outlet at which to purchase Dominican cigars, which some aficionados prefer to Cuban cigars. Those considering purchasing a box of cigars can smoke one for free.

A particularly attractive outlet for jewelry is **La Canoa,** Calle Beller 18 (© **809/586-3604**). If you drop into this place, you can wander around, noting the difference between what's in front (a well-ordered, glossy-looking jewelry store) and what's in back (a much more workaday and less glossy series of workrooms where a crew of locals actually polishes and sets amber and larimar into gold and silver settings.) Prices for most of the jewelry here range from US$50 to US$3,500 (£26–£1,842), although some pieces in the US$14,000 (£7,368) range have been spotted. Although there are the predictable array of gold, diamonds, and precious colored stones, our favorites are the chunks of amber—some pale, some tawny, and some of them blue—set into gold frames and configured as pendants, brooches, earrings, or rings.

PUERTO PLATA, PLAYA DORADA & COSTA DORADA AFTER DARK

Casino action dominates the night. Newest with the most imaginative decor is the **Casino at Ocean World** 😊😊, Calle Principale 3 at Cofresi (© **809/291-1111**). Its cabaret show staged here, with gorgeous dancers, is the best in the D.R., rivaling some of the spectaculars in Las Vegas. A well-recommended way to experience the charms of this place involves booking a place on the "Ocean World Magical Nights," wherein, for US$69 (£36) per person, you'll get round-trip transfers by minivan from most of Puerto Plata's hotels, unlimited access to a well-stocked dinner buffet, access to a dolphin night show and a sea lion night show, access to the casino and the location's many bars, and access to a Las Vegas–style revue replete with views of performers artfully outfitted in a minimalist style. Your hotel desk can usually book such tours for you. Less modern, but within the Playa Dorada hotel complex, is the sprawling, block-buster-style casino at the **Holiday Village Golden Beach** (Playa Dorada, © **809/320-3800**).

The Playa Dorada Hotel complex contains about 14 hotels, some of which have **discos** that welcome anyone, guest or not, into their confines. These after-dark diversions tend to be filled mainly with foreign visitors, although they occasionally attract locals looking to hook up with tourists. None charge a cover, and the almost-universal drink of choice, Presidente Beer, costs RD$110 (US$3.35/£1.70) a bottle.

At least three discos pulse out dance music every night of the week within the Playa Dorada complex beginning at 10pm. (Be aware that, in the words of one Dominican night owl we know, "Things don't get interesting till around 11:30pm.")

The hands-down most entertaining disco at Playa Dorada, the one that everyone says is the wildest, most animated, and most rau-cous, is **Mangú,** Playa Dorada (© **809/320-3800**). Its designers positioned it adjacent to the Holiday Village Golden Beach Resort, but with separate entrances. You'll find an attractively balanced blend of both local residents, many eager to score with an off-island visitor, and holiday makers, who merge and mix in an animated blend of hot bodies and hot merengue. Entrance is free for residents of the Holiday Village, but around RD$100 (US$3.05/£1.55) for nonresidents. Expect flashing lights; hundreds of writhing bodies; and a skin, glitter, and feathers show that begins at 11:30pm.

Mangú's most visible competitor is the **Roadway Western Bar and Mix Grill,** in the Playa Dorada Plaza (© **809/320-4502**). Set within a simulated recreation of a log cabin, on the back side of the resort's busiest shopping center, its walls are outfitted with gringo/gringa slogans like "Gringas are forever." There's no cover charge, but a Presidente beer goes for RD$120 (US$3.65/£1.85).

A final contender for the nightlife circuit in Puerto Plata is **Crazy Moon,** adjacent to the lobby of the Paradise Hotel (© **809/ 320-3663**). Though not as sweepingly popular as either Mangú or the Roadway Bar, it can be a lot of fun, and the music is always danceable.

2 Sosúa

24km (15 miles) E of Puerto Plata

This emerging resort boasts one of the finest beaches in the Dominican Republic, **Sosúa Beach.** A strip of white sand more than .8km (½ mile) wide, it's tucked in a cove sheltered by coral cliffs. The beach connects two strikingly disparate communities, which together make up the town known as Sosúa. As increasing numbers of visitors flock to Sosúa, mainly for its beach life, it is quickly becoming a rival of Puerto Plata. You don't come here for history, but oh, those soft, white sands and crystal-clear waters, all to be enjoyed when many northern climes are buried under snow. Sosúa also has a well-deserved reputation for resorts with much more reasonable rates than similar accommodations at Puerto Plata. You won't find the super-deluxe resorts that are commonplace in Puerto Plata, but prices in Sosúa are half what they are at the big resorts. And the beaches are just as lovely.

At one end of the beach is **El Batey,** an area with residential streets, gardens, restaurants, shops, and hotels. Real-estate transactions have been booming in El Batey and its environs, where many villas have been constructed, fronted by newly paved streets.

At the western end of Sosúa Beach lies the typical village community of **Los Charamicos,** a sharp contrast to El Batey. Here you'll find tin-roofed shacks, vegetable stands, chickens scrabbling in the rubbish, and warm, friendly people, many of whom are expatriate Haitians.

Sosúa was founded in 1940 by European Jews seeking refuge from Hitler. Trujillo invited 100,000 of them to settle in his country on a banana plantation, but only 600 or so Jews were actually allowed to immigrate, and of those, only about a dozen or so remained on the plantation. However, there are some 20 Jewish families living in Sosúa today, and for the most part they are engaged in the dairy and smoked-meat industries, which the refugees began during the war. Biweekly services are held in the local one-room synagogue. Many of the Jews intermarried with Dominicans, and the town has taken on an increasingly Spanish flavor; women of the town are often seen wearing both the Star of David and the Virgin de Altagracia. Nowadays many German expatriates are also found in the town.

GETTING THERE   To get here from Puerto Plata, take the autopista (Rte. 5) east for about 30 minutes. If you venture off the main highway, anticipate enormous potholes. Taxis, charter buses, and *públicos* from Puerto Plata and Playa Dorada let passengers off at the stairs leading down from the highway to Sosúa Beach. Most rides cost RD$60 to RD$100 (US$1.80–US$3.05/90p–£1.55).

GETTING AROUND   Most visitors walk to where they want to go in Sosúa. Most of the taxis wait for passengers in the center of town at the intersection of calles Pedro Clisante and Arzeno. *Motoconchos* run up and down the town and all around all day long, most rides costing RD$60 to RD$100 (US$1.80–US$3.05/90p–£1.55), which is about one-third the price of a typical cab. You might want to pay the added *dinero*, however, since these motorcycle drivers are reckless and dangerous, speeding through traffic as if they didn't hold your life in their maniacal hands.

FAST FACTS: SOSUA

In lieu of a post office, you can go to **EPS Sosúa Business Services,** Calle Pedro Clisante 12, El Batey (© **809/571-3451**), open Monday to Friday from 9am to 5pm. The business service promises delivery to your destination within 5 business days of mailing. For currency exchange or ATMs, go to **Banco del Progreso,** Calle Pedro Clisante 12 (© **809/563-3233**), open Monday to Friday 8:30am to 4pm and Saturday 9am to 1pm. Another choice is **Banco León,** Pedro Clisante 73, Plaza Perdomo (© **809/476-2000**), open Monday to Friday 8:30am to 5pm and Saturday 9am to 1pm.

For Internet access, go to **ALF Internet Café,** Calle Pedro Clisante 12 (© **809/571-1734**), open daily 9am to 10pm, charging RD$50 (US$1.50/75p) per half-hour or RD$80 (US$2.40/£1.25) for 1 hour.

For a medical problem, head for **Centro Médico Dr. Quiroz,** Calle Eugenio Kunhardt 57 (© **809/571-2060**). For an ambulance, dial © **911.**

The best pharmacy is **Farmacia Sosúa,** Calle Pedro Clisante 10 (© **809/571-2350**), open Monday to Friday 8am to 9pm and Saturday 8am to 8pm. The local office of the **Western Union** is at Calle Duarte 2 (© **809/571-3800**), open Monday to Saturday 8am to 7pm. For the police, go to Calle Principal Cabarete (© **809/571-0810**).

WHERE TO STAY
THE ALL-INCLUSIVES
Amhsa Casa Marina Beach 🏖   This sprawling all-inclusive opens directly on a private beach set against a lush backdrop of vegetation. It is similar to its sibling (see below), but older, dating from the late 1980s. The bedrooms (almost too many of them) are stacked up against two big swimming pools. Each of the accommodations opens onto a small balcony with a view. Rooms are midsize for the most part and furnished in a typical Caribbean style, with rattan furnishings and vivid colors on the spreads and draperies. Each comes with a tiled bathroom with a tub and shower. A combination

of Creole and international cuisine is featured in the hotel's dining venues, and it's quite creditable without ever rising to the sublime. To escape the curse of all those buffets, savvy guests book a table in one of the specialty restaurants, featuring seafood or Italian cuisine. The usual array of activities from windsurfing to sailing is offered, and management tries to keep its captive audience amused at night with bands or live shows.

Calle Dr. Rosendo, Sosúa, Dominican Republic. (C) **809/571-3690.** Fax 809/571-3110. www.amhsamarina.com. 300 units. US$174–US$260 (£92–£137) double. Children 7–12 US$60 (£32) extra. Rates are all-inclusive. AE, DC, MC, V. Free parking. **Amenities:** 3 restaurants; 5 bars; nightly entertainment; 3 outdoor pools; tennis court; watersports equipment; bikes; salon; massage; doctor on call; photo shop; 24-hr. medical services. *In room:* A/C, TV, safe.

Amhsa Casa Marina Reef 🐵🐵

Constructed right before the turn of the millennium, this all-inclusive is built on a private reef. On palm tree-studded grounds, it's one of the best all-inclusives in town and better than its sibling (see above). Well-rounded facilities and affordable rates fill up its rooms all year. Each midsize guest room comes with tropical furnishings, mostly rattan, brightly painted Dominican colors, and the use of local crafts throughout. Two full beds come with each bedroom, and all units contain a private bathroom with tub and shower. There's the invariable buffet restaurant, but such monotony is relieved by a series of specialty restaurants for which reservations are required. The by-now-familiar round of outdoor activities are featured here as well, including windsurfing and snorkeling.

Calle Dr. Rosendo, Sosúa, Dominican Republic. (C) **809/571-3535.** Fax 809/571-3104. www.amhsamarina.com. 378 units. US$174–US$260 (£92–£137) double. Children 4–12 US$60 (£32) extra. Rates are all-inclusive. AE, DC, MC, V. Free parking. **Amenities:** 2 restaurants; 4 bars; 3 outdoor pools; health club; watersports equipment; salon; massage; 24-hr. medical services. *In room:* A/C, TV, safe.

Sosúa Bay Hotel 🐵🐵

Launched in 2002, this is the most appealing, the best-designed, and the most up-to-date hotel in Sosúa. It's a handsome, colonial-style complex, serving some of the finest cuisine in Sosúa. The resort opens onto the often tranquil waters of Sosúa Bay. This is one of Sosúa's attempts to attract more upmarket clients who might normally patronize Playa Dorada. The pillared lobby is the most impressive at the resort. As the management states, you can start your breakfast with a mimosa and be wined and dined throughout the day, staying up late dancing to the sound of merengue. The midsize bedrooms, scattered across a three-floor building, are decorated with colonial-style wood furnishings and colorful bedspreads and draperies. Each comes with a tiled bathroom with tub and shower. If available, opt for one of the superior doubles with ocean view; others open onto lushly planted gardens. Your choice is of one king-size bed or else two double beds; most accommodations come with private balconies.

Breakfast and lunch buffets are lavish. At night you can dine more formally—and much better—at various venues that feature the likes of Italian or international cuisine. The resort also has some of the best entertainment at Sosúa, and offers one of the most diversified activities programs.

Dr. Alejo Martínez 1, Sosúa, Dominican Republic. ©️ **809/571-4000.** Fax 809/571-4545. www.starzresorts.com. 193 units. US$192–US$348 (£101–£183) double. Children 4–11 pay 50% of adult rate. Rates are all-inclusive. AE, MC, V. Free parking. **Amenities:** 3 restaurants; 2 bars; 3 outdoor pools (1 for children); health club; watersports equipment; bikes; laundry service; dry cleaning; aerobics; yoga. *In room:* A/C, TV, fridge, safe.

INEXPENSIVE

La Puntilla de Piergiorgio ★ *Value* This hotel lies in a residential neighborhood, within a 10-minute walk from the bustling commercial center of Sosúa. Built on a rocky promontory high above the beach, it has a neo-Victorian design that includes lots of enticing gingerbread, lattices, and whimsical grace. Accommodations are bright, large, well maintained, and outfitted with white-tile floors, flowered chintz upholsteries, and a semicircular veranda with views of either the garden or the ocean. Each accommodation comes with a small but neatly arranged tiled private bathroom with shower stall.

Calle La Puntilla 1, El Batey, Sosúa, Dominican Republic. ©️ 809/571-2215. Fax 809/571-2786. 51 units. US$75–US$110 (£39–£58) double. Rates include breakfast. AE, MC, V. **Amenities:** Restaurant; bar; outdoor pool; room service; babysitting; laundry service; dry cleaning. *In room:* A/C, TV, hair dryer, safe.

WHERE TO DINE

La Puntilla de Piergiorgio ITALIAN A 10-minute walk west of Sosúa's center, this place serves the best Italian food in town, attracting an animated clientele of Europeans looking for a change from Creole and Dominican cuisine. Alas, although the setting is gorgeous, sweeping out over the coastline and the sea, the food isn't always as glorious, generating some complaints for its uneven cookery. The setting, located in the hotel of the same name, is a series of outdoor terraces, some of them covered, most of them open-air, that cascade down to the edge of a sea cliff. There's enough space to allow conversational privacy for virtually any intimate dinner, and a pair of gazebo-style bars that provide an ongoing supply of mimosas and rum-based drinks. It's true we've had better versions of every dish served here, but for the area, it is reasonably competent, especially the different preparations of fresh fish caught off local waters, which you can even order barbecued. Sometimes the chef gets fancy, as when he flames the prawns with cognac, or goes continental with his filet steak in green-peppercorn sauce. The cannelloni Rossini (chopped meat and spinach) isn't bad at all.

Calle La Puntilla 1. © **809/571-2626**. Main courses RD$190–RD$395 (US$5.75–US$12/£2.90–£6.10). AE, MC, V. Daily noon–midnight.

Morua Mai INTERNATIONAL   This is the most visible, and most deeply entrenched, restaurant in downtown Sosúa—the "dining flagship" of the town. Established by German entrepreneurs in the 1970s, and set at the town's busiest intersection, it manages to remain somewhat aloof to Sosúa's burgeoning sex industry, thanks to a location in a neighborhood that's a few blocks removed from the densest concentration of *putanas* and their pimps. It was designed of timbers and palm thatch like an enormous Taíno teepee, under which ceiling fans slowly spin, and wicker and wooden furniture help create an ambience conducive to the leisurely consumption of tropical drinks and well-prepared food. Steaks and seafood are staples here. Depending on the arrival of fresh supplies that day, the menu might also include four different preparations of lobster; several kinds of shrimp, including a version with spicy tomato sauce and fresh vegetables; four different preparations of sea bass, including a version flavored with Chablis; orange-flavored chicken spiced with ginger; steak Diana, flavored with bacon; and pork in mustard-flavored cream sauce. An excellent version of paella contains chunks of lobster and fresh shrimp.

Pedro Clisante 5, El Batey. © **809/571-2966**. Breakfast RD$75–RD$85 (US$2.25–US$2.60/£1.15–£1.30); pizzas and pastas RD$175–RD$225 (US$5.30–US$6.80/£2.70–£3.45); main courses RD$100–RD$1,275 (US$3.05–US$39/£1.55–£20). AE, MC, V. Daily 8am–midnight.

On the Waterfront ✶✶ INTERNATIONAL/SEAFOOD   The memory of Marlon Brando's Oscar-winning 1954 movie, *On the Waterfront,* is perpetuated here. This informal yet elegant restaurant sits on a cliffside, serving the finest cuisine among the independent restaurants of Sosúa. To everyone's delight, especially the owners, in 2005, ocean currents and tides unexpectedly deposited vast amounts of sand at the base of this restaurant, creating an "instant beach" which has added considerably to its allure. As you peruse the menu, take in sweeping views before deciding on the best of the catch of the day, which might feature fresh lobster, sea bass, conch, calamari, or red snapper, the latter tasting delectable when perfectly grilled as it is here. If you don't want fish, opt for a tender steak in pepper sauce or some lamb chops grilled with aromatic herbs. Other menu highlights include filet of sole in a tangy orange sauce or fettuccine primavera.

Calle Dr. Rosendo 1. © **809/571-2670.** Reservations recommended. Main courses RD$540–RD$1,200 (US$16–US$36/£8.30–£18). AE, MC, V. Daily 7am–10pm.

SPORTS & THE GREAT OUTDOORS

There are watersports kiosks about every 90m (295 ft.) along the beach, any of which will rent you snorkeling gear and tell you the best spots for seeing fish. You can also rent sailboats, windsurfers, and other watersports gear at any of the kiosks.

Gipsy Ranch, Carretera Sosúa–Cabarete, opposite the Coconut Palm Resort (© **809/571-1373**), is the region's largest and best-recommended **riding stable,** home to about 20 horses, which can be hired for equestrian treks of between 1 and 4 hours. You'll begin your experience at the stone corral about 7km (4⅓ miles) from Sosúa and 5km (3 miles) from Cabarete. A half-hour jaunt goes for RD$448 (US$14/£6.90); a 4-hour excursion through forests and along beaches costs RD$1,596 (US$48/£25). Reservations are strongly recommended.

Many divers are attracted to the waters off Sosúa. In town the best outfitter is **Northern Coast Diving,** Calle Pedro Clisante 8 (© **809/571-1028;** www.northerncoastdiving.com). There are more than a dozen diving sites off the coast, including a wreck, a canyon dive, and a wall dive. Northern Coast offers PADI-certified divemasters or instructors, featuring a two-tank boat dive for RD$1,960 (US$59/£30) with equipment, RD$1,680 (US$51/£26) without. For RD$9,800 (US$297/£151) you get 3 days of diving and certification training. The outfitter also offers 3-hour snorkeling excursions for RD$1,120 (US$34/£17) per person.

Several adventure tours are offered by **El Tour Tours,** corner of calles Dr. Alejo Martínez and Duarte (© **809/571-4195**), founded in 1999. River rafting is an exciting pastime costing RD$1,820 (US$55/£28). They can also arrange horseback riding for RD$896 (US$27/£14) and catamaran sailing for RD$2,100 (US$64/£32).

SHOPPING

Patrick's Silversmithy, Calle Pedro Clisante 3 (© **809/571-2121**), was established by British expatriate Patrick Fagg in 1973 as a showcase for his unusual jewelry designs. At least half of the inventory here is made within his studios, and each incorporates such local stones as larimar and amber. About 80% of the inventory is made from silver, making these one-of-a-kind creations affordable.

The best art gallery is **Viva,** Calle Dr. Alejo Martínez 10 (© **809/ 571-4222**), which sells local art and giftware. An excellent selection of Dominican masters is on sale; the giftware includes beautifully crafted wood sculptures in mahogany and *guayacán* (ironwood). Many ceramic "faceless" dolls are also for sale.

3 Cabarete

The winds that blow constantly southward off the Atlantic swept in a hip young crowd in the 1990s, as Cabarete emerged as the premier windsurfing site in the Caribbean. But only a small portion of the visitors who come here today are actually interested in the waves and jumping on a board. Many bask in the glory of the surfers by day and strut their stuff in the hyper-hip town bars by night.

There's also a lower percentage of all-inclusive hotels in Cabarete than within most of the other resorts of the Dominican Republic. The mood here is youthful, extroverted, and bold, with the majority of visitors moving without any particular loyalty to any individual dining venue, sometimes preparing meals within their rooms, and barhopping at whim after dark. There's a strong sense here of a radical counterculture devoted to sun, fun, watersports, good times, and hard drinking. But at least some of that might change as large-scale developers eye the community for the setting of a new generation of large-scale hotels, resorts, and condos.

To service the needs of the growing number of visitors, the town has attracted some of the most aggressive prostitutes in the Dominican Republic; all ages, all skin tones, all degrees of blatancy. If you're a heterosexual male in Cabarete, you'll absolutely never, ever, lack for female companionship, paid or unpaid.

News of Cabarete's allure has spread among the 20-something populations of Europe. Especially prevalent are visitors from France, Holland, Germany, and some of the Eastern European states like Poland and Bulgaria. There are fewer North Americans here than you'd expect, and a growing number of French and German expatriates.

The big attraction is **Playa Cabarete,** with its white sands and ideal wind and surf conditions. Cabarete isn't particularly distinguished architecturally, consisting of a series of relatively small-scale hotels, restaurants, and gift shops lining either side of the highway that parallels the north coast. Virtually everything in town lies along

---

Serious Windsurfing

Cabarete hosts an annual weeklong windsurfing tournament every June. Only amateurs are allowed to participate. For more information, contact the **Happy Surf School,** Hotel Villa Taína, Calle Principal (© **809/571-0784**); the **Carib Wind Center,** Calle Principale (© **809/571-0640**); the **Fanatic Windsurfing Center,** in the Café Pitu, Calle Principale (© **809/571-0861**); or any staff member at the **Azurro Club** (© **809/571-0808**).

---

this street (Calle Principal), with the exception of small-scale shops that are found on narrow alleyways that bisect the main street.

In November of 2006, the government paid for the deposit of many tons of sand to the local beachfront, thereby adding considerably to its allure. Cabarete, incidentally, is one of the very few places in the entire Caribbean that offers as wide a variety of wind- and wave-driven sporting venues. Primary among them are surfing, windsurfing, kite surfing, and wakeboarding. (Its aficionados compare it to snowboarding behind a powerboat on the still waters of a river.)

GETTING THERE   To reach Cabarete from Sosúa, continue east along the autopista (Rte. 5) for about 13km (8 miles). Taxis and *públicos* from Sosúa will also take you here.

WHERE TO STAY

Azurro Club (Azurro Club Estrella and Azurro Club Cabarete) ⭐

One of Cabarete's more deeply entrenched resorts was built in the late 1990s in a stylish, avant-garde design. It has been bought, reconfigured, and expanded by the well-recommended Azurro chain of resorts. Today, you'll find slightly more upscale accommodations in the Azurro Cabarete, and lodgings that are just a notch less comfortable across the road, in the Azurro Estrella. With direct access to a wide sandy beach, on the outskirts of Cabarete's main commercial core, it's noted for a soaring network of steel girders, and an attempt on the part of the staff to keep its guests amused with a variety of organized although somewhat haphazard daily activities. Despite a slightly disorganized staff, this is one of our favorite large-scale hotels in Cabarete, thanks to its convenient location and sense of style. The respective buildings of this resort rise in four-story designs, usually around well-landscaped central courtyards. Bedrooms are well maintained, attractive, and airy, usually with white-tile floors and large bathrooms with tubs and showers.

Calle Principal, Cabarete, Dominican Republic. ⓒ **809/571-0808.** Fax 809/571-0904. www.starzresorts.com. 272 units. Winter US$175–US$240 (£92–£126) double; off season US$125–US$140 (£66–£74) double. Rates are all-inclusive. AE, MC, V. **Amenities:** 3 restaurants; 3 bars; 3 outdoor pools; gym; room service; babysitting; laundry service; dry cleaning; nonsmoking rooms; rooms for those w/limited mobility. *In room:* A/C, TV, hair dryer, iron, safe.

Natura Cabañas & the Attabeyra Spa ★ *Finds*

This is the ultimate eco-sensitive boutique hotel, and if you enjoy a return to nature and an abandonment of the comforts that some travelers wouldn't want to do without, it might be your cup of tea. Positioned midway between Cabarete and Sosúa, 4km (2½ miles) from either, it occupies the site that was conceived as the owner's (a Chilean expatriate named Lole Sumar) private home. In 1990, she opted to improve her acreage with a series of artfully rustic wood and concrete structures for the shelter and amusement of like-minded New Age friends. Some are mushroom-shaped organic-looking structures whose curved lines might have been inspired by Catalan architect Gaudí; others are more functional structures of wood clapboards and thick beams. Regardless of the shelter you select, you'll get a sense of living on a sunny, not particularly stressful summer camp for adults and their children. None of the units has air-conditioning, a TV, or telephone, but there are yoga classes conducted without charge for residents twice a week (the venue is a Taíno-inspired wooden structure in a forest adjacent to the beach). Don't come here looking for upscale flair and urban style, since you really won't find it. Instead, you have an almost defiant sense that people are in Cabarete to get their lives back in order; read quietly in the sun, often in hammocks; and communicate with the great outdoors. Meals are served in different replicas of outbuildings inspired by the tenets of Taíno design. Main courses cost RD$420 to RD$860 (US$13–US$26/£6.45–£13), and are likely to include Creole-style braised octopus, langoustines with mushroom sauce, grilled tuna steak with pistachio, and dorado with coconut. The on-site spa is New Age–centered, small-scale, personalized, and artsy.

In the La Perla Marina Complex, Cabarete, Dominican Republic. ⓒ **809/571-1507.** www.naturacabana.com. 11 units. US$160 (£84) double; US$210 (£111) triple; US$240 (£126) quad. MC, V. **Amenities:** 2 restaurants; bar; outdoor pool; spa; free use of mountain bikes; jeep rental facilities; massage; horseback riding; yoga classes. *In room:* Kitchen (in some), no phone.

Tropical Hotel Casa Laguna *Value*

One of the better lodging values in Cabarete is this 1980s hotel, just across the street from the beach, within a pleasant walled-in garden. Each of the rooms has a refrigerator, mahogany louvers, and lattices, plus functional furniture. Most have sparsely equipped kitchenettes, and each has a tiled bathroom with a combination tub/shower.

Calle Principal, Cabarete, Dominican Republic. © **809/571-0725**. Fax 809/571-0704. www.tropicalclubs.com. 127 units. US$55–US$95 (£29–£50) double. AP (full board) US$25 (£13) per person extra. DC, MC, V. **Amenities:** 3 restaurants; 2 bars; 3 outdoor pools; salon; massage; babysitting; laundry. *In room:* A/C, TV, minibar, fridge, hair dryer, iron, safe.

Velero Beach Resort ⑭ *(Finds)*   Pleasant and well maintained, with a history dating back only to 2000, this small but charming boutique hotel occupies a buff-colored complex of three-story buildings set directly astride the beach at the extreme eastern end of the resort. The architectural components of this place enclose a manicured lawn dotted with palm trees, a rather small swimming pool, and an open-to-the-breezes bar and restaurant covered with palm fronds. You're never far from the sound of the crashing surf at this place. At least half the clientele here is European, many of them checking in for 3 to 4 weeks at a time as part of their annual holidays. Bedrooms open onto verandas or patios, and each is attractively and comfortably furnished with modern tropical pieces; each unit also comes with a tiled bathroom with tub/shower combo.

Calle La Punta 1, Cabarete, Dominican Republic. © **809/571-9727**. Fax 809/571-9722. www.velerobeach.com. 58 units. US$75–US$110 (£39–£58) double; US$95–US$140 (£50–£74) junior suite; US$155–US$310 (£82–£163) suite. Children under 12 stay free in parent's room. Rates include breakfast. AE, DC, MC, V. **Amenities:** Restaurant; bar; exercise room; massage; babysitting; Internet access; gift shop. *In room:* A/C, TV, fridge,

WHERE TO DINE

Casa del Pescador ⑭   SEAFOOD   Since 1988, Casa del Pescador has served sophisticated seafood in an engagingly hip environment that's the domain of a Swiss expatriate. It's right on the beach, in the heart of town. To begin, sample the chef's flavor-filled fish consommé. He does very well with shrimp, too, either with pastis sauce or more zestily, with curry and fresh garlic. On a hot day, the seafood salads are a welcome relief and tasty, too, as are the grilled octopus in spicy Creole sauce and fresh lobster in garlic sauce (unless you love garlic, you might find the latter overpowering; ask for butter instead). Although there's a full wine list, Presidente beer seems the best accompaniment to the fish, especially on hot, sultry nights.

Calle Principal. © **809/571-0760**. Reservations recommended for dinner. Main courses US$8–US$23 (£4.20–£12). AE, DC, MC, V. Daily 10am–11pm.

Onno's Bar INTERNATIONAL Established in 1999 by an expatriate Dutchman, this restaurant is one of the most visible and popular hipster hangouts in town. It occupies substantial mahogany-trimmed premises that sit directly on the beachfront, with one end opening onto the town's main thoroughfare. Inside a woodsy-looking and heavily timbered interior, you'll find scaled-down models of sailing ships, and a staff and clientele that's mostly European. You can chill out here for hours with a drink or two, but if you want food, the menu lists well-prepared versions of salads with chèvre or Camembert cheese, filet of beef with pepper or garlic sauce, Indonesian-style satay skewers of beef or chicken with peanut sauce, and a spicy version of spare ribs.

Calle Principal s/n. ⓒ **809/571-0461.** Main courses RD$230–RD$495 (US$6.95–US$15/£3.55–£7.60). No credit cards. Daily 8:30am–1am (till 2am Fri–Sat).

SPORTS & THE GREAT OUTDOORS

Not surprisingly, Cabarete is home to one of the Caribbean's best **windsurfing schools, Carib Wind Center,** Playa Cabarete (ⓒ **809/571-0640;** www.caribwind.com). It's devoted to teaching proper techniques and to renting state-of-the-art equipment. Equipment rental costs US$45 (£24) for 5 hours, and instruction is US$35 (£18) per hour. Clients who book a week or more in advance receive discounts of around 20%. A worthy competitor, located just a few doors away, is the **Fanatic Windsurf Center,** Calle Principale (ⓒ **809/571-0861;** www.fanatic-cabarete.com). Fanatic sometimes offers rates a bit less expensive than those at the Carib Wind Center.

Although windsurfing attracts more media attention than any other sport in Cabarete, conventional surfing is also big and getting bigger. Because of the prevailing tides and wind patterns, it's best undertaken at **Playa Encuentro,** a 2km (1¼-mile) stretch of beachfront that's 4km (2½ miles) west of Cabarete and 5km (3 miles) east of Sosúa. Here, surfboards are rented from a crowd of active aficionados at the **Club M-Endy,** Playa El Encuentro, Carretera Sosúa–Cabarete (ⓒ **809/571-1625**). (You'll turn off the main coastal highway at the Coconut Palms Resort, then follow the signs, driving along dirt roads through cow pastures, to Club M-Endy.) M-Endy's centerpiece is a soaring, thatch-roofed bohío that's the site of a simple bar and restaurant. Burgers and grilled fish cost from RD$160 to RD$750 (US$4.85–US$23/£2.45–£12). Renting a surfboard costs US$20 (£11) per day and lessons can be arranged for around US$35 (£18) an hour.

Iguana Mama at Cabarete (📞 **800/849-4720** in the U.S. or 809/571-0908; www.iguanamama.com) offers the best **mountain biking** and hiking. Going strong since 1993, it features a trek to Mount Isabel de Torres with experienced guides that lasts a full day and costs US$65 (£34) per person. If enough people book, this tour is offered daily. Another trek involves a 900m (2,953-ft.) downhill cruise, costing US$40 (£21) per person and held only Monday, Wednesday, and Friday.

Finally, **Gipsy Ranch** (📞 **809/571-1373**) is the most complete riding stable in the Dominican Republic; they'll take you **horseback riding** at a cost of US$20 (£11) per person for an hour or US$60 (£32) for a 4-hour ride.

CABARETE AFTER DARK

Las Brisas, Calle Principal Cabarete (📞 **809/571-0614**), is the most popular nightlife venue in Cabarete. Arrive after 10:30pm when the dance club action begins. From 8am to 10:30pm daily, food is served. The dance floor is illuminated with strobe lights and lasers, and the bar is always busy. Many patrons arrive with dates of their own, but if you're a man flying solo, never fear, as a bevy of attractive working women are invariably on hand to provide companionship.

Hip nightlife is also found at the little bars—shanties, really—along the beach. There's live music every night after sunset. Tuesday nights it's salsa and merengue at **Onno's Bar** (📞 **809/571-0461**). **The Bamboo Bar** (no phone) is the place to be on Friday night, and on Saturday the new **Wave Bar** and **Tribal Café** (no phone) draw the most patrons. On virtually any night of the week, you can find dialogue and a sense of cosmopolitan hip at the **Café Pitu,** Calle Principal (📞 **809/571-0861**). Set a few steps from the also-recommended Onno's Bar, and radically upgraded late in 2006, it's the bar that's almost always cited as a centerpiece of Cabarete nightlife. It serves 25 kinds of pizzas, priced at RD$80 to RD$300 (US$2.40–US$9.10/£1.25–£4.60); breakfasts priced at RD$80 to RD$150 (US$2.40–US$4.55/£1.25–£2.30); and platters of rib-sticking food priced from RD$150 to RD$400 (US$4.55–US$12/£2.30–£6.15). It also offers wireless Internet access throughout its premises, thereby creating a sometimes studious venue of scantily clad athletes swigging rum punches and surfing the Net. *Note:* Only some of these bars have phone numbers, and none bears an individual street number on the Calle Principal, but each of them is easy to spot as you walk up and down either the beach or the town's main street.

Index

See also Accommodations and Restaurant indexes below.

CLOSED
due to
accidental demolition

WEGEN BISSIGEN
EICHHÖRNCHEN GESCHLOSSEN

CERRADO
CABRAS

Κλειστό
Μετεωρίτες

POOL CLOSED

プール も

ELECTRIC EELS

閉鎖中

Hotel
closed for
facelifting

FERMÉ POUR
RAISON
DE GRÈVE
DES BONNES

FECHADO!
POR CAUSA DE
ATAQUES DOS CROCODILOS

I don't speak
sign language.

A hotel can close for all kinds of reasons.

Our Guarantee ensures that if your hotel's undergoing construction,
we'll let you know in advance. In fact, we cover your entire travel
experience. See www.travelocity.com/guarantee for details.

✱✱ travelocity

You'll never roam alone.

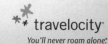